# Hooked on
# Hockey

*Chicken Soup for the Soul: Hooked on Hockey*
*101 Stories about the Players Who Love the Game and the Families that Cheer Them On*
Jack Canfield, Mark Victor Hansen, and Laura Robinson

Published by Chicken Soup for the Soul Publishing, LLC    www.chickensoup.com
Copyright © 2012 by Chicken Soup for the Soul Publishing, LLC. All Rights Reserved.

The publisher gratefully acknowledges the many publishers and individuals who granted Chicken Soup for the Soul permission to reprint the cited material.

Front cover photo courtesy of Webstockpro.com/UpperCut-RF. Back cover and interior photos courtesy of Photos.com.

*Cover and Interior Design & Layout by Pneuma Books, LLC*
For more info on Pneuma Books, visit www.pneumabooks.com

Distributed to the booktrade by Simon & Schuster. SAN: 200-2442

**Publisher's Cataloging-in-Publication Data**
*(Prepared by The Donohue Group)*
Chicken soup for the soul : hooked on hockey : 101 stories about the players who
love the game and the families that cheer them on / [compiled by] Jack
Canfield, Mark Victor Hansen, [and] Laura Robinson.

    p. ; cm.

Summary: A collection of 101 true personal stories from hockey fans, hockey players
of all ages and rankings, and hockey parents, discussing why they love hockey, how
hockey has changed their lives, and anecdotes from playing or watching hockey.
Includes stories by NHL players and Olympians.
ISBN: 978-1-61159-902-2

1. Hockey--Literary collections. 2. Hockey--Anecdotes. I. Canfield, Jack, 1944- II.
Hansen, Mark Victor. III. Robinson, Laura. IV. Title: Hooked on hockey

PN6071.H63 C45 2012
810.8/02/03579                                    2012943519

PRINTED IN THE UNITED STATES OF AMERICA
on acid∞free paper
21 20 19 18 17 16 15 14 13 12          01 02 03 04 05 06 07 08 09 10

# Chicken Soup
## for the Soul®

# Hooked on
# Hockey

### 101 Stories about the Players Who Love the Game and the Families that Cheer Them On

## Jack Canfield
## Mark Victor Hansen
## Laura Robinson

Chicken Soup for the Soul Publishing, LLC
Cos Cob, CT

Chicken Soup for the Soul

www.chickensoup.com

# Contents

## ❶
## ~Fresh Air & Ice~

## ❷
## ~Game On!~

## ❸
## ~FAN-tastic!~

## ❹
## ~Heroes Among Us~

**❺**

# ~Family Ties~

**❻**

# ~Global Games~

**❼**

# ~Dreams & Inspiration~

# ❽
## ~Life Lessons~

# ❾
## ~Spectacular Spectators~

**⑩**

# ~Slice of Ice~

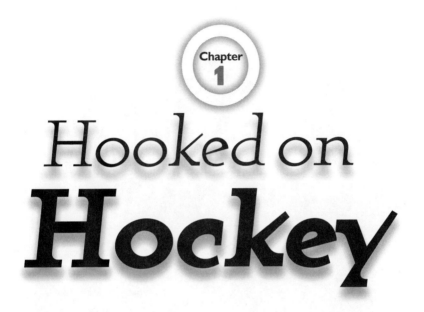

# Fresh Air & Ice

# The Dawn Patrol

*Winter must be cold for those with no warm memories.*
*~From the movie* An Affair to Remember

I n the frigid glow of dawn, seated on stumps around the remains of the previous night's bonfire, we laced on our skates. Then we sat hunched, toques pulled low over our ears, warming our numbed fingers above the embers, awaiting sunrise.

The Credit River emptied into Lake Ontario just west of Toronto. In the 1960s, it froze solid. Parks and Recreation staff plowed the snow from its surface and re-flooded it nightly, creating a public skating rink that stretched for miles. A mecca for pleasure skaters and shinny players of all ages, who came to enjoy nature's beauty and bounty. Fires were built along the banks to warm them and coloured lights were strung from shore to shore to add ambiance at night. Thousands spent their afternoons and evenings enjoying the ice.

This was our time. We were "the dawn patrol."

As the sun began to creep above the horizon, my friend Bill and I would slip our hands into our hockey gloves, take up our sticks and abandon the fire. Clumping our way through the bulrushes and shell ice to the river's edge we paused, poised for the moment. Then the first golden rays would strike, unveiling an unblemished sheet of glistening blue-white ice, stretching farther than our eyes could see. The invitation to fly on our booted blades of silver steel had been issued.

A few short strokes to test balance and edge, then with longer more powerful strides, our blades began carving the virgin ice, leaving a trail of diamond chips in our wake. No boards to confine us, no blue lines to restrain us; we challenged imaginary opponents, deking them with our best moves, turning, spinning, stopping, starting and winning every time.

The sub-zero nights made river ice very hard and this, combined with the water flowing just a foot beneath our skates, created a distinct hollow sound each time our blades cut into it. We were breathing hard now as the frigid air tugged at our lungs, but we warmed to the task.

The first puck dropped. It was game on. No coaches, no officials and no line-changes, just the two of us, skating side by side, exchanging short passes, getting the feel. Then, "Go Bill!" and I would fire a long lead pass challenging him to snare it. He in turn would test my mettle. If we missed a few, no matter—our rink was endless and our energy boundless. We had but one rule. Follow the fresh ice.

Full sunlight now and the reflection from the gleaming surface made our eyes water as we skated leisurely up river, on patrol, still sliding passes, backhand, forehand, sharp or soft and then suddenly, "Dump and chase!" Bill firing the puck straight up river and the race was on. Impossibly, that skittering black disk seemed to gain speed, as with heads down, legs driving and sticks extended, we vied to be first to snare it.

Crack! The sound of a shot? No, just ice and sunlight interacting, and magically a fissure appeared in our rink. A two-inch wide crack opened at our feet and ran from shore to shore. It was the first of many that would form as the day unfolded, and one of the hazards of river skating. We glided on, passing the central bonfire area where the general public would soon begin to intrude on our sanctuary.

Then in the distance we saw a familiar figure moving rapidly toward us: a fellow pathfinder who shared our passion, but in a different way. Hunched forward, arms clasped behind his back, balanced on incredibly long blades, a speed skater approached. Freed from the endless circles and crossovers of competition, his powerful legs drove him forward at remarkable speed and he flew past us. We lifted our sticks in salute; he nodded without breaking form. He would return and pass us again before we reached our goal.

Our destination was the end of the fresh ice. It was our passion to leave our mark from beginning to end of that wonderful rink and we always did. We knew during our downriver return, as we added to the cuts and curves we had already made, that the magic spell of being first comers, of it being our ice and ours alone, would be soon broken.

The families were gathering near the fires, preparing to join us, and groups of shinny players were starting pickup games. We would play in several as we trekked back downriver.

When we reached our starting point we had to search to find our boots, now mixed amongst scores of other pairs, left by those who came later. As we sat warming them over the fire, readying them to accept our tingling toes, we often got strange "quitting so soon?" comments or looks from those just lacing up. Bill and I would just smile, hang our skates on our sticks and shoulder them for the walk home.

Little did they know! We would return on the morrow, in the darkest hour, to repeat our ritual. We were "the dawn patrol."

~John Forrest

Chicken Soup for the Soul

# Playing Shinny on Macamley Street

*Growing up, if I hadn't had sports, I don't know where I'd be.*
*God only knows what street corners I'd have been standing on and God only*
*knows what I'd have been doing, but instead I played hockey*
*and went to school and stayed out of trouble.*
*~Bobby Orr*

We didn't have ice skates or an ice rink, but we kids were blessed by the gods of hockey with the perpetually snow covered streets of south Buffalo winters. Heck, we had taped up hockey sticks, a puck (sometimes a tin can), and goals marked with old sneakers. What else did we need? We played with heart and a passion known only to eleven-year-old boys crazy in love with the game of hockey.

It was the mid-forties. Our Buffalo Bisons hockey team, American League farm club of the legendary Montreal Canadiens NHL team, was burning up their league. Buffalo won the coveted Calder Cup several times in the forties.

We kids listened to every game on the radio (no TV yet) and would take turns sharing tear sheets from the sports pages of the *Buffalo Courier-Express* newspaper. We'd pore over the stats of each game at school. "Did Pargeter get the hat trick last night? Wow! That's twice this month already."

My best pals—Dave "Murph" Murphy and "Bones" Miller—along

with Don, Bernie and myself were the hard-nosed ones. We played when Macamley Street was slick with ice or loaded with two feet of snow. We played in the sleet and the rain and right through some of Buffalo's biggest snow squalls. Bring it on. We were ready.

Our uniforms were jeans, winter coats and earmuffs. Playing in our overshoes, we didn't look much like hockey players but we played with the intensity of pros, right through the icy winds that blew off Lake Erie and the black and blue hurts on our shins. We checked our opponents into the snow banks that lined Macamley Street. The only local rule we observed, in deference to our complete lack of protective gear, was no lifting the puck.

The only time we stopped playing was when a car made its way down the street and we had to pause to let it go by. Otherwise, our games went on for hours or until the street lights went on. That was our signal to call the game and return to the mundane world of family life, homework and cleaning up for dinner.

Two or three times a season, our gang managed to get the money together to take the bus downtown to see the Bisons play at Memorial Auditorium. We lived for those days. The Aud, as we called it, was a first-class indoor sports arena with seating for about 12,000 fans. We could only afford the cheap seats so we sat way up in the higher regions of the auditorium, but we felt lucky just being part of the raucous crowd cheering on our beloved Bisons.

Just before the breaks between periods of the games, we would hustle down from the cheap seats to the lower floor where the teams had their locker rooms to catch our team coming off the ice. Just to see our heroes up close was a thrill. Sometimes, we'd get brave and yell out our encouragement: "Hey, Al way to go" or "Nice game, Pargeter." If we were rewarded by so much as a grunt from one of the players, we felt graced by the Almighty.

But nothing prepared us for the time one of the Buffalo players came off the ice carrying a hockey stick that had a crack in the shaft. He apparently had just noticed the crack and was about to hand it to the manager for disposal. I was right there in front of him. Summoning up all the courage I had in my eleven-year-old body, I said, "Can I have it?" The player looked down at me for a second. "Sure kid, it's yours." He thrust it into my waiting hands. It was a miracle. I had a real professional hockey stick.

Oh My Gosh! Dave and Bones crowded around me. "He GAVE it to you?" exclaimed Bones. "Wow! Are you lucky." Everything was a blur after that. We watched the final period of the game but I was lost in a haze of unexpected good fortune. My hands clutched the stick tightly, but my soul was already in paradise.

We played shinny again at home but it didn't take long for the already-damaged stick to break into two pieces. I taped it up the best I could and kept it for a while in the cellar of our house on Macamley Street. All too soon, our hockey crazy period ended as we grew into adolescence and went our separate ways to different high schools in the Buffalo area. Eventually, the Buffalo Bisons morphed into the Sabres of the National Hockey League. Alas, I find myself living in California now, far from the snowy streets of south Buffalo.

Ah, but the memories remain.

~Hank Mattimore

# Watch Out for the Diving Board!

*If you carry your childhood with you, you never become older.*
~Tom Stoppard

Chip. Chip. Chip.

My dad — brandishing a long, heavy spud bar — lorded over a tiny hole in the ice on the northwest corner of our farm pond.

Chip. Chip. Chip.

With each downward stroke of the spud bar, the hole in the ice grew a little bigger.

Chip. Chip. Chip.

Three of my brothers and I knelt around the hole, eyeing the progress.

Looking up, I asked "Now Dad?"

"No, John, not yet," he replied.

Chip. Chip. Chip.

Eventually, my dad stopped cutting the ice with the spud bar. Then he knelt down next to the hole and stuck his bare hand into the freezing water.

We watched him grope around.

I repeated, "Now Dad?"

"Yep," he returned. "The ice is thick enough for you boys to go onto the pond."

"Whoo Hoo!"

That was all we needed to hear.

Four boys leapt up and ran to the tool barn. Our next task was to remove the snow from the top of the ice. Of course, the fact that we only owned two snow shovels didn't deter us. Joe and Jeff grabbed those two snow shovels and ran straight to the pond. Standing side by side, they began traipsing across the surface, pushing snow to the side. Being older, Jerry and I grabbed two benches from the picnic table. Laying them on their sides, we pushed those benches across the ice, cutting a swath in the snow that was twice as wide as that of the snow shovels. Within an hour, the four of us had cleared a rough, rectangular rink that was so large the swimming board on our dock protruded into the playing area. But that was okay... we would just remain vigilant so as to not skate into it.

Next, Joe ran into the house to get all the hockey sticks and our puck, while Jerry and I continued to set up the rink. The picnic benches that we had used as snow plows would now double as our goals. Again laying them on their sides, Jerry and I placed the picnic benches at each end of the rectangle.

Next, three of us returned to the tool barn, for up in the mow was a metallic box that contained our skates. But therein laid the rub—there wasn't a single pair of hockey skates in the box. Instead, they were all hand-me-down figure skates! Some were even white, having been given to us by our Aunt. We didn't care—skates were skates. We wrestled that metallic box down—being careful to not hit Dad's lawnmower—and placed it on the snow in front of the tool barn.

About that time, Mom opened the back door and stepped onto the house's back deck, yelling "Boys?"

"Yeah, Mom?"

"Aunt Betty is bringing over Dave and Dan."

"Whoo Hoo!"

My cousins David and Daniel were the same ages as Jerry and I, and lived a short ten minutes away. They would give us enough boys to play three-on-three.

About that time, Joe returned with a hodge-podge mixture of

hockey sticks that we had purchased over the years from Ace Hardware in town. Wanting to look like professional hockey players, we had wrapped black tape around the blades and also rigged a black knob on the end with the same tape. Joe also had our puck, which we had placed in Mom's freezer—much to her objection.

Joe laid everything down, and immediately eight hands began rummaging through the metallic box for skates that would fit. Right there in the snow we sat down, kicked off our boots, and put those figure skates on over white athletic socks. Blisters be damned!

As we stood erect on figure skates for the first time since last winter, Aunt Betty's Rambler pulled into our gravel driveway and parked. My aunt exited the car and went into the house to visit with her sister, but Dave and Dan bolted straight toward our outdoor locker room.

Dave and Dan sat down in the snowy spots that we had just vacated, only to see that the white figure skates were the only ones left.

After Dave and Dan donned their skates, the six of us walked to our makeshift rink, reviewing the standard ground rules of farm pond hockey:

1. Since we had no referee, there would be no opening face-off. Instead, we would toss a coin to determine which team got the puck first. Then, the losing three would simply throw the puck down the ice to the winning three to start the game… like a football kick-off.
2. In three-on-three pond hockey, there was no goalie.
3. Likewise, there was no penalty box. We obeyed the rules.
4. When the puck got whacked onto land, the first player to skate there, run up on the snow, and retrieve it received a free start at the point where the puck exited the ice.
5. If anyone was skating with the puck down the north side of the rink, it was a common courtesy to yell, "Watch out for the diving board!"

~John M. Scanlan

# The Endless Rink

*Ice hockey players can walk on water.*
*~Author Unknown*

I grew up in the far reaches of northern New York State in a little hamlet comprised of ten houses, a church and a one-room schoolhouse. I have fond memories of an idyllic youth spent playing in the woods, biking for miles on country roads and spending hours exploring the shores of a brook at the bottom of the hill behind our house.

Especially the brook. It was a playground and oasis that served our youthful needs for all four seasons. In the spring, it was the place to build dams to reroute the fast-moving water. In the summer, it was a berth for our series of homemade rafts, only one of which, if memory serves me well, could actually float with one of us standing on it.

The fall was a time for quiet reflection by the brook. We would wile away hours traveling up and down its banks and play Pooh sticks on the narrow bridge that carried the small blacktop road up the hill to our hamlet.

But the best time of all at the brook was winter. As Christmas approached and the temperature dropped, my brother and I eagerly awaited the formation of the first layer of ice. By January, the ice was thick enough to skate on and that's what we did, every chance we got.

On weekends, our friends and us raced down the long hill behind our house with skates, hockey sticks and shovels in hand. For it was almost always necessary to shovel snow from the surface to make our own private hockey rink.

Once the rink was cleared, we struggled with frozen fingers to lace up our skates. Two pairs of discarded boots served as makeshift goal posts for our rink of dreams. Hockey sticks that had earlier been stuck upside down in the piled up snow were now retrieved and pucks were dropped so everyone could play.

Eventually we would break into two teams and play a pickup game until the score became too lopsided or the sun was too far below the horizon to see the puck anymore. The score was often secondary; the joy was in playing the game.

When we finally stopped for the day, we could feel our toes tingling as we took off our skates. We trudged back up the hill and into our warm house, our cheeks glowing like embers, our damp hair flattened against our foreheads and our bodies enveloped in fatigue.

As the winter progressed, our rink would become more sophisticated as we added makeshift nets and carved out seats from the snow banks. If we had ever figured out how to string up lights and run a 500-foot extension cord, we surely would have continued to play well into the night.

Sadly, the rink's days were numbered. If we were lucky, we would continue to shovel off the next snowfall and continue playing. But if we faced freezing rain or a quick thaw, our rink would disappear for days or weeks at a time.

We knew our outdoor hockey season was short, which is why, I guess, we made the most of it. We packed in as many games as we could.

And once in a while, there would be a magical occurrence on our brook. Every few winters, we would be treated to a huge midwinter melt that swallowed up all the snow and was quickly followed by a flash freeze that turned our little brook into a clear perfect ice surface from shore to shore.

On those magical days, there were no makeshift nets or pairs of boots doubling as goal posts. We simply skated on our smooth glassy brook as far and as long as we wanted to, passing a puck back and forth until we finally had to turn around and skate home.

I remember the days of morning-to-night hockey with fondness. But there's a special spot in my memory reserved for those few magical days when we skated on our own endless rink.

~David Martin

# Uncle!

*October is not only a beautiful month but marks the precious yet fleeting
overlap of hockey, baseball, basketball, and football.*
~Jason Love

I was one fortunate kid, let me tell you. Growing up in Michigan's
Upper Peninsula, we never worried about traffic jams, unless
you counted the deer crossing areas, or the occasional lineups
to buy pastries at the Finnish bakery. The air was clear, the lakes cool
and clean, and the scenery spectacular. If it weren't for the mosquitoes, you would have thought you had already made it to heaven.

Summers were spent playing baseball, and winters belonged to
basketball. I loved those two sports with a passion that couldn't be
matched, and spent many a day as the hero of my imaginary teams.
And then one winter my father dug a hole in our back yard.

"What's Dad up to?" I asked Mom on a cold November day. He
had borrowed a backhoe and was digging a very large hole behind
our house.

"He decided he wants to put in an ice rink for the winter," she
explained, with a bit of a sigh.

Well, my father never did anything small. This rink was nearly
the size of a stadium facility, or at least if looked like that to my eight-year-old eyes. Dad got the volunteer fire department to come out and
flood the area, and we had one of the biggest patches of ice short
of Lake Superior. Coincidentally, that Christmas Santa brought us all
skates as presents.

After getting over the initial wobbles (and cutting open my brother's lip with my blade on a bad fall), I started to really like the rink. Then Dad came home with some hockey sticks and a puck, and a new winter sport was born in our family. I found that this was not only a lot of fun, but using the stick really helped out my beginner's balance on the skates. I loved hockey!

But alas, basketball beckoned. My little town was crazy about basketball—even won two state titles back in the fifties—and there wasn't a local hockey team to be found within reasonable driving distance. So the hockey gear was stuffed into the back of my closet, and rarely considered. The ice rink was eventually filled back in, and my father moved on to building a ski lift down our back hill, which is a story for another day.

Years passed, and I went away to college. It wasn't until I arrived at Michigan Tech that I learned that they had won the NCAA Hockey Championship the previous year. I guess you could say that the locals and students were a bit excited. I didn't have a choice—once again hockey ruled the day! My roommate turned out to be a raving lunatic of a hockey fan, and he introduced me to the finer art of his own pre-game warm-up. We would stand behind the net and shove our faces against the glass, and as the practice shots ricocheted off the glass next to our heads, we tried to see who could last the longest without flinching.

Man, did I ever love going to those hockey games! We had a great scorer on the team named Zuke, and my favorite fan sign read, "Jesus Saves. But Zuke scores on the rebound!" Once our archrivals came to town, and a huge brawl broke out before the puck even dropped to start the game. It was the most incredible fight I ever witnessed. The officials just let them go at it until they all finally got too tired to keep swinging their arms. Everyone was fighting—even the goalies were pummeling each other. Well, as much as two men in all that protective gear could actually pummel. And once again, I loved hockey!

Then life happened, and I moved away from my beloved Michigan once I graduated from college. In Denver, the Broncos and football ruled the sports scene. Later, in Salt Lake City, it was the Jazz and the NBA. Hockey? Forget it!

Then I did something I never imagined in my life. I married a Canadian! And once again, hockey came back into my life, this time for good.

Looking back, it seems that each time I shoved hockey aside in my life, it found a way to creep back in. Now I stand up and scream like a crazy man, especially watching the Stanley Cup. I love the action, intensity and grace of the game. I love the speed, passing, checking, penalties, pain, fighting, scoring and winning. Yes, I'm an American with little experience playing the game, but I sure can appreciate the incredible skill of those who do.

So hockey, to you I say "Uncle." As much as I tried to ignore you and put you out of my life, you kept coming back, again and again. And for that, I thank you. Baseball? Too long and slow. Basketball? It's okay. But hockey? Now you're talking. Drop that puck and let 'er rip! What could be more wonderful?

I wonder what my wife would say if I start digging up her flower beds this fall?

~Bruce Mills

# Backyard Games

*My father used to play with my brother and me in the yard.*
*Mother would come out and say, "You're tearing up the grass."*
*"We're not raising grass," Dad would reply.*
*"We're raising boys."*
*~Harmon Killebrew*

**W**e live in a small town in Manitoba where, in winter, the rink becomes the centre of the community. My husband Luc and I were blessed with three boys—Danny, Ian and Robert—and we naturally became "a hockey family." From November to March our lives revolved around hockey practices and games at the rink. But of even more importance on a daily basis was the hockey played regularly in our own backyard.

For fifteen years or more, in addition to coaching various teams most years, Luc also created our own rink for our sons' hockey games—using the hose to flood a large section of the backyard garden. Ice making would begin as soon as the temperatures were consistently below freezing, usually by early December. Many frosty evenings Luc would pull on his snowmobile suit or parka several times a night and retreat to the backyard to add another thin layer of ice—thin layers being better for smoother ice. Creating a backyard rink truly became a labor of love for him. With three boys clamoring for him to finish, we prayed the weather would remain cold. If a warm spell occurred, the ice making was put on hold, only to resume when the temperature was cold enough again. Of course, the boys played neighbourhood street hockey all year long, summer and winter, but for "real" hockey, skates and ice were considered necessities.

Once the backyard ice was ready, if they weren't at the rink, one or all of the boys were usually playing hockey after school and weekends—often with the addition of several neighbourhood children. Our backyard would ring with cheers, with shouts of "He shoots! He scores!" and sometimes with arguments about the legitimacy of a goal. After a break for dinner, the youngsters often continued their hockey until bedtime, because Luc erected a floodlight to illuminate the rink. I think our boys usually enjoyed their backyard games more than the "real" games at the rink—and it didn't matter how low the temperatures were! If feet or hands became too cold, someone would suggest a short break inside for a mug of hot chocolate.

One photo in my collection shows the two younger boys—Robert, aged four, and Ian, aged six, at the time—warmly dressed in snowmobile suits, facing off against each other at centre ice. Robert is wearing a Toronto Maple Leafs toque, while Ian's toque appears to be in New York Islanders colours. (In actual fact, our family has always supported the Montreal Canadiens, but we didn't have the right-colored toques that winter.)

Our youngest son was particularly keen about hockey. The winters Robert was four and five, when his brothers were at school, he would often spend the afternoon skating on his own, always with hockey stick in hand and puck on the ice. "He shoots! He scores!" resounded from our backyard—loud enough for our next-door neighbour to hear. Before the single-player game, though, one traditional event occurred: the singing of the national anthem. I remember standing at my kitchen window watching as one small boy dressed for an outdoor hockey game stood at attention and loudly sang "O Canada"—not always in tune, but with great pride and enthusiasm. I like to think of that as a quintessential hockey moment.

Our yard no longer sports a backyard rink. Our children are all grown now, away from home, and our grandchildren live too far away for Grandpa to make them a rink. Still, some days, I hear in my imagination the sound of skates on ice and shouts of "He shoots! He scores!"

~Donna Firby Gamache

# Rink of Dreams

*Childhood is measured out by sounds and smells and sights,*
*before the dark hour of reason grows.*
*~John Betjeman,* Summoned by Bells

I t seemed like a good idea at the time. We thought so highly of it, in fact, that we acted before my twelve-year-old brain could find a shred of fault in it. One wouldn't normally look at a rough patch of asphalt and picture, in its place, the freshly-Zambonied surface at Madison Square Garden. But we were dreamers and, worse, we played hockey.

"Go in the back yard," I told my brother, "and grab the big trash can. I'll find the shovels."

Nick's boots and much of his legs below the knees disappeared in the snow as he waded through the back yard. "It's full of leaves," he shouted when he reached his destination.

"Just dump it out," I told him, "and bring it over to the hose." The hose itself was hard and brittle, like a long thread of dried pasta before it hits the surface of a boiling pot of water. There was nothing odd about this, given the fact that the mercury had barely risen above twenty degrees in at least a week. So I attached the end to the faucet with my gloved hand and twisted the nozzle to full blast.

At first, only a slow trickle of slushy liquid drizzled out, but in a minute or two the water gushed forth as it would on any spring day. I placed the hose inside the industrial-sized can and then handed Nick one of the shovels.

"Let's clear a spot while it fills up," I told him.

Since Nick and I lived on a cul-de-sac, our block had always served as an impromptu street hockey rink for the entire neighborhood. What began as small pickup games with the position players in their Converse All Stars and the goalies wearing old baseball mitts, had graduated over the years into Cup-style blood matches on roller blades and with full line changes. Now, with a little help from our trusty snow tools and Mother Nature, we were about to give our game the ultimate advancement.

Nick and I worked quickly, shoveling out a large, rectangular area in the center of the court. On more than one occasion, a smiling neighbor peered from his driveway with appreciation, no doubt admiring what he initially perceived as a public service to the entire block of morning commuters.

We shoveled off just enough snow so that a two-inch layer covered the surface of our fledgling rink, and we piled the rest of the white stuff neatly around the outside to form a set of makeshift boards. Then we trudged back up to the house to retrieve our homemade Zamboni. The shoveling had apparently taken longer than we'd anticipated because a frigid waterfall was overflowing the can and forming a slushy puddle next to the entrance to our garage. If you watched closely enough you could almost see crystals forming right before your eyes.

"It's working," I said to Nick.

"Awesome."

"Help me lift it," I told him, and that was probably the understatement of my life. You never realize how much water weighs until you're carrying a thirty-gallon drum of the stuff through a foot of snow. By the time we got the can down to street level, it probably held closer to twenty-five gallons of fluid since large portions of it had sloshed off the surface in monsoon-like waves and soaked through our gloves.

When the journey was complete and the can was positioned in the center of the rink, I gave the order. "Let's pour it out." We tipped the can on its side and a torrent of water streamed onto the street and dispersed itself evenly within our boundaries. We repeated the process maybe four or five times until there was a three-inch layer of rapidly hardening slush all across the surface. "Let's go have a cup of hot chocolate and warm up while we wait," I suggested.

We drank the cocoas with our faces pressed against the front window so that we could stare at our masterpiece. It mingled with the cold air and made dangerous transformations on the street that only a hockey player could love. Then I picked up the phone and called every kid in the neighborhood. My message to all was brief and clear.

"Hockey game in twenty minutes... Manassas Court... bring your ice skates."

Within minutes, the street was teeming with mini hockey players in their sweaters with names like "Tocchet" or "Hextall" or "Gretzky" sewn across the back. Each one of them approached the rink with eyes as wide as hockey pucks before plopping down in the snow banks to lace up their skates.

Being the master engineers, of course, my brother and I took the honors of cutting the first blades across the ice, and I'm happy to say that Madison Square Garden held not a candle to our Manassas Court Marvel. Our edges gripped the surface like high-performance radials and paid not a passing gesture to the stony shrapnel beneath. And when Nick feathered a lightning-quick pass across the imaginary neutral zone and I heard the pleasing click of corrugated rubber slapping tape on the end of my stick, I could almost feel the frenzied hush of fans all around me.

But when I snapped back to reality, I noticed the shouting was not coming from an overpacked set of stands. In fact, the scolding came from a man who, at that moment, was not a big fan of mine at all.

"Are you guys crazy?" he screamed from my front porch. It wasn't often that my father raised his voice. When he did, you could rest assured there was a monumental catastrophe at hand—like the sun was about to collide with the Earth, or a couple of overeager kids had unwittingly turned a quiet, snow-capped street into a retirement community for any vehicle with wheels. "Enjoy your game," he said under his breath as I approached. "As soon as it's over get rid of that ice. I don't care how you do it, but make it disappear."

I followed his instructions quite nearly to the letter. We skated like rising NHL stars until our legs were weary and the streetlights winked their soft glow. But I didn't have the heart to destroy our masterpiece. So I left it, in all its glory, to enjoy a full night of sub-zero temperatures.

"Did you destroy the rink?" my father asked over dinner.

"Yes," I said.

"Good. I'm proud of you." But the sudden pride he had in his son was about to melt away more quickly than any sheet of ice.

The next morning my alarm clock, probably the wake-up call for an entire blocks-worth of startled slumberers, was the slipping and grinding of my neighbor's rear wheel drive as he attempted to exit his driveway and traverse the daunting stretches of our rink.

Dad was not happy.

While my friends spent their snow day sledding at a nearby hill, I was stuck chipping away two days worth of ice with a hammer and a rusty chisel until the masterpiece was nothing more than dirty snow and a cobbled patch of asphalt.

For hockey, it was worth every second of grueling labor.

~C.G. Morelli

# The Hockey Skate Thief

*What we have done for ourselves alone dies with us;*
*what we have done for others and the world remains and is immortal.*
~Albert Pike

"Hey, want to play with us?" The wind came sliding down over the ice, carrying the high-spirited sounds of the players' anticipation. Each time the puck neared the opposing goal, the cheers and jeers grew louder. I stood at the edge of our town pond and watched the neighborhood kids' hockey game. I wished I could play too, but I didn't have skates.

"No, maybe later...." I said, trying to discipline my voice to show indifference. We were poor, but we were also proud. World War II had just ended, and we were refugees in the small town of Osterode, Germany. Barely enough to eat, and as if poverty was a disgrace, we veiled the truth. Instead of pride, disappointment and loneliness walked with me on the way home.

With my head low and drooping shoulders, I entered through the kitchen door. The aroma of simmering potato soup greeted me. Miss Gertrude, our landlord's maid, sat at the table opposite my mom, in front of her some bread and jam. She often brought us food. Knowing my mother would not accept stolen goods she always insisted, "Don't worry... it's from my ration," or "Don't worry... it was a gift."

"What's wrong?" my mother asked seeing my brooding posture.

"I wish I had skates," I blurted out, falling into the chair between them. "So I could play in the hockey game."

"But, you know my child..." my mother was stopped by Miss Gertrude.

"Guess what?" Jumping from her chair with an unexpected vivacity for someone so plump, the maid repeated, "Guess what? Just today I had to clean out the landlord's attic and among the many things he no longer needs was a pair of hockey skates." She headed for the door shouting over her shoulder, "I will go and get them right now."

My mother bit her lips and started to put the bread and jam away. "She is too good," she mumbled, walking to the stove to stir the soup. "I don't know how we will ever repay her.

Ten minutes later, Miss Gertrude returned with a pair of skates under her apron. "Hurry," she said. A smile played around her lips as she handed the skates to me. "Hurry, hurry, go and play."

My mother drew her eyebrows together but before she could question her, Miss Gertrude assured her, "Yes, yes, it is all right. They were headed for the garbage pile."

I marveled at my new possession, the adjustable screw to the shoe skates with its glistening sharp edges. No longer able to contain my delight, I gave my mom and Miss Gertrude each a quick hug. Grabbing my coat, gloves, and skates, I ran for the door.

A light snow began to fall, turning the town into a winter wonderland. When I arrived at the pond, the hockey game was still on.

"Hey, you can be on my team," one of the kids yelled, his cheeks red from the wintry air. I hastened to fasten the skates to my shoes. Somewhat out of breath, I joined the game. And while the snow-flakes danced all around us, we played until darkness came and lights glimmered in windows of nearby houses.

The exhilaration of that first hockey game, almost a lifetime ago, and the joy of the many games that followed, will always stay with me. And so will the lingering question of whether that kind, generous maid, Miss Gertrude, was a hockey skate thief.

~Christa Holder Ocker

# The Arena of Life

*Canada is hockey.*
*~Mike Weir*

Hockey, people say, is what defines us as Canadians. I don't know if I totally agree. Granted, the game's image has been copied onto our currency, but we are a more diverse lot than that. I have to admit, however, that hockey did play a defining role in my life back in the 1960s.

As young children, it was pond hockey that my brothers and I enjoyed. A similar scene is enshrined on the back of Canada's five-dollar bill, in a painting entitled "The Pond." Two such surfaces lay within walking distance of our childhood home. Nestled amidst the rolling hills of Northumberland County, these frozen platters offered considerable protection against the bitter winds of winter while we played the game we learned to love. One pond even came with its own warming hut — an ancient, abandoned, navy blue Chevy. Bereft of windows and doors, stripped of its motor and wheels, the car had been dragged to the marshy water's edge in order to function as a duck blind for a group of hunters in the mid-forties. It provided the perfect place to sit and chat while we laced up our skates... mine, the lone white pair among all the black and brown ones.

There was plenty of pleasure to be found playing pond hockey:

- The ethereal beauty of a wintry landscape when robed in ice and snow.

- The camaraderie created as we shovelled off the snow-covered ice.
- The sheer joy of making up our own rules, with no adults around to enforce theirs.
- The serene quiet of the outdoors as a backdrop to the pleasing clicketty-clack of stick on ice.
- The ecstatic feeling of freedom as we raced over the ice, cool, crisp air rushing over ever-reddening faces.
- The clean, clear smack of the puck on a perfectly executed give-and-go.
- The euphoric invigoration of strenuous outdoor exercise and the blissful sleep that followed later that night.
- And occasionally, the glorious magic of pristine, clear ice when a flash freeze followed a January thaw.

Of course, we experienced our fair share of frostbitten fingers and toes, and the odd unintentional clip to the head or other minor injury, but all this paled in comparison to the delight offered by puck on pond. Cast-off boots became goaltender's pipes, the sun overhead the time clock, snow banks the boards.

In mid-winter, our one-room schoolhouse offered more of the same icy enchantment. On Friday afternoons we experienced physical education at its finest. With sticks and skates slung over our shoulders, we often walked with our teacher to a nearby farmer's field for a game of shinny.

And then, the inevitable—change. Our school closed and my brothers and I transferred to one in the nearby village. This was nothing, however, compared to what happened one fateful Saturday.

"I think we'll register the boys in organized hockey this year," my father announced.

Of course, I too expected to play.

"Girls aren't allowed to play hockey in town," my father said.

How could this be? I had always played hockey with my brothers.

The next weekend I stood in the driveway, tears in my eyes, while my father loaded the boys into our old Studebaker and drove off into the big, bustling town of Cobourg to sign the necessary forms and pay required fees. That winter I watched with my mother on the outside of the boards while my brothers zoomed over the ice, experiencing "the thrill of victory, the agony of defeat."

"Why can't girls play?" I asked one day.

"It's just the way things are," my mother explained.

This exclusion was one of the great disappointments of my childhood.

My great letdown did serve a valuable purpose, however. It was an initiation of sorts, a defining moment in the arena of life. I came to an abrupt realization that male and female opportunities were not necessarily the same.

Eventually, I did get to play organized hockey, helping start a women's team during my final year at university. It was even more exciting and fulfilling than I had anticipated.

It was only a club team, not a varsity squad like the boys had. That meant we had to pay our own way. But that was okay. At least we finally got to play. And although we never won a game that year, in our minds, we had scored a major victory.

~Judi Peers

**10**

# The Graham Hockey League

*Memory is a way of holding onto the things you love,*
*the things you are, the things you never want to lose.*
*~From the television show* The Wonder Years

Trudging through the snow, calls of "Branch!" ring out through the woods as we crunch our way over the drumlins around Wenham Lake. We all know the shorthand for protecting our faces from the long prickly twigs that line the path that we know by heart even though it's covered in ice and snow. We're heading to Little Cedar for pond hockey, and the conditions are perfect.

Cedar Pond is the sister of Wenham Lake, famous for the pure, crystalline water that spawned a thriving ice industry into the 19th century until the invention of refrigeration. Queen Victoria is said to have been particularly fond of Wenham Ice, demanding a huge supply to cool royal refreshments for herself and her friends. The same bubbling springs that produced such rare, desirable Wenham Ice keep us off the wide-open expanse of the big lake. Locals know that the sheet of unbroken ice on Wenham Lake is pocked with deceptive chasms of open water covered by a thin sheen of ice where the springs keep the water from freezing solid. Little Cedar Pond is nestled beside the big lake like a teaspoon beside a bowl, carved out of the rocky New England soil by a mile-thick glacier thousands of years ago.

The cold, crisp air smells of winter and pine, and it's dark in the woods despite a brilliant blue sky. I'm in my early twenties, but I still feel a chill in these woods that has nothing to do with the February freeze. The history of this area is ancient, from the Agawam tribe that lived on the shores of Wenham Lake to the early settlers who survived the devastation of the Salem Witch Trials. John Greenleaf Whittier's poem, "The Witch of Wenham," is set in these woods, and the ghosts of the past seem to linger behind the thick pines and towering oaks.

But the laughter and chatter of our group keeps my imagination at bay, and we're choosing teams before we even reach the edge of the pond. Our teams are made up of players who range from beginners on borrowed figure skates to college and semi-pro athletes in Super Tacks, the current rage in hockey skates in the 1970s and 80s. What matters in the Graham Hockey League is sportsmanship, a sense of adventure and a love of the outdoors.

Little Cedar is just the right size for the games in the league, named for our family because we supply the most players. If Mother Nature had been a hockey mom, she couldn't have laid out a more perfect hockey rink. Surrounded by tall, graceful cedars and boulders just the right size for putting on skates and sipping hot cocoa, the pond is remote, quiet and breathtakingly beautiful. My younger sisters, Pam, Kar and Trishy, are in great demand when teams are chosen along with our friends, and my brother Rob is one of the stars. Our mom declines the invitation to join us, probably because she has already spent enough years in the heavy manmade cold of hockey arenas while my brother played youth and high school hockey. She is content to let us go, and she will listen with rapt attention to our stories later on.

Our dad had us on skates as soon as we could walk. Although he joked that he never got the five sons he really wanted, he raised four girls and one boy who spent many hours on the small rink he built in our back yard. We could all hold our own in a hockey game when most girls in that era were told to stand on the sidelines and cheer for their brothers or stick to learning figures. We called Dad our fearless leader, and he was happy to suit up with us to join our games, dazzling the crowd of younger players with his skill, and leaving newcomers staring after him open-mouthed as he whizzed by to score a goal.

If the planets are in alignment and the weather cooperates, pond ice is as smooth as a sheet of glass. The conditions must be right: weeks of arctic temperatures with no snow are the key to perfect pond ice. Days before the game, my boyfriend, Scott, would watch the weather and if it looked hopeful, calls would go out. And by Saturday morning, friends from all over New England would head to Little Cedar.

On this particular weekend, an unusually long stretch of frigid, snow-free days and nights produced the rarest of rare, the holy grail of pond hockey: black ice. Black ice is free of the frothy air bubbles that color it cloudy or light. Black ice is so translucent that leaves swirling toward the bottom are captured in their descent, suspended as if in a crystal ball. Hapless fresh water minnows and the occasional perch are frozen in stark relief against the murky depths, giving the ice an otherworldly look. Black ice is as smooth, hard and sleek as tempered steel. Skate blades etch clean white loops and spirals across the dark surface, leaving a trail that sparkles like diamonds in the sunlight.

The game is underway, and the air is filled with shouts of "Awesome ice," or "I'm open!" The steely clink of blades carving the ice mixes with the heavier clack of wooden hockey sticks fighting for the puck, punctuated by the crack of a slap shot or hoots over a good lift. Soon, jackets and hats are tossed into a huge pile at the edge of the ice despite the cold. Vivid reds, blues and greens in the pile add a welcome burst of color to a landscape locked in shades of gray for so many months. The game heats up and we fly up and down the ice, wheeling and spinning as the puck changes hands.

We are a no-check league, but it doesn't stop some good-natured jostling. My sisters and I can't resist taunting our brother as he skates circles around us, so fast, confident, and graceful on the ice. Secretly, though, we are proud of his skill and we laugh when our dad's team beats us and he comes over to chide us with his favorite line, "Shake hands with a winner." Our hockey friends become an extended winter family, reuniting when the ice is prime. We welcome anyone who wants to play, but one jealous girlfriend finds the game too intense and retreats to dry land with a feigned injury. Sulking on the sidelines, she christens my sisters and me "The Hanson Sisters" after the stars of the cult movie, *Slap Shot*. Although her remarks were probably not made with a compliment in mind, my sisters and I laugh and thank her because we're honored to be compared with real hockey players.

After the game, we break out the lunches, hot cocoa and snacks. Sitting around on coats, rocks and tree stumps, we dissect the game like broadcasters on the Sports Network, reliving the highlights and teasing each other over less-than-stellar moves. It doesn't matter if we're executives, college kids or teenagers, we're all out there for the love of the sport, the camaraderie, and the wonderful memories we created on those picture perfect winter days.

A friend took a photo of my dad with my brother, my sisters and me in our sweats and hockey skates on one of those extraordinary black ice days. Over thirty years later, it still brings back the joy of the game and the boundless freedom of flying across the ice, hockey stick ready, in hot pursuit of the puck. It would have been so easy to just hunker down and ride out the winters inside during those years, but I'm so glad we didn't. The memories from those carefree days and wonderful games have become more precious through the years.

~Susan Winslow

# 11

# Hockey Memories

*Winter is not a season, it's an occupation.*

~Sinclair Lewis

In 1963 when our son was four years old, my wife and I decided that since we lived in Minnesota he should be exposed to hockey. So, we put up sideboards around the back yard and proceeded to flood it. Flooding and waiting for it to freeze was a complicated and time-consuming task. It took a lot of work, patience and maintenance. But, it paid off. Our back yard became a gathering place for the neighborhood kids.

Many cold winter nights, after we had gone to bed, we could hear the swish of skates on the rink. Looking out we would see one of the older kids skating, stick handling and shooting pucks all alone. This young man went on to play hockey in high school, college hockey at the University of Minnesota and professional hockey with the New York Rangers and Hartford Whalers. We like to think that, in some small way, we helped him in his hockey career. His name is Warren Miller.

We moved to another Twin Cities suburb when our son was eight. There was an outdoor rink in our neighborhood, but no indoor rinks nearby. We spent many nights nearly frozen watching little league hockey out in the elements. Many cold Saturday mornings we would hear the front door shut about 6:00 a.m., look out, and see our son heading for the rink with his hockey gear over his shoulder.

The younger kids would have to get to the rink early, before the older kids came and took over. When the older ones arrived, they would still let the younger ones play, but it was harder for the younger kids to get the puck. This actually worked to the younger ones' advantage, but they were not aware of it at the time. Early in the day they could work on stick handling—the art of moving the puck with a hockey stick. When the older kids came, in order to keep up, the younger ones would have to improve their skating ability. Some days our son would only show up for lunch and supper, and to warm up. After thawing out, and with a full stomach, back he would go.

Our son did not go on to an illustrious hockey career, although he played high school and small college hockey. We believe we instilled in him a love of the sport that carries on today. Hockey helped him to build character and learn valuable social skills.

There are very few outdoor hockey rinks in the Twin Cities today. Almost every town in Minnesota has its own indoor rink. Those old days were great, and we have many fond memories of being nearly frozen while watching little league games with friends and neighbors. I hope our grandchildren and great-grandchildren play indoors, but the love of the sport and our desire to watch the next generation might just entice us back to the outside rinks if need be.

~David K. Overlund

# 12

# Hockey Détente

*Hockey is figure skating in a war zone.*
*~Author Unknown*

Growing up in New England in the sixties, every winter our neighborhood's frozen pond was transformed into a war zone. The dividing lines were clearly drawn: boys versus girls, hockey players versus figure skaters. For kids like me who spent all winter on any form of frozen water, the turf battle over this rutted, slushy, stick-imbedded surface was critical. Boys in black hockey skates would flash by, circling the girls in a low-slung crouch, inching closer like a wolf pack. Girls in skating skirts and pom-pom festooned white skates would pirouette and spin in the middle, pretending to ignore the circling pack. When tempers flared, a boy would do a sliding stop in front of a girl, sending up a spray of frozen ice crystals, marking her like a dog. The girls would retaliate by dumping the boys' hockey bags in the snow, or pulling down the goals. The boys accused the girls of chipping the ice with their toe picks, the girls accused the boys of making ruts with their sticks. The battle raged, challenges were hurled:

"Get off the ice, we were here first!"

"You can't tell me what to do. We aren't in Russia you know!"

Ah, Russia. With our preteen minds filled with fallout shelter drill instructions and threats of communist takeovers, Russia loomed large as the great frozen wasteland of oppression. We were familiar with the strategies of a "cold war," which we had been watching play out internationally, as well as a local cold war over the rights to our small, frozen piece of turf. Threats escalated, and no one was winning.

Until one day in the late afternoon when the unimaginable happened.

Fewer and fewer kids were showing up at the pond, victims of the Hong Kong flu, and the hockey players could not stand up a scrimmage with so few boys on the ice. That afternoon, when I looked up from the sidelines, I watched as one of the older boys skated up to me and stopped. He asked me if I wanted to play. To play hockey!

"Me?" I asked. Maybe he had mistaken me for a boy. My hair was tucked up under my ridiculously long stocking cap, the pom-pom of which gently bobbed against the small of my back. No, he couldn't have, I thought, looking down at my figure skates.

"Yeah, you wanna play or not?" he asked, impatiently wiping his nose with the back of a gloved hand. He didn't wait for my answer, but instead handed me an old stick. "Take my little brother's stick. We need a wing."

Then he turned and skated to the center of the ice, not checking to see if I followed. I hastily unlaced my skates halfway down to free my ankles and wrapped the extra length of laces around and around. When I glanced up, my girlfriends' faces stared back at me, their mouths formed into little "O"s. I gripped the stick, feeling tacky from the wrap of old black electrical tape, and skated onto the ice. It felt good, this stick held in front of me like a tripod, skating down low in a crouch, picking up speed... swapping the stick from my left to right hand, back and forth, back and forth. It felt natural.

That afternoon tipped the balance in the "boy versus girl" mind-set; it signaled a change in the dynamics of the frozen pond feud, which had raged for generations. By the time the moon appeared over the frozen pond, some other girls had joined the game and we played as equals. We even got a few begrudging compliments from the guys, noting that we could indeed skate well and that we did know a thing or two about hockey. When the full moon was high and bright in the sky, we shucked off skates, pulled on snow boots, found our castoff skate guards, and trudged along the wooded path towards home, still feeling as if ghost blades were attached to our feet. We never had another mixed game of hockey again, but ever since that day we somehow found more room on that small patch of ice in the woods for all kinds of skaters. It was the beginning of a thaw in the war of the sexes—an era of détente—at least for the time being.

~Lisa Trovillion

# Small Town Hockey

*Every day is a great day for hockey.*
~Mario Lemieux

Minor hockey—those two words conjure up all sorts of images and memories for me.

Allow me to take you back to hockey framed by a simpler time. A time before Tim Hortons' commercials, composite sticks, even artificial ice. Minor hockey that came without the expensive hockey gear and its modern day trappings. Hockey the way it was meant to be played: for the pure fun of it.

I loved going to the local outdoor rink, nestled behind my school, in small town Manitoba—Pinawa, to be precise.

The early 1970s were a simpler era. It was a time that pre-dated satellite TV, where few had cable TV and no one had video games.

On a typical winter afternoon, your mother pushed you out the door to play boot-hockey with the neighbour boys, and then, two hours later, had to coax you back in for supper.

Saturday nights were reserved for watching hockey on the old Sylvania TV (though it was new to us then). We sat on a couch in the den and followed the skilled play of NHLers, like Bobby Orr, Darryl Sittler and Jean Béliveau. But even better than watching hockey, I loved playing Canada's favourite winter sport.

On school days, I recall walking to my neighbourhood outdoor rink, carrying my Sher-Wood stick over my shoulder, the blade shoved through my Bauer skates, laces dangling free.

Coming to the rink, I'd hurriedly shed winter boots in favour of my skates, anticipating which of my friends was already there. This was all done within the confines of an outdoor shack—no indoor changing rooms back then.

Then, there was the exhilaration of being the first one to step onto newly flooded ice, of chasing the puck to the end boards, and then skating into the wind hoping to beat your best friend to the net during impromptu games of shinny.

If you decided to imitate Bobby Hull by taking that risky slap shot, you hoped you hit the mark and that it didn't fly over the steel-mesh netting behind the net, burying itself in the deep snow.

But that kind of thinking is lost on a twelve-year-old boy. We fired those slap shots as hard as we could, thinking only of hitting the back of the mesh—and hoping the blade wouldn't break. Every once in a while an errant shot would fly over the net, and three or four of us would scramble over the boards to find it in the snow. We had no choice—it was the only puck we had.

The best times, though, were the Saturday morning hockey games.

First up was a quick breakfast provided by my mom. Then, while my dad went out to warm the car, I would head down to the basement, collect my gear and stuff it into an old hockey bag—the one with the draw string at the end—and lug it up to the car.

Huddled in the front seat beside my dad, we would drive to the local arena to meet the other dads. Four or five of us would pile into a mid-sized car or station wagon—there were no minivans back then—and in convoy style follow the lead vehicle to the host town.

Sitting in the back seat, I would listen to my teammates recount an overblown story from a previous game or debate strategy for the game yet to be played, overlooking the fact that it was these same guys from the paper mill town that had beaten us so soundly three weeks ago.

All talk would suddenly come to a stop as the convoy pulled into the parking lot. We'd arrive, excited to be playing a formidable rival, one of the best teams in our league. We'd scramble out and head to the back of the car, retrieving our sticks and hockey bags.

Back then, many southern Manitoba towns didn't have arenas, much less artificial ice. The smaller towns only had outdoor rinks, the dressing rooms situated outside resembling big shacks with little heating provided. I recall my father helping me lace up my skates and ensuring I was adequately dressed for the weather.

Some mornings, the temperature hovered at minus twenty degrees Celsius—with the sun shining. The coach made sure everyone played every second or third shift so no one sat too long on the bench and got too cold.

Between periods, off came the skates. My dad would rub my socked feet between his hands, returning a measure of warmth to my semi-frozen toes. Now that I think back, it was a special time between father and son. After the game, regardless whether we won or lost, my dad would come to the dressing room. While I was excitedly recounting a good play or a missed penalty by the referee, he would help me remove my sweaty gear.

Sometimes I would look up and notice that not every boy was as fortunate as I was. Some dads didn't come to the dressing room, preferring to smoke in the lounge and talk to their friends. Sadly, some didn't come out to the games at all.

Once I'd finished dressing, my dad would hand me a couple of dollar bills and I'd rush to the canteen to wait in line for that well-deserved hot dog and Coke.

It's funny that all these years later I can barely remember how many goals I had scored or which line I'd played on, but I can vividly recall my dad patiently listening to an excited twelve-year-old recounting a breakaway while taking bites from his lukewarm hot dog. I was in pure hockey heaven.

But all too soon it was time to head home.

By the time we hit the highway, each one of us would be lost in his own thoughts, interpreting the outcome of the game his own way.

As we retraced our way back home, we would drift off one by one, tired from the exertion of the game.

Then, after being dropped off at home, I would run in the back door and up the stairs, into the arms of my smiling mom, eager to recount the highlights once again and leaving Dad to carry my hockey bag inside.

And the next week I'd be ready to do it all over again.

~Robert J. Stermscheg

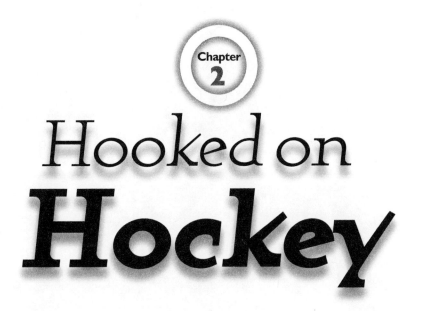

# Hooked on Hockey

## Game On!

# Shooting Star

*Being the best that you can be is possible only if
your desire to be a champion is greater than your fear of failure.*
~Sammy Lee

My husband Manny and I went to as many Chicago Blackhawks games as we could in the mid-1980s. We both loved the fast pace and physicality of the game. Manny has always said that for his money hockey is the best spectator sport out there. I have to agree. One of the teams at the top of Chicago fans' hate list was the Minnesota North Stars. It could get very ugly when they came up against the Hawks, but it made for an exciting game.

Fast forward ten years and we were living in Texas with our two children Dominic and Francesca. It had been decided the Lone Star State needed a hockey team, and guess which franchise they bought? Yes, the Minnesota North Stars became the Dallas Stars. In our hearts we would always be Blackhawks fans, but we had to embrace a hockey team in Texas. It was a piece of home. That was our rationale for buying season tickets that first year. Different name… different team!

Our eight-year-old son Dominic had never seen a hockey game and Manny decided the games would be a father/son bonding time. At the first game, Dom was hooked. He was amazed how fast a bunch of guys on skates maneuvered a little round disc up and down the ice. He was determined to stay until the end. Since it was a school night, I told Manny not to come home too late. It was the third period, a close game and Manny tried to convince Dom it was time to leave. "Dad," he said. "We can't leave now! No one else is." Dom won out.

Dominic loved wearing his Stars jersey even though it came to his knees. Coming through the turnstile one night, all decked out, he was noticed by one of the attendants. He asked Dom if he wanted to go down on the ice between periods and shoot the puck in a contest. He was too stunned (and a little scared) to answer. He was a shy boy who liked to observe things going on around him and never wanted to be the center of attention. He stood frozen as Manny jumped in with both feet for him. "Sure," said Manny. "He'd love to." Dom was relieved when Manny told him he would take him to the ice after the first period and be there the whole time.

Towards the end of the first period, Manny walked Dom down to the ice, all the while telling him how much fun it would be. Dom gingerly took his place on the ice and looked small as the youngest competitor out there. The three contestants were introduced and the games began!

Standing ten feet from an open net, they each took their shot. Everyone was successful, but the crowd cheered loudest when Dom took his shot and made it. A piece of plywood covered the front of the net for the second attempt on goal. The target would be a twelve-inch slot cut in the center of the board, and the contestants would stand at the face-off circle twenty feet away. The first competitor took his shot: no goal. Anticipation grew in the crowd as the second competitor lined up to shoot. Again, no goal. The crowd was in a frenzy as Dom lined up to shoot. They were with him. Dom took his shot and everyone watched as the puck slid easily through the slot. Goal! The little man in the Stars jersey made it, and the crowd went crazy. Dom was amazed at their reaction.

There would be two more shots on goal. One from the blue line sixty feet away and one from center ice about ninety feet away. Dom's competitors would not come anywhere close to the goal with their two attempts. To the delight of the crowd, Dom came within inches of the goal with each shot he took.

Dom didn't just win the prize that night. For a moment in time this shy little boy had the undivided attention of an entire arena of hockey fans. He was a Dallas "star!"

~Catherine Pendola

# The Best Seat in the House

*Get your children and small pets away from the TV,*
*'cause the NHL is in your living room!*
*~Doug McLeod*

Perhaps my love affair with broadcasting booths, and one in particular—Foster Hewitt's famous gondola at Maple Leaf Gardens—began when I was six or seven years old. My father, Leslie McFarlane, was a guest in the gondola one night in the mid-thirties. It was the night the Chicago Blackhawks came to town with half a dozen American-born players in their lineup and gave the Leafs quite a battle before losing 3-2.

I'm not certain why my dad was invited to be in the gondola that night, participating in the radio version of Hockey Night in Canada. Perhaps it was because he had a reputation as a skilled writer of hockey fiction. He was also engaged at the time in writing many of the Hardy Boys books under the name Franklin W. Dixon for $100 per book and no royalties. But few people knew about that. When I told a couple of my teenage friends that my dad was F.W. Dixon they looked at me strangely. One of them said, "Oh, sure. And my dad's Turk Broda."

Perhaps, subconsciously, listening to him on the radio that night, I considered the possibility of someday following him along the cat-walk that led to that mysterious and magical place where Foster Hewitt made Saturday night the most exciting night of the week. Growing up, along with millions of Canadians, I thrilled to Foster's descriptions of the exploits of Syl Apps, Gordie Drillon and Red Horner. The Leafs were my heroes and I had the Bee Hive Corn Syrup photos to prove it.

One year I wore an old blue hockey jersey to my games of shinny on the local pond in Whitby, Ontario. I asked my mother to cut out a number—two numbers actually, a one and a zero—from a piece of white felt and I had her stitch them side by side on the back. Number 10 was for Apps—my favourite player.

One night, my dad said, "Come with me, you're going to meet one of the great stars of hockey." He took me by the hand to a smoke-filled hall in downtown Whitby. In this hall filled with large men puffing on cigars, my eyes stinging from the vile smoke, I met Syl Apps, captain of the Leafs. He wore a huge overcoat and a fedora. Over the hubbub I asked him for his autograph. He looked down and smiled, then signed my scrap of paper. When I looked at it I was thrilled. "Dad, Dad, look! He signed, 'Best wishes, Syl Apps.' He gave me two extra words." Many years later, I found myself sitting next to Apps in the Gardens' press box and he chuckled when I reminded him of that night in Whitby and how meaningful those extra words were to a young fan.

In the thirties and forties, the hockey broadcasts on radio were mesmerizing. At house parties, the men gathered in the living room around the radio while the women chatted in the kitchen. The party began when the game was over and Foster had selected his three stars. I enjoyed the intermissions, featuring hockey-wise regulars around the Hot Stove, men like Wes McKnight (later to become my boss at CFRB radio in Toronto) Elmer Ferguson, Bobby Hewitson and Baldy Cotton. I envied these men with the authoritative voices. They got in to see all the Leafs games… for free! I was even more impressed when my dad told me the Hot Stove Leaguers actually were paid to sit around a microphone and talk hockey. What a fascinating way to make a living. Even a part-time living.

Perhaps the broadcasting seed was planted then. If I failed to become another Apps, perhaps I could become an announcer! In the meantime, wearing my ragged blue sweater, I skated circles on the pond.

In time I would get to play three years of junior hockey where I would learn that checking Jean Béliveau or scoring a goal against Glenn Hall were daunting tasks. Then followed four years of U.S. college hockey at St. Lawrence University (where I set some records that still stand six decades later) and one brief tryout (I had to ask for it) with the Chicago Blackhawks. By then I had realized I was never going make it to the NHL so I turned my attention to broadcasting.

After two years with a TV station in Schenectady, New York (not much hockey there, folks, so we started a team called the Schenectady Generals and played outdoors on a rinky-dink rink), I put all my belongings in a U-Haul and moved with my family to Toronto. Surely I was ready for a role, any kind of a role, with Hockey Night in Canada.

No such luck. In 1959, there was an audition for the host's job and I was asked to try out. My interview with King Clancy went quite well I thought (who wouldn't look good talking to Clancy?), but Ward Cornell got the job. "You're too young," I was told. That same week, there was a stunning offer from CBS in New York. I was asked to conduct interviews (on skates) and handle commentary for CBS on the NHL Game of the Week. "We're looking for a young announcer, a fresh face," they told me. "And one who can skate." God bless America! I became the first Canadian to work NHL games on a U.S. network and was paid $200 per game. I commuted to the games from Toronto and was able to keep my job with CFRB, a CBS affiliate.

Four years later, there was another opening on Hockey Night in Canada. In those days, Bill Hewitt worked with a different commentator each week, usually a sportswriter. Somehow a decision was made to add a permanent man to the crew and I got the job.

For the next seventeen years I had the best seat in the house—a chair in the gondola—sitting next to broadcast legends Bill and Foster Hewitt and providing commentary to Bill Hewitt's play-by-play.

I chuckle when I recall some of the oddball things that were said and done in those early days. Prior to my very first game, my boss stuck his head in the gondola, called my name, held up three fingers and said, "Brian, I think you should speak three times a period. That'll be a nice balance between you and Bill." I was stunned. I couldn't believe he'd set a quota on the number of comments I was allowed to make. Sorry, boss, but I broke that edict in the first five minutes of my first game.

At the end of each game, I left the gondola and hustled to a place on the catwalk high over the crowd. There I would interview Foster Hewitt and ask him for his three star selections. Perched on the catwalk, above the fans in the green seats, fans would often crane their necks and hoot and holler at us. Occasionally, I'd hear someone shout, "Jump, McFarlane, jump!" Years later, when Gary Dornhoefer joined our crew, and made his debut on the catwalk, he was appalled to hear the fans urge me to jump. "I can't believe they taunt you like that," he said.

I said, "Gary, broadcasters, like referees, have to be thick-skinned."

Dornhoefer was even more shaken during his second trip to the catwalk. The fans below ignored me and began shouting, "Jump, Dornhoefer, jump!"

I told him later, "Gary, that's nothing. Years ago, I was making my way through the crowd one night when a guy yelled at me, 'McFarlane, you're the reason I come to the games. I can't stand listening to you at home.' I gave the loudmouth fan a big wave, indicating he'd come up with a good line, a line I used at banquet appearances at least a hundred times."

I witnessed some amazing sights from the old gondola. How we thrilled to the introduction of color television, preceded by the installation of huge banks of lights to illuminate the ice and to make the colorcasts a spectacle. Then there was instant replay. How we gaped at our monitors the first time a goal was scored and seconds later it was magically replayed on our screens. Later, we were able to bring our viewers highlights from games at the Montreal Forum — all within seconds. People everywhere watched in awe and said, "How in the world do they do that? It's amazing."

Sometimes, amazing things happened on the ice below. Hunched forward on my chair, I helped describe some of the greatest events in Toronto's hockey history. One night, February 7, 1976, Darryl Sittler set a record of ten points in a game. His mark has lasted almost forty years.

Ten years earlier, when there were only six teams and 120 NHL players, there was a dramatic Stanley Cup triumph of the Leafs. Imlach's team of old-timers stunned the Montreal Canadiens in the 1967 finals. It was the end of an era because the NHL was about to double in size and many of the Leafs would not be back the following season.

I often wonder how many people are able to say, "I was at the Gardens that night." It's a dwindling number—a few hundred perhaps—while the number of fans who've never witnessed a Leafs Cup win keeps rising—in the multimillions.

There was no better vantage point than the gondola to appreciate the magic of Orr, Hull, Howe and Béliveau, the antics of Eddie Shack, the artistry of Keon, Kelly and Mahovlich, the awesome strength of Tim Horton, the magnificent goaltending of Bower, Sawchuk, Plante.

All too soon they were gone. All too soon, so was I.

~Brian McFarlane

# Hockey Heart Ties

*A daughter is a little girl who grows up to be a friend.*
~Author Unknown

"Let's go Rangers!" my cousin, dad, uncle, and I chanted from our seats all the way up against the back wall of Madison Square Garden. I must have been around eight years old at the time, but I still remember that night like it was yesterday.

We were bundled up and giddy with excitement as we piled into our family station wagon and headed into New York City for a great night of family, love, fun, and ice hockey. I think it was the second game I had ever been to, and I knew this would be great because my cousin was my best friend, and her dad was my dad's twin. We both looked up to our fathers, longing to bond with them over something no one could take away from us. I'd soon find out that ice hockey was exactly what would always tie us together.

We didn't have on T-shirts or team attire, but we knew who we were rooting for and couldn't wait to get there. Two little girls on an adventure with their daddies was just what a Saturday night called for. The car ride seemed short. We arrived in the center of Manhattan, parked and trekked to MSG. Other fans bounced out of their cars and walked the streets wearing hats, sweatshirts, and jerseys. It felt like a mass of red, white, and blue, and the energy that pumped through our veins was indescribable.

I felt butterflies in my stomach as we moved with the other happy fans. I had a tie with these people, these strangers, and I began to understand what it meant to be a fan. I was only a little girl, but I was a Rangers fan too.

As we entered the stadium, I wondered if we'd ever find our seats. We passed stands of food and memorabilia before riding up escalators that took us up flight after flight after flight. When we finally reached those coveted seats where we'd share an unforgettable night with our dads, it hit me. I was here to watch the Rangers, and it felt so cool.

For dinner, we got hot dogs and soda, which was a very special treat because neither of our households allowed the sugary drink. And to our delight, we each received a foam finger to wave in the air while we cheered. Who would have thought that an overpriced red and white hand could provide us with such utter joy?

As the game went on, we bounced in our seats as we watched skaters race around the rink working their hardest to put the puck in the goal. Sometimes, my eyes couldn't keep up with the puck. Even if I blinked, the puck would no longer be where I thought it was the moment before.

We booed loudly when a goal was scored by the other team or when a referee made a bad call. We cheered even louder when the rest of the stadium cheered. Sometimes, we didn't even know why we were cheering at all.

The best moments were when the Rangers scored a goal. The entire stadium would leap to its feet, and there we were, two little girls, chanting alongside our fathers with sheer and uncontrollable happiness because our team was winning, and our team scored a goal.

I couldn't tell you who the New York Rangers played that night, but I can tell you that they won. It was the joy of sharing this experience with my family that I'll always hold near to my heart. Ice hockey brings back amazing memories for me, and it ties one of my heartstrings to my dad's.

Now that I'm much older, it's such a pleasure to sit in front of the TV and watch games together. It was an even better feeling when I brought my father to a game last year. Even though we lost that night, it was still a memory that I'll treasure. We may both be adults now, but I'll always be my dad's little ice hockey-watching girl. And ice hockey will always tie us together no matter where we are in our lives. It always has and always will.

~Amanda Romaniello

# Winning with Gretzky

*You miss 100% of the shots you never take.*
~Wayne Gretzky

Sunday, April 18, 1999 was Hall of Fame inductee Wayne Gretzky's final official game with the New York Rangers. He would retire from an illustrious career at the end of the season. That day would also turn out to be a memorable one in my son's life... one that we'll never forget.

My son Spencer was no stranger to hockey. He was a member of two evening pickup teams, playing only when the ice was available, sometimes at 3:00 or 4:00 a.m. We often crossed paths while I was going to work and he was returning from a late-night game.

Earlier in the hockey season, Spencer, an avid Rangers fan and season ticket holder, was selected from thousands of hockey fans at Madison Square Garden to be a contestant in a hockey shootout. His 6' 7" frame made him stand out in the crowd and he was chosen by a member of the Rangers' promotions staff to be a participant in the contest. He would attempt to shoot a hockey puck into a small circle on the goal line from center ice, hoping to win the coveted prize of a brand new Mercedes Benz. Accuracy would be the key to winning.

Spencer's first attempt to qualify for the sports car was right on target. The puck slid into the circle as if guided by fate. At the time he had no idea how many other contestants would be competing against him. When he had successfully left the qualification round, he was guaranteed a phone call and two tickets for the night of the final shootout, on the last game of the season. At that time Wayne Gretzky hadn't yet announced his retirement, which ironically, was to occur that same evening.

Spencer, a firefighter, had the backing of the entire department and encouragement from his buddies. If anyone can do it, he could, was the consensus. I was nervous for him, hoping he would at least shoot the puck near the circle and not be affected by the overzealous sell-out crowd. If the puck flew into the stands, he would never live it down.

The time had come. During intermission, Spencer and two other contestants were brought into the center of the rink and handed five pucks. Beads of sweat formed on my son's forehead. He effortlessly made the first two out of five shots, but missed the others. The crowd cheered. The second contestant missed all five shots. The insensitive crowd booed. The third contestant missed the first three shots but luckily made the last two. Everyone gasped! It was a dead heat, which called for a shootout. My nails had already been chewed down to the cuticles. I placed my shaking hands over my eyes, wanting to look, yet dreading to see my son lose the contest. A roar broke out from the arena when Spencer's name was announced. Stamping feet and clapping hands ensued as the captivated audience rooted for the popular firefighter.

The best of three shots would win the car. Spencer was up first. He took a deep breath and fired the puck. Miraculously he got two of three shots in the circle. Next up was his competitor. He made only one shot. The Garden exploded. The sounds were deafening.

Flashbulbs popped and pandemonium erupted. Hockey fans chanted Spencer's name, much like they had done earlier for Wayne Gretzky. My son came up a winner, keeping his cool on the ice, unlike his mother, who was falling apart in the stands. In this, the most sought after season game, Wayne Gretzky and Spencer's name were mentioned in the same sentence and in the news. They shared the spotlight, winners on that unforgettable Sunday.

To be in attendance at this final game alongside one of the greatest living hockey players in the world would have been enough of a prize for my son. To be on the ice and take part in this celebration along with the Rangers players in the locker room was an extraordinary experience. I'm proud to say that Firefighter Maran had nerves of steel and the talent of a professional hockey player. He won the Mercedes and received a true hero's welcome at the firehouse the next day. What he treasures most was the handshake from his idol, Wayne Gretzky, and not the car. What I treasure most was seeing his winning smile and a sigh of relief.

~Irene Maran

# Welcome Back Clark

*Welcome back, your dreams were your ticket out.*
*Welcome back, to that same old place that you laughed about.*
~Welcome Back, Kotter *theme song*

I have the greatest job on the planet. I get to perform live music for twenty thousand diehard fans every home game for the Toronto Maple Leafs. My name is Jimmy Holmstrom and I am the Maple Leafs organist. It is a job that I perform with enthusiasm, pride and respect. I have executed my duties for twenty-five years now and I have never missed a game. Every night is filled with unexpected, unscripted excitement. I try to sense the feeling of the crowd and anticipate the movement of the game and supply appropriate music.

One particular night in March 1996, the city of Toronto erupted in elation. Cliff Fletcher, General Manager of the team, had traded a draft pick for the return of former Leafs captain Wendel Clark. The Kelvington Cowboy/Captain Crunch was coming back! The Hound Line, with Russ Courtnall and Gary Leeman, was long gone. Clark had new line mates to gel with: Sundin, Gilmour, Domi, Kypreos and Muller to name a few.

During the pre-game intermission I played the Thin Lizzy tune "The Boys Are Back in Town." In an earlier interview Wendel had admitted to being a nervous, eleven-year veteran rookie. The crowd was so excited about his return that there were no line-ups at the concessions during the warm-up. The seats were full!

As the team left the dressing room and skated out to the ice I turned up AC/DC's "Back in Black." The crowd began cheering and continued nonstop throughout the warm-up. They sustained it right up to puck drop, the beginning of the Dallas Stars-Toronto Maple Leafs game. On Wendel's first shift he threw a big hit. The Gardens fans went crazy! The crowd was cheering insanely as Jiggs McDonald, the TV announcer, declared "Guess who's on the ice?" He later pronounced, "The crowd will let you know every time Clark takes the ice." It seemed that Wendel was hot-wired to the city of Toronto.

Fletcher was hoping for results from his trade for Wendel. Well, he got those results immediately; "Clark to Gilmour to Clark—HE SCORES!" I had to stop any music when I got the audio signal, but I couldn't hear my long-time friend and associate in game operations Paul Morris as he tried to announce the goal over the pandemonium!

The crowd never let up throughout the entire game, cheering on every Clark shift. You just don't see crowds reacting to players like that anymore. As we approached the midway mark of the game we all seemed to sense we were witnessing something extraordinary, a game we would never forget. When Clark stepped onto the ice in the late stages of the game there was an eerie quiet in the rink. It was as though everyone realized just how special it was to have the heart and soul back on our team.

I decided this was the moment.

Before the game, I had prepared a special song for Wendel's return. It was time. I put in the CD and played the television theme song, *Welcome Back, Kotter*. The music filled the arena... but only for a second. As one, over seventeen thousand in attendance suddenly rose to their feet and cheered wildly! After a moment the cameras focused in on Wendel. He gave the impression that he was taken aback, which inspired us to even greater adulations. The officials skated away from the face-off circle and leaned on the boards. They too were caught up in the moment. The game froze. We all stood together and as if for the first time actually comprehended the tribute.

It was a phenomenon. The crowd's spontaneous cheering continued until the last lyric ended with "Back here where we need ya." A close-up of Wendel showed his eyes glassing over, and we fans all knew that he loved us as much as we did him. Even some press members in the gondola, along with me, were caught off guard and perhaps humbled by the spectacle.

I could never have imagined a moment like this. It was a case of preparation meeting opportunity with the stars aligned. After the delay, everyone collected themselves and the game resumed. Even though the Leafs won a shutout victory, the score was anticlimactic. The night unfolded as if it were a movie script! Goalie Felix Potvin got the shutout, but was deemed the second star of the game. This game was about the return of our captain. It was the return of desire. It was a good ole Saskatchewan boy "kickin it" again for the blue and white! It was the return of hope for another Stanley Cup run and yes, that year we made the playoffs.

Wendel Clark, the heart of the team, was delighted to be home where he was treasured, cherished, respected and most of all belonged. He was named the first star.

For all of us, it was a game we'll never forget. The night was a magical, electrifying and historic moment in time.

~Jimmy Holmstrom

# Hockey, You Had Me at Face-Off

*The manner of giving is worth more than the gift.*
~Pierre Corneille, Le Menteur

The "hockey stick present." According to Urban Dictionary, it's "a gift given another that is really a present that the giver wants for him/herself." I received my first hockey stick present the Christmas after I was married. My husband gave me a sleeping bag. To me, "camping" means staying at a hotel that doesn't have room service. I thanked him warmly, but added that I wasn't really interested in camping. "No problem," he replied quickly. "I'll use it myself. Mine is pretty worn out."

I recently received a variation of the hockey stick present from my son. He had just graduated from college in New Jersey, where he had developed an interest in college and professional ice hockey. For Mother's Day, he handed me a ticket to a Washington Capitals' hockey game; he even included an Ovechkin T-shirt.

Just as I am not a fan of camping, I am also not a fan of watching team sporting events. In fact, I'd much rather be watching a Broadway show. Like all good parents, I sat through my children's many sports activities: baseball, soccer, and the most boring of all, high school crew. But voluntarily attend a professional sporting event? Well, football is just too silly for words and a dentist's drill sounds better to me than that annoying "squeak, squeak, thud, thud" of basketball.

But what could I say? My son explained that the ticket was expensive and hard to come by because it was for a playoff game. I wasn't sure what it was a playoff for (I later learned it was for the Stanley Cup), but I feigned enthusiasm. Then he showed me that he had a ticket to the game as well. And I understood. It wasn't a true hockey stick present because he didn't want my ticket for himself. But it was similar—what he wanted was someone to go to the game with him!

Everything changed the minute I entered the Verizon Center and was engulfed in a sea of red hockey jerseys. I felt the crackling excitement of the fans and the friendliness that comes with a shared passion. And I soon discovered that hockey fans are simply a different breed of sports fans. They cheer louder and with more energy than any other fans. Total strangers become instant friends as soon as they sit down. My son proudly told everyone sitting around us that this was my first game and a Mother's Day present from him. I was welcomed to the fold.

And then I heard the sounds of hockey: the swooshing of the skates; the thwack of the stick hitting the puck; the bang when the players hit the glass; and, most amazing of all, the siren when someone "lights the lamp" and scores. And sometime during the game, they showed the Capitals' *Unleash the Fury* video—a montage of scenes from sports movies designed to whip up the crowd, and the team, even more. True, hockey is just a variation on the theme of "keep away" found in most other team sports. But it's played on ice! I have enormous respect for anyone who can stand up on ice skates, let alone play a game. I was mesmerized.

The game was thrilling! Sadly, the Caps didn't win. But I did—I became hooked on hockey. Now I follow goal counts for Carlson, Backstrom and the "Great Eight" Ovechkin. I read hockey blogs like Russian Machine Never Breaks. I've only missed one game since that first one. I even watch the games on TV when no one is at home and I scream all by myself. And I know what a power play and a PK (penalty kill) are!

And most importantly, that first hockey game ticket turned out to be the "Stanley Cup" of presents—it gave me a way to bridge the transition into an adult relationship with my son. He and I have a shared passion—we talk and watch and cheer hockey. He even got me to try ice-skating with him. I don't get far from the rail while he skates all around me, but I look great in my Washington Capitals sweatshirt. And for Christmas, not only did we give our dog a Capitals' collar and a road kill penguin (mascot of the Caps' rival team), but my son and I unknowingly gave each other identical *Unleash the Fury* T-shirts!

I may get another hockey stick present some day... certainly I hope I do!

~Moira Rose Donohue

# 20

# Hockey
# with a Side of Ice

*I like vending machines, because snacks are better when they fall.*
*If I buy a candy bar at the store, oftentimes*
*I will drop it so that is achieves its maximum flavor potential.*
*~Mitch Hedberg*

here's much to love about the typical hockey arena. The speed of the skaters, the roar of the crowd, the pulsating music and the dazzling light show are all part of the excitement. There is one aspect about the hockey experience, however, that often gets overlooked by many hockey fans. But I'll bet it's as much a part of the fun for you as it is for me. I'm talking about hockey arena food! Sure, you won't find the finest cuisine at a hockey rink, and your average cardiologist may have a minor infarction just reading this story, but you don't have to look very far to find something to keep your body warm and your taste buds tingling when you go to the arena.

For a three-year stint in the late 1980s, I was lucky enough to be the arena announcer for the United States Hockey League's North Iowa Huskies. These talented nineteen- and twenty-year-old skaters played their hearts out in front of sparse crowds in a tin building on the frigid North Iowa Fairgrounds. There were times during a deep, dark Iowa winter when it was actually colder inside the building than out, but the concession stand kept the crowd and the employees toasty warm with delicious, snappy, Iowa-bred hot dogs in warm buns.

Even now, I can almost get a whiff of the steam that rose from between my hands as I tore into the hot, silver wrapper to get to the delectable flavor inside. Many a time I nearly missed announcing a penalty call due to my culinary adventures, but somehow I always managed to blurt out: "At 4:13 of the third period, two minute minor for interference on Sioux City's #23, Edgar 'The Fudgie' McFlugie." Now, try saying THAT with a mouthful of mustard, bread and banana peppers. Seems like I was always lucky enough to choke out the words over the arena's cranky PA system just as was I swallowing my last bite.

My travels have taken me all over the upper Midwest since those days long ago, but mostly I've spent time here in my home state of Minnesota, and that means I've had a chance to see lots and lots of hockey games and enjoy some great food along the way. I've watched some thrilling matchups in Mankato, for example, where for years I've stood cheering on the Mankato West High School Scarlets to many a victory, all while enjoying the crisp nachos at All Seasons Arena (ASA). The ASA, by the way, is where they're quite generous with the melted cheese, something you'd have to expect here in the land of Minnesota nice. Add to that one of the tallest and tastiest cups of hockey arena coffee you'll find anywhere, and you've just discovered a little slice of heaven right here in the state of hockey.

The MSU Mavericks, one of the best mid-sized Division One hockey teams in the nation, call the Verizon Wireless Center home. I, however, prefer to call the facility the "Dough Dome" in homage to the wickedly wonderful, salty and sensational soft pretzel that you'll find there on game nights. One of those babies and a large cup of Vinnie's Shaved Ice is enough to make even the toughest Maverick fan forget an overtime loss to the despised Minnesota Golden Gophers.

If you move on up to the pro ranks in my neck of the woods, you'll find just about any kind of food you want at St. Paul's Xcel Energy Center, where you can enjoy Minnesota Wild hockey and some truly good eats. The upscale patron can feast on the good stuff like yellowfin tuna and Yukon Gold mashed potatoes. My tastes, though, run a bit more toward average arena fare. On my last visit the menu consisted of an ice-cold cola, the Wild Dog smothered in mustard and onions, nachos and cheese with jalapenos, and the endless supply of popcorn in the souvenir bucket. You'd be quite proud of me—I only went back for a refill once.

There's more to enjoy about hockey than just great food of course. Ice arenas are just cool places to be in general, regardless of whether the venue is high school, college, amateur or pro. Who doesn't feel the excitement when seeing the players' slashing skates, punishing checks into the boards and lightning fast slap shots? I've come to appreciate good defensive play just as much as an aggressive offense with a line that can put up points. Hat tricks are fun too… but they're even better when the hat is of the plastic souvenir variety, filled with hot, melted cheese, suitable for dipping! You could say a night at the hockey arena is something I enjoy, but I prefer to think of it as something I will always love, with *relish*.

~Mark Spangler

# 21

# Pass the Puck!

*No one can whistle a symphony. It takes a whole orchestra to play it.*
*~H.E. Luccock*

I could barely skate, knew next to nothing about the game and couldn't really follow the puck during a game.... and not just on TV, but live! Still, after moving to Toronto from California and watching my son Jack get seriously into hockey, the day soon came when the other hockey dads, not knowing how little I knew, looked at me and asked if I was going to "ante up" and do some coaching for house league. Wanting to fit right in, I heard myself saying "Sure!"

At the beginning my son had to constantly explain the rules to me, to his embarrassment. Heck, I didn't even know what a "shift" was. Still, I loved being with Jack and spending that time with him and the other kids on the team. And along the way something occurred to me while I watched the boys play. Something that ended up making me a pretty good coach. I think *because* I didn't know anything it was relatively easy for me to see the most important aspect of the game: passing the puck.

Soon I was known by that trademark. I was forever drilling it into my players, whether they were quite accomplished or had just started the game. "Pass the puck! Pass the puck!" Over and over, game after game, I was relentless. As far as I could tell, it overshadowed every other aspect of the game.

Let me explain.

House league teams have many different levels of players because of two rules. Number one—everyone who wants to play gets equal ice time. Number two—in order to play on the elite Select teams, you *had* to play on a house league team. With such a disparity of expertise, there were always certain players who were much, much better than other players. To many of these guys this meant that they could be stars, getting the puck and taking it all the way up the ice and attempting to score whenever they had the chance. These players were our "prima donnas" and sometimes they were more than a little difficult to get through to. Very often they thought they were better than they actually were.

As my son and I watched the NHL games on TV, I was struck by the passing. When it was good, the team did well—when it wasn't, they didn't. Either way these guys passed the puck all the time. When I brought this argument into the locker room, I knew the "stars" on the team weren't really listening, and with the equal ice time rule, there wasn't much recourse for me. If they didn't want to pass, there wasn't much I could do about it. Nevertheless, I pushed my mantra.

I remember one night a new player on our team had come to me before the game and was concerned because his grandparents were in from out of town and were in the stands. He told me he had never even had the chance to score a goal because the "star" on his line just never passed the puck. I told him that this player was always thinking he could score alone, but rarely did. I said that the next time the "star" started up the ice he should simply skate as fast as he could behind him and stop in front of the net and wait for an inevitable rebound. Three shifts into the game he got his very first goal! After the game he brought his grandparents back to meet me. I can still see the smiles and pride emanating from them all!

Gradually my teams saw that passing was indeed the key and that the more they passed, the more they scored, and perhaps even better, the more they looked like real hockey players. They loved that they could actually frustrate the other team by passing back and forth and keeping control of the puck. I even found a way to get through to some of my "stars." I got them to play a little game (after they scored a few times of course, that is). The idea was to see who could get one of the novices to score by passing to them at the last moment. They ended up loving this because all the good players in our league knew each other well; many of the opponents in house league were often teammates on the all-star, Select team. They liked being able to tease a buddy after the game by saying, "Hey, you mean that new kid scored on you guys?"

It's been close to ten years since I first came to Canada from sunny California and the dad who can't even skate has coached many teams, several of them to league championships. What I have found is this. The kids have the most fun in house league, not in competitive hockey. And it's good-natured fun. Hockey at its best. It's only about the game, nothing else. There are more laughs, closer scores, no hard feelings and nobody really cares who wins. Because of the equal ice time rule and the absence of checking, nobody is left out and no one gets hurt.

I've also found that the spectators—usually only parents—seem to love the house league games the most too. There's no overzealousness from the stands, like in the more competitive games, and the overall atmosphere is lighter and more enjoyable. Hockey is, and always should be, first and foremost, a game, and games should be fun! Fun to play and fun to watch.

Just remember—"PASS THE PUCK!"

~Mark Ettlinger

# Got Teeth?

*You're not really a hockey player until you've lost a few teeth.*
~Bill Gadsby

"Brrrr," I said to my husband Jeff as we hurried toward the Scottrade Center, home of all our Stanley Cup dreams. Despite chill-to-the-bone temperatures and winds that chafed on contact, we couldn't wait to watch our beloved St. Louis Blues play. Finally inside, we went our separate ways, but not before Jeff offered me a winning smile.

"See you after practice," he said. "If I get a puck, I'll give it to one of the kids. Always kids down by the ice, you know."

"I do know," I answered, smiling back.

Now I really wasn't patronizing him. It's just that we had this conversation every game, about pucks and practice and kids down by the ice. Still, I loved that hockey gave him such joy. He especially liked the pre-game drills, and we always arrived a good thirty minutes early so he could observe rink-side before joining me in our upper-bowl seats. As I settled in upstairs, I caught sight of Jeff below. I could well envision the twinkle in his eye as he watched the team rehearse their dekes and slap shots. There was an ease to him now that hadn't been present an hour before, when he was fraught with worry over his stressful job. Hockey was already working its magic.

We were truly a hooked-on-hockey family. While none of us had ever played the sport, we had held Blues season tickets for many years. We'd been fans since the Brett Hull era, fallen in love with Kelly Chase, and counted our lucky stars when we were blessed with a half-season of Wayne Gretzky. There was something about hockey that even I found enticing. Though not a fan by any means before I married my sports-crazy husband, I now couldn't wait to attend a game. I loved the international feel of it all, of hearing two national anthems sung when the Blues played a Canadian team. I loved pee-wee hockey at period break, the shimmer of the ice, the thwack of the puck against glass and how our whole arena of impassioned fans broke into a silly power-play dance when the opposing team committed a penalty. But there was one small thing that had always given me pause: some of the players' startling lack of teeth.

"It's kind of a badge of honor, Mom," remarked my older son one day in his penalty-for-roughing voice. "Those guys are thinking about scoring goals, not about losing their teeth."

"It's part of the game," concurred my younger son, though with slightly more sympathy than his brother. "But I can see how those missing teeth might bother you, Mom."

Bother, indeed.

As someone who'd been involved in a long-ago car accident that had resulted in enough dental work and jaw surgery to put me in the maxillofacial Hall of Fame, I guess you could say I was obsessed with teeth. I loved a full, beautiful set of them, and the hockey moves that proved detrimental to those pearly whites—elbowing, boarding, high-sticking, to name a few—made me a wee bit squeamish. "I don't reward bad behavior," I often told my boys during particularly vile fights on the ice, when everyone else was cheering wildly and I would sit waiting for the referees to intervene. I was a mom, after all, and I didn't think fighting set a good example.

Not that my boys shared my sentiment. No, they just indulged me, all the while shouting things like: "Hit 'em again!" "What? They started it!" "Five-Minute Major? No way!"

Not that my favorite usher, Christine, echoed my sentiment either. "There's no whining in hockey, baby," she told me the night we first spoke. "I see you here every game, all bundled up, not complaining about the cold. Shoot, that's the sign of a good fan. That's what we do."

Not that my older son's favorite player, Keith "Big Walt" Tkachuk, could relate to my squeamishness whatsoever, yet he was living proof that my worries at least had merit. One of our team's most celebrated stars, Tkachuk was a tough-it-out forward who had recently retired, though not before suffering serious facial injuries in his last year, the result of a flying puck that cost him five teeth and infinite trips to the dentist. Ever the professional, he'd scored a goal for his efforts on that play, but as I later watched highlights on the news, I couldn't help feeling his pain. Certainly, I knew what he faced. There would be root canals and implants, bite problems and chewing difficulties, not to mention significant jaw involvement. I hated that he would be ending his fine career minus his five front teeth.

Surprisingly, however, it was Big Walt's injury that made me realize why I loved hockey so much. The understanding came during a game when the Blues were honoring Tkachuk for his recent Hall of Fame induction. From out on the ice, he waved to the crowd, and as Jeff and I saw him on the Jumbotron, Jeff turned to me and said, "Hey look, hon. Walt's got teeth again!"

"Oh my gosh," I replied, doing a quick double take. "He does!"

Big Walt was, in fact, sporting his new pearly whites, but I hadn't even noticed! It dawned on me then that maybe what I had focused on all these many months when I'd seen him on the news or featured at games wasn't his lack of teeth, after all. Maybe what had caught my attention was how his blue eyes sparkled with love for his sport, how his dedication and can-do attitude seemed to touch every fan. Sure, his toothless grin had been on display for all the world to see, but it was his larger-than-life smile that had captured our hearts.

"Brrrr," I said to Jeff as we left the arena, wind whipping through our coats at every turn. Finally inside our car, we cranked on the heat, our conversation still peppered with hockey. There had been some awesome moments, some thrills and spills, and end-to-end action that had delighted. There had been laughter and high-fives, Christine's warm hug, and the playfulness of her fellow usher, Ophelia, as she delivered her usual fist-bump hello. Somehow, it never seemed to matter who I was, what I did, or what kind of day I'd had. When I entered that arena at game time, it felt like coming home.

Which I think, in the end, is what hockey does for us; it makes fans feel like family. I'm grateful for the experience of that, and to be able to share that experience with my husband and sons. I'm grateful for our boys on the ice, who not only make the whole experience possible, but who give us their all, every game, every night, for their camaraderie and sportsmanship, and okay, even for their occasional "bad behavior" — with or without teeth!

~Theresa Sanders

# Hooked on Hockey

## FAN-tastic!

# All Hockey, All the Time

*How beautiful a day can be when kindness touches it!*
~George Elliston

"Close your eyes, Jordan, and don't peek," I said, leading my six-year-old son up the stairs to his room. "Your dad has been working on your room all day."

I led Jordan into his room and instructed him to open his eyes. My son gasped and said, "My room looks like a hockey rink!"

It was true. His dad had painted the baseboards yellow and the chair rail red. The floor was complete with center ice and the blue lines on each side. It probably wasn't the best thing for the resale value of our home, but my son positively loved it.

"I did the walls and the floor," his dad explained, "but there's still some decorating to do."

Jordan grinned. "It has to be hockey stuff. I want my room to be all hockey, all the time."

He already had the NHL sheets and comforter set. He had a shelf full of pucks from games he'd been to and dozens of miniature Zamboni machines of various sizes. He even had a trophy he'd won when his own hockey team had had an especially good season.

Jordan looked around. "There's already a lot of hockey stuff in here," he said. "But I need something to hang on that wall."

Our family held season tickets to the local minor league hockey team, the Indianapolis Ice. Jordan loved to wait outside the locker room after games so he could talk to the players.

"Maybe I should get all the players' autographs and hang them up in my room," Jordan said.

But his dad went one step further. After the next game, he snapped a photo of Jordan with each player, printed them out, and then asked the players to autograph the pictures. We hung up the photos in Jordan's room. They were among his prized possessions.

But his room wasn't finished yet. During one of our post-game sessions, Jordan was telling one of his favorite players about his new room.

"Well, how would you like a game stick to hang on your wall?"

Jordan's mouth dropped open. "You'd give me your stick?"

"Sure, after the last game of the season, remind me and I'll give it to you," he said. "I'll even sign it for you."

Jordan jumped up and down and hugged the player.

He talked about little else in the coming weeks. But on the day of the final home game of the season, Jordan woke up with the stomach flu.

"Buddy, we're not going to be able to make it tonight," I said softly.

"But what about my stick? If I'm not there, Nate will give it to another kid. He might think I forgot or I didn't want it after all."

"I know, buddy," I said, stroking his hair. "But you're too sick to go to the hockey game."

Jordan tried playing "Let's Make a Deal" with me all day. "If I eat lunch and keep it down, can we go tonight?"

"I'm sorry, honey, but you're just too sick," I said.

"But my stick, Mom," he said. "I have to be there. That stick will be the most important part of my room."

Through sheer willpower, Jordan managed to control his tummy for the rest of the day.

So against my better judgment, I took him to the game. I could hardly focus on the game because I was so concerned about him.

But he was fine, and when the final buzzer sounded he practically ran to the locker room to collect his prized stick.

When Nate came out, he was already holding his stick. He winked at me and said, "Got a marker, Jordan?"

Jordan handed him his well-used Sharpie and watched as his favorite player signed his game stick and handed it over.

"I went through a lot to be here tonight," Jordan said, telling the story of his stomach bug.

"I hope it was worth it," the player said with a grin.

"Are you kidding me?" Jordan said. "This is the best day of my whole life! Between your stick and all my pictures of the players, I have the best room in the whole world!"

Jordan's room, like Jordan's life, was indeed all hockey, all the time.

~Diane Stark

# Orange and Black

*High sticking, tripping, slashing, spearing, charging, hooking, fighting,*
*unsportsmanlike conduct, interference, roughing...*
*everything else is just figure skating.*
*~Author Unknown*

One day my dad walked in the front door and handed me a brown paper bag. I knew what was inside—the best sandwich in South Philly – A Nick's Roast Beef. Then I saw an envelope underneath the wrapped sandwich. I opened it and found the only thing that could knock a Nick's down to second place: hockey tickets. Not just any hockey tickets. Orange and black tickets. Flyers tickets. At the Spectrum. The noise, the sold-out arena. Bobby Clarke. Bill Barber. The Hound. The Hammer. The Watson Brothers. Dorny. Moose. And my all-time favorite: Bernie Parent.

I became interested in hockey through a friend I met in middle school in South Jersey. Her family was a big fan of the Flyers, and they got me hooked. Flyers tickets weren't always easy to get back then, but sometimes my dad would manage to snag a pair and we would go to a game. I don't think he was all that interested in the games, and I'm sure the noise bothered his sometimes-problematic ears—17,000-plus screaming Flyers fans didn't help him hear any better. But family meant everything to my dad, and spending a few hours at a hockey game with his youngest child was worth the extra ear ringing.

I went to college a little farther north, in central New Jersey. During my four years there, I encountered a slew of hockey fans but they were mostly Rangers or Devils fans. I survived a lot of teasing during those years but it builds character. One of my sisters married a Rangers fan with two brothers and a dad who are Rangers fans as well. I've taken a lot of ribbing over the years from them too. Family—you can't spray paint their house orange and black no matter how much you want to. I understand passion for a team, so I accept their dedication, misguided as it is.

I share my Flyers fandom with our children. Our middle child has cerebral palsy and is in a wheelchair. An orange and black wheelchair. I haven't figured out how to hook up the "Let's go Flyers!" theme so it plays when his chair is moving, but I am still trying.

My husband has to go to games directly from work if I am not going with him, otherwise I will try to steal his ticket. The joke between us is that if he ever gets invited to a Flyers Stanley Cup Final Game 7, and there is only one ticket, I get it. I have promised to think of him the entire time I'm drinking beer and talking masonry construction with his game buddy.

One day, a few years ago I answered the ringing telephone. "Someone here wants to say hello." I thought it was a coworker of my husband's. Except none of my husband's coworkers is a French-speaking Quebecer. It turned out Bernie Parent was golfing in the group ahead of my husband, so he asked Bernie to say hello to his hockey-crazed wife, and Bernie, being the gentleman he has always been, agreed. I can't honestly tell you what he said to me. I just remember the accent.

I watch the Flyers in the new arena now. It is much bigger and it doesn't have the nostalgia of the Spectrum, but the game is still the same. Maybe a little more sane than the games of the 1970s, but no less exciting to a young girl, now a grown woman, who still lives and breathes for the orange and black.

~Laura Guman Fabiani

# The Glory Days

*No man is an island, entire of itself; every man is a piece of the continent.*
*~John Donne*

They called it a "Dynasty." That was the New York Islanders as they swept the Stanley Cup finals and brought the trophy to Long Island four years in a row—1980, 1981, 1982 and 1983.... and we were part of it! Thirty years later and my throat still gets constricted when I think of the excitement of the games.

My husband Bob and I watched the Islanders get their "skating legs" from the early 1970s. But in 1977, as they were getting serious about good game performance, we got serious about joining their supporting cast and signed on for season tickets. First row seats behind the Islanders home goalie! And there we sat for every home game until 1985 when we moved away.

How do I begin to describe "The Glory Days" that the New York Islanders brought to Long Island? "Glory" in the smooth precision game they played. "Glory" in the good family relationships they presented. "Glory" in the local pride the game instilled in Long Island residents.

I'll start with the "glory" of their game. Oh to see the finesse in team work... like Eddie Westfall winning the puck off the boards, John Tonelli picking it up to Bryan Trottier who skates a precision quick shot to Mike Bossy and it's in the net. The sticks go up and "SCORE" rings out! Then there's the memory of how the Islanders were called a "choke" team when it came to Stanley Cup playoffs.

"Choke" called the Bruins' fans in a playoff game in 1980; Clark Gillies dropped his gloves and fists went up. No fans ever called "choke" to the Islanders again. And oh-the-memory of seeing Bobby Nystrom speed skating down the ice, his golden hair flying high, a quick stick and the puck going in—the overtime win of the first Stanley Cup to come to Long Island. The crowd exploded. The Island came alive. Horns honked on the expressway. Fans waved out car windows to each other on Northern and Southern State Parkways. Dr. Generosity restaurant in East Meadow was filled to overcapacity with frenzied fans and players!

The Islanders "glorified" family life on the Island. They lived among us. Their wives and girlfriends worked locally and came to the games. Most players were visible to their fans off the ice on the Island—quick to volunteer their time in supporting local needs. Coach Al Arbour's wife sat six rows behind us, waved a cheery hello each game as we gave her the thumbs up sign. Their high school age daughter liked to come down to chat with us between periods, exchanging team news and getting our feedback to take to her dad.

There was local pride and spirit in Long Islanders that wasn't there before and has not been seen since. We lived just fifteen minutes from the Nassau Coliseum, home of the Islanders. We arrived at each game wearing our official NY Islander jerseys, a present to us from our daughter Jeanne. We were there in freezing rain, ice and snow. There was just no missing an Islander game. Our whole section became fast friends—"a little family"—a result found in each section throughout the Coliseum. Season tickets were a prized possession. It was said that divorce settlements revolved around who would get the Islander tickets. Long Island *Newsday* fed our interests daily with local news, reviews and pictures, and labeled the winning years of the New York Islander Dynasty "The Glory Days."

In January of 1980 it was announced that the U.S. Olympic hockey team would arrive to practice at the Nassau Coliseum on their way to play in the Olympic games at Lake Placid, New York. We were also told that one of the players, Ken Morrow, would be returning to Long Island after the Olympics to become an Islander. Well, my good hockey friends and I were at the Coliseum to welcome and cheer the Olympic team on their way. Who can forget—the 1980 U.S. Olympic hockey team went on to become known as "The Miracle on Ice" as they swept the Olympic games, beating Russia in the final game. The spirit that came alive throughout our country with the hockey win of that night is similar to the spirit that brought Long Islanders to their feet in celebrating the Stanley Cup wins of the "glory days" of the Islander Dynasty.

What was it like to be a New York Islander fan during these years? We were so involved with the game that it was like living on an emotional roller coaster. I can remember swinging from heights of exhilaration to depths of extreme agitation as I watched our beloved Islanders execute unbelievable finesse and teamwork one game and be on the brink of elimination the next. I'll never forget a 1982 playoff game when we were one score down with only one minute to play; I saw the Stanley Cup fading away. I "white knuckled" the arms of my seat. But somehow the puck got into the net. We were alive for an overtime win. The Islanders pulled it out again!

Islander hockey love took over our family. Our teenage daughter, Jennifer, became a hockey statistician—with notebooks filled with player facts and figures. Our oldest daughter, Lisa, became an Islander fanatic and developed crushes on many of the players. As for Bob and me, they were truly "glory days" of intense shared love of hockey—of the game, the players and one another.

~Martha Helen Cotiaux

# Road Apples

*You find that you have peace of mind and can enjoy yourself,*
*get more sleep, and rest when you know that it was a*
*one hundred percent effort that you gave—*
*win or lose.*
~Gordie Howe

I grew up in the 1950s in a small city—Prince Albert, Saskatchewan. Junior hockey was played fast and hard. Our Prince Albert (PA) Mintos played the Moose Jaw Canucks, the Regina Pats, those terrible "goons" from Saskatoon, and the dreaded Flin Flon Bombers. The boys from the mining town of Flin Flon were tough, always ready to drop their gloves and fight. We Minto fans had watched our players grow up competing at local neighborhood rinks. Our loyalty was fanatical and ferocious.

The small junior hockey league arenas brought the spectacle so close that fans felt involved in the action. We sat on frozen benches in unheated arenas. Our steaming breath mingled with that of the players. Shouts and cries of players and fans, the whacks of stick on pad, and smashes into the boards merged into one sound, one sense of being in the game. Flashing blades scraped showers of white powder from once gleaming ice as two accelerating opponents hurtled to an inevitable meeting at mid ice. A collision felt in the bones of each fan created a shocked split second of stopped motion. Instantly the players separated, twirled, regained speed, and the pell-mell rushing and crashing continued; the uniformed gladiators pulled by the powerful magnet of the small black puck.

Back then I never wondered what inspired those young players. Pondering is for later times in life. Clearly, they were bursting with the exhilaration of playing this greatest of games, of being young and invincible, skating as fast as they ever would. I realize now another reality—good jobs out on the prairie in the fifties were hard to find. These lads were playing for their lives to make it onto the rosters of an NHL hockey team. Back then, there were only six NHL teams to provide the promise of fame and fortune.

Where did this hockey skill and speed begin? It started behind our homes, where parents saw winter's deep snow as the gift of yards and gardens needing no work, and youngsters pictured center ice in Toronto or Boston. Dads helped out, and after much tamping and shaping with snow shovels, and hours of flooding with the garden hose, our back yards became ice rinks. Small rinks, sure, and usually too small to use skates, but perfect for scurrying frantically in boots, brandishing our hockey sticks, improving our puck handling—and giving Dad a workout in goal.

Then off to school on a cold winter's morning. Boys in my town played hockey on the way to school. We would not have cared if it was uphill, five miles to school, both ways. Most mornings the temperature was well below zero. Twenty to forty below was not uncommon, but we never felt the cold. Not while racing along, swiftly passing ice pucks back and forth across the snow covered roads. I remember that the best pucks were frozen "road apples." Delicately put, these were dropped by the horses that still pulled the milk wagons in our town. Ice chips weathered away, but the "material" in road apple pucks, once frozen, withstood a hundred hard slap shots on the way to school. Plus, you could see them during a blizzard.

Nights at the neighborhood hockey rinks allowed us to put on skates and play the real game. Clumping out of the clubhouse on sharpened skates, wood fire smoke clinging to winter jackets, we pretended to be pros coming out for a game. The first hour on the rinks was for us "normal" kids, those blessed with average talent.

Temporary goal markers were placed, usually three sets facing across the ice, not lengthwise, so three games could be played at once—with up to seven or nine players a side. The rushes each way were fast and furious, the scoring absurdly frequent, the goalies chosen more for their courage than skill.

After our hour of enthusiasm and energy, we scrubs gave way to hopeful future junior hockey league stars. The goal posts were now regulation, as were the rules. Older teens of proven talent showed their stuff. In PA the best players from my East Flat rink vied with the best from the West Flat, and up on the Hill, and the surrounding farming communities for openings on the Minto team. We all had pals and favorites to cheer on. What joy when one of "our" lads eventually made the Mintos! Even better—some of those Mintos stars occasionally made it to the NHL. In our small frozen town, on Saturday nights, we might hear their names called out during radio broadcasts of Hockey Night in Canada.

Does hockey have idols like Babe Ruth, or Michael Jordan? Absolutely. To me, the greatest is the incomparable Gordie Howe, who starred with the Detroit Red Wings. Gordie, at the peak of his career in the late fifties, was my idol. I traded most of my hockey cards and one younger brother just to get his hockey card. Mom made me get my brother back.

In the summer of my fifteenth year, I caddied at a prestigious golf course in a national park north of our city. In walked Gordie Howe with his clubs. In caddying, you take turns, and it was my up. "Halderson!" I heard the golf pro yell my name. I went to heaven and back a dozen times in about two seconds. Gordie walked over to me. I was small to the barrel at fifteen, just pushing five feet, and skinny. I looked up, and up, and up at a smiling giant some ten feet tall. He kindly spoke, pointing to a bag of golf clubs weighing more than I did. "Think you can carry these for eighteen holes, son?" I would have sold that same little brother to the devil to say yes, but he was not handy, so I had to admit that, no sir, I didn't believe I could.

Gordie shook my hand and the next caddy in line, some kid my age with Neanderthal genes and hair sprouting from the muscles bunched on his forehead, picked up Mr. Howe's clubs. No, I was not jealous. I forever retain the glorious memories of road apple street hockey games, the PA Mintos, and almost—almost—caddying for Gordie Howe. Life's great opportunities missed, I have learned, are often more memorable and meaningful than those achieved.

~William Halderson

# 27

# Hooked

*When you're out on that floor cheering, you don't worry about the judges or the other teams. All you need to worry about is cheering your heart and soul out and knowing that you are doing the very best you can.*
~Corey Phillips

Growing up in North Dakota, I learned to ice skate when I was young. But I didn't know anything about hockey until I was exposed to the game as a student at the University of North Dakota. The Fighting Sioux lived up to their name and the fast-paced game quickly fascinated me. During my years at UND, I cheered the team on—thrilled when they won a national championship one season. But after graduating and moving away from North Dakota, my hockey-watching days were over. And it was not until I met my husband two decades later that I renewed my interest in the game.

When I started dating Steve, the NHL teams were in the middle of the Stanley Cup playoffs. Instead of excluding me when he watched his favorite team's games, Steve managed to find restaurants with large screen TVs—where of course, the playoffs were shown. As a result, many of our dates included watching games. I didn't mind. I loved the sport, which pleasantly surprised Steve.

We spent many nights cheering on Steve's team, the Red Wings. He not only helped me learn players' names, but he filled me in on their history as well. Over the next months, we cheered for the Red Wings as they defeated their opponents and went on to win the Stanley

Cup. Just like any hockey fan after a win, I was thrilled. "My" team had won and the players' names would be forever engraved on the coveted Stanley Cup.

The Red Wings season that year had been dedicated to Vladimir Konstantinov, a former Red Wings defenseman whose career had ended the year before after a car accident. I remember Steve and I watching this championship player wheel his chair onto the ice and touch the Cup. The crowd in the stadium clapped and cheered and we felt honored to witness his unexpected appearance. The loyalty of his former players and the fans' reactions spoke volumes to me about this team I'd chosen as "mine."

The Red Wings' championship was certainly a highlight during our dating. And though I can't say for sure, that big win might have helped prompt Steve to make a pretty important decision. He proposed to me—less than three months after we started dating! We were married six weeks later and my new in-laws made sure the two of us had matching Red Wings national champion T-shirts—which we still wear to this day. And my wedding gift to my husband? His own Red Wings jersey, of course. Over the years, we've managed to collect more T-shirts, hats, Christmas decorations, and other Red Wings paraphernalia, but one item has been especially well used. When our first grandchild was two, we bought her Red Wings pajamas, and that set has been passed onto each of our three grandkids over the past nine years. What fun for us to see our little ones clothed in our favorite team's logo.

Like any true hockey fan, we prefer watching games in person. But because our city doesn't have a professional hockey team, live games have been rare for us. The ones we've attended, though, have all been memorable.

Perhaps the most memorable game for us took place the week of my husband's fiftieth birthday. For months, I planned my surprise for him. Then, on his birthday, we drove to the airport and flew from Florida to Flint, Michigan where his family had a surprise party planned. During the flight, I presented my birthday gift—tickets to a Red Wings game in the Detroit Joe Louis Arena. His happy reaction couldn't have been more rewarding. And when we attended the game two days later, seeing players like Lidstrom and Shanahan up close couldn't have been more exciting—except, of course, watching our beloved Red Wings claim victory over the opponent.

Now we are looking forward to our next memorable Red Wings game—we are taking our eleven-year-old granddaughter. She's become a Red Wings fan too. In fact, much to our surprise, she announced last year that she wanted to play hockey. It didn't matter that she didn't know how to skate. She'd only been on ice once, but she was determined to play the game. Fortunately, our area has an indoor skating rink and my granddaughter signed up for lessons. By Christmas, she was learning the skills of hockey. Of course, my husband knew just the appropriate Christmas present for her—a Red Wings jersey with her name on it. Now she proudly wears that to all her lessons. And in the next few months, because she's learned to skate well, she will join a hockey team. We can hardly wait to see her in action.

And we can hardly wait to see her reaction when she watches her first live game. She might think she's a fan now, but we're sure she'll really be hooked on hockey, and especially hooked on the Red Wings. What more could any fanatical Red Wings grandparent ask for?

~Georgia Bruton

28

# The Edmonton Oilers Get Even

*Life is too short not to do a little practical joking.*
~Krista Allen

Imagine that you, an ardent hockey fan, were offered a job to work for your favorite NHL hockey team. Where you'd get to know all the players, go to all the home games, drop into the dressing room after a big win. How thrilling would that be? That's where I was in 1985, months after "Lord Stanley's Cup" had visited.

In the mid-1980s the dominant team in the NHL was the Edmonton Oilers, led, of course, by superstar Wayne Gretzky. The players were considered "gods" in Edmonton because of their Stanley Cup wins in 1984 and 1985. The city was electric with Oilers' fever.

Though an Oilers' fan since Gretzky started with them in 1978, I learned to love the rest of the players too as they molded into a dominating force in the early 1980s. So imagine my excitement in November 1985 when I was hired to be Promotions Manager of the Oilers!

Me, an average Joe AND a Gretzky and Oilers fan! My friends couldn't believe it. Even my dad had trouble believing it until the weekend he visited me from the east and I got him into a game and up to the press box for a look behind the scenes.

It may sound funny that a two-time Stanley Cup winning team would need a "promotions manager." How tough could it be to "promote" a team in its own market when everyone already loved them? But coach Glen Sather knew what he was doing as much with the front office as he did the team. My job was to garner corporate support for the team in the form of sponsorships, giveaway items at games, advertising in the game program, community relations activities and intermission on-ice fan entertainment.

One of the giveaway items I worked on was a poster of the Oilers that we could hand out to all 16,000 fans as they arrived at a future game. We had a sponsor and needed a theme for the poster. Two years earlier the team had done the traditional "winner" poster showing everyone lined up in jerseys and the Stanley Cup out front but we wanted something new.

At the time the Oilers' home rink was the Edmonton Coliseum and their occasional practice rink was at the massive West Edmonton Mall, home to 800 stores plus an arena, water park, amusement park, hotel, bird sanctuary and lake with a pirate ship. I suggested we play on the Disney attraction, Pirates of the Caribbean, and use the mall's pirate ship to theme our Oilers' poster "Pirates of the Coliseum."

The idea was approved and we outfitted the players and coaches as pirates aboard the mall's full-size pirate ship. The players actually had fun dressing up, adding fake moustaches and beards and stomping around the ship saying "Arrrghh" as pirates are known to do. Glen Sather was hilarious with a fake parrot sitting on his shoulder.

The photo shoot took a couple of hours, stretched out only because of the antics of players who were just like "kids" when all together with no pressure to score goals. Just after I announced that the shoot was "wrapped," I was lifted in the air by four players who shouted, "This is for making us come here!" and tossed overboard into the fifteen-foot deep lake.

I don't know if they knew or cared if I swam, but fortunately I did and hauled myself back on the ship where I threatened the guilty parties with inane promotional activities. Everyone was highly amused and the incident and a photo even made the paper the next day.

The poster was a huge hit when given out at a game weeks later, delighting fans who tried to figure out who was who in this rare glimpse of the "gods" in a down-to-earth pose. At least as down-to-earth as swashbuckling, dangerous pirates can be.

~Michael Brennan

# Warming Up to Hockey

*God could not be everywhere and therefore He made mothers.*
*~Jewish Proverb*

I've never been much of a hockey fan. For someone living in northern Minnesota, this is a bold confession—not usually shouted from rooftops, but whispered discreetly on dark street corners.

I'm not a winter person. The cold month of January is enough to get my long underwear in a bunch. The one thing worse than January is realizing I've still got February to endure—and everyone knows February is the longest month.

It's only logical—sitting in a cold, ice-filled arena didn't make my bucket list.

Life has a way of throwing us a flying puck every so often. I'm a mother to four kids. Two already play hockey and a third is on the horizon. Can you say icing?

Any parent will attest, once you have children, your life is no longer your own. You share it with your kids. This is why you became a parent. If your kids want to explore a certain hobby or sport, and it is in your means and interest to help them, you do so. Mine wanted to play hockey. Ambivalent or not, I was along for the ride.

During my son's first year of play, I had to help him suit up a couple of times. I couldn't believe the complexity of the garb. There were pads and socks and protectors all held together with white tape. There were funny looking pants called breezers. The helmet, in and of itself, was a sight to behold. I believe there were three or four snaps, a chin guard and a mouth guard attached with plastic.

It still astounds me: we suit our little ones up like this, put sharp steel blades on their feet, give them a long stick and say, "Go for it!" And they do. That's the amazing part. They do.

These little people, who can hardly stand up on skates at the beginning of the season, are able to skate fluidly a few months later. They learn the coordination of handling the stick and puck at the same time. They learn to skate as fast backward as they can forward. They learn to pass and dig and stay onside. They learn to rely not only on themselves, but their teammates and coach as well.

As important as anything else, they learn to enjoy our long, cold winter. And they help their moms do the same.

A few years ago, I entered the world of hockey as a novice. I've learned a lot since then, and am proud to say I no longer consider myself a total rookie. I understand my fair share about a world where Zamboni is king. I've learned to appreciate a perfect pass and a well-executed play. I've learned about breakaways, blue lines, high sticking, the five hole, icing, hat tricks, going top shelf and weekend jamborees.

I've learned the importance of thick socks and good boots. I've learned those hand warmer things really do work. I've learned hot cocoa tastes better when you're cold.

I've also learned that when my kids enjoy something thoroughly and entirely, it's hard for me not to feel the same way. I started out as an ambivalent parent, but that's changed. I have become a fan. I may not shout my sentiments from the rooftop, but I have been known to join the hockey moms in a team cheer. It's fun. And besides, the clapping and yelling helps keep the blood circulating to my extremities.

~Jill Pertler

# 30

# The Littlest Bruiser

*What is a hero without love for mankind?*
*~Doris Lessing*

"Are they coming out soon?" my six-year-old son Jordan asked for the sixteenth time.

I smiled and tousled his hair. "They've got to take showers, buddy, because playing that hard makes them really sweaty and stinky. So after they get cleaned up, they'll come out of the locker room and you can congratulate them."

"And get their autographs too," Jordan added. He waved his program through the air and grinned.

"Don't you already have their autographs?"

"Yeah, but not on a program." His grin grew bigger as the players began to trickle out of the locker room. Many of them had damp hair, several sported bruises, but all of them wore grins as big as Jordan's. And it was no wonder. They'd won tonight in a real nail biter, complete with a shootout.

The team was the Indianapolis Ice. They might have played in the minors, but to my young son, they were huge stars.

Huge stars who actually knew his name.

As season ticket holders, standing outside the locker room had become an every weekend event for our family. It wasn't long before a few of the guys began to recognize Jordan and even call him by name.

The first time it happened, my little boy grew six inches right before my eyes. "Did you hear him, Mom? He knows my name! A real live hockey player knows my name!"

It wasn't long before Jordan knew each player's name, number, and position. He had his favorites, and they weren't always the best players on the team. They were the ones who paid him the most attention.

"Hey, Jordan, did you see my goal tonight?" They would ask him. And, "Jordan, did you like it when I smashed that guy into the boards?"

Jordan just soaked it up. When he began to play himself, he shared the details of his games with his favorite guys. And even better, a few of them even remembered to ask him how he did.

The end of the season was a sad time for our family. We'd enjoyed the games and talking with the players afterward. We really hated to see it end.

As a last hurrah, the Ice sponsored a thank you dinner for all of the season ticket holders. After we ate, the coach took the microphone and thanked everyone for a great season. "And now, we've got some special awards to hand out to our guys."

The coach announced the team's MVP and motioned for that player to come to the stage. Our table was toward the front, so as he walked by us he high-fived Jordan and said, "There's my favorite fan."

I thought Jordan was going to hyperventilate.

The coach announced the player who'd scored the most goals, as well as the one who had saved the most goals. Both guys high-fived Jordan on their way to the stage. The coach handed out an award to the guy who'd spent the most time in the penalty box. He then grinned and gave an award for the player who'd eaten the most Big Macs throughout the season.

It soon became obvious that every player was going to head to the stage to receive an award. And it seemed that each one was going to acknowledge my son on their way.

Jordan was turned around backwards in this chair, kneeling so that he could see each player as he made his way to the stage. The coach announced the award for the team's Biggest Bruiser, the guy they could always count on to start a fight and win. As the guy headed to the stage, he high-fived Jordan just as the other guys had done. But he put a little more force behind it and he ended up knocking Jordan backwards out of his chair. Jordan hit the floor and popped back up, unhurt. But when he realized the entire crowd was laughing, he began to cry.

"They're not laughing at you, Jordan. They're laughing at me," the player told him. "They think it's funny that I'm getting an award for being the Biggest Bruiser on the team, and now I just beat up a five-year-old kid."

Jordan wiped his face and smiled. "I'm six, and you didn't beat me up." He puffed out his chest and said, "It didn't even hurt."

Bruiser grinned at Jordan and then went up front to collect his award. On the way back to his seat, he oh-so-gently patted Jordan on the head.

"Be careful," one of his teammates yelled. "Don't hurt him again!"

"He didn't hurt me," Jordan yelled back. "I'm way tougher than that!"

Bruiser handed Jordan his certificate. "I think you deserve this more than I do."

For weeks afterward, Jordan refused to answer to his name.

What did he want us to call him?

Bruiser, of course.

~Diane Stark

# 31

# The Making of a Hockey Fanatic

*Realize that now, in this moment of time, you are creating.*
*You are creating your next moment. That is what's real.*
*~Sara Paddison,* The Hidden Power of the Heart

If someone had told me ten years ago that I would become a hockey fanatic, I would have told them they were crazy. And if someone had told me that I would find myself standing outside of the Detroit Red Wings locker room shaking hands with Drew Miller, I would have told them they had lost their mind! But, both things did in fact happen.

Don't get me wrong—I love sports, but hockey had been nowhere near the top of my list. I grew up watching football, baseball and auto racing with my dad. He didn't like hockey because he didn't like "all the fighting." So I formed the impression early on that hockey was a divisive sport and not worth my time. That all changed when I met my would-be husband Andy.

Andy loved sports, Andy loved hockey, and despite living in Pennsylvania, Andy loved the Detroit Red Wings. As his new girlfriend, it was my duty to show an interest in the things that he liked. On Halloween night in 2001, Andy took me to see a minor league hockey game. The Grand Rapids Griffins—the Red Wings' minor league team—came to town to play against our local team, the Hershey Bears. I was open to the idea of trying something new, and

I must say that it was quite exciting. I don't remember much about the game, but the highlight for me was watching Andy as he joyfully taunted the Bears' players who served time in the penalty box. Hockey was proving to be pretty fascinating after all, and I think I scored a few points with Andy that night!

Andy's passion for hockey continued and so did our courtship. We were married in 2003. With marriage came change—the birth of our daughter, moving (a few times), and new jobs for each of us. But hockey was still ever present in our lives. I enjoyed sitting and watching the Wings' games on television with Andy. It was a chance for us to unwind and spend some time together at the end of a long day. I learned more about the game and the players, and Andy could tell that I was really starting to enjoy it, almost as much as he did.

In 2009, we went to our first Red Wings game in Columbus. Andy was all decked out in layers, sporting a Red Wings hat, T-shirt, sweatshirt and Datsyuk jersey. The game against the Blue Jackets was great (Wings won!) and I found myself cheering, screaming and jumping out of my seat with Andy and the rest of the fans. I could feel the excitement in the air. It was as though the arena had come to life, and so had I. Was this really happening? Had I become a genuine hockey fan?

It was clear to me that my interest in hockey was no longer about impressing Andy—I was hooked! Almost immediately after the game, Andy and I began scheming about our next hockey game. But this time, we had to go to Detroit, to Joe Louis Arena. We knew there would be nothing like watching a Wings home game at the Joe. We planned our trip to Detroit for the following February to celebrate our anniversary. Andy wore the usual layers, but this time with a Franzen jersey. I had not yet committed to a favorite player, and I decided it was time to choose. I didn't want to choose a popular and well-established player. I've always favored the underdog, the new guy.

The Wings hosted the Buffalo Sabres and their star goalie Ryan Miller. Andy mentioned that the Wings had signed his younger brother Drew earlier in the season. In the program for the game, there happened to be an article about Drew Miller. It talked about his time at Michigan State, his disappointing start in the NHL, and his desire to contribute to the success of the Red Wings. I told Andy, "That's him—that's the guy!" And so I found myself even more connected to the game by choosing a player to follow and committing my loyalty to him as a fan.

Andy and I decided to continue with our new anniversary tradition and went to Detroit again in February 2011. In addition to celebrating our marriage, we were also celebrating another important occasion—I had just reached the five-year benchmark of being free of breast cancer. Unfortunately, the celebration did not last long. Shortly after returning home from our trip, I learned that the cancer had recurred. The news was devastating and the timing seemed too ironic. Our feelings quickly turned from joy to sorrow. We took our time processing this sad news; however, it did not take Andy long to come up with the ultimate plan to lift my spirits. He told me that he had contacted the Detroit Red Wings and shared my story. They would be hosting us for a game in the fall, and I would soon be meeting Drew Miller!

I spent my spring and summer dealing with surgeries and chemotherapy, but the anticipation of going to Detroit kept me encouraged. Finally September arrived, and the new hockey season was upon us. We were contacted by Christy Hammond from the Red Wings' Community Relations Office. She invited us to come up for their Breast Cancer Awareness Night in October. This time Andy and I decided to take our daughter Kaitlyn with us to share in the fun. The seats were amazing and the game was thrilling, but I was anxious the entire time waiting for what would happen after the game!

The game ended and we quickly headed downstairs where we were escorted to the Red Wings locker room. My heart and my thoughts were racing as we walked down the hallway. What a difficult year this had been, and now I was being treated to a very special evening! I was so grateful to be sharing it with my precious daughter and my loving husband, who had been so thoughtful.

Drew and Christy greeted us outside the locker room. They were very kind and gracious hosts. We were given a personal tour of the locker room, we had several pictures taken with Drew, and we left with some great gifts and autographed memorabilia. It was an amazing and unforgettable experience!

It may have taken many years, but I finally discovered that my first impression was far from the truth. Hockey is about much more than "all the fighting." Hockey does not bring division but unity. It fosters a connection between a husband and wife. It shows that community extends far beyond the boundaries of a city or state. And it can bring healing when your spirit is broken. Thank you Andy, thank you Detroit Red Wings, and thank you hockey for bringing joy to my life and for being there when I needed you most.

~Brandi South

# The Cursed Jersey

*Superstitions are, for the most part, but the shadows of great truths.*
~Tryon Edwards

Sports fans tend to be superstitious. Maybe it's crazy, but we can't help it. So much about sports comes down to luck, a good hit, a lucky catch, a bad angle. One can't help but believe in bad luck and good luck, and that certain rituals, like not shaving during playoff time or wearing socks of a certain colour, can affect the outcome of a game.

For my mother, it's the deep-rooted belief that her Toronto Maple Leafs jersey is cursed.

My father bought her the jersey in 1994, as an anniversary present. At the time, the Leafs were playing in the conference finals and she couldn't wait to wear her jersey as she watched her beloved Maple Leafs on television.

The first game she was able to watch, the Leafs lost and then the next. Suddenly, the Leafs were down three games in the series and on the verge of elimination. Every time she wore the jersey, they lost. My mom decided to not wear it and instead she left it in her room, on her bed.

The Leafs rallied and took the lead in the game; it began to look like all hope was not lost. I was eleven at the time and I happened to go into my parents' room. I saw the jersey there and I couldn't figure out why my mother wasn't wearing it, so I took it down to her. "Mom, you forgot to put on your jersey," I said, handing it to her.

My mother nervously took it and as soon as she did, the Vancouver Canucks scored. The tide of the game changed, and the Leafs were eliminated that night.

"It's the jersey," my mother declared to my father and me. "It's bad luck."

My father rolled his eyes at her and grumbled about how it was a wasted gift if she wouldn't wear it, but my mother was convinced and she banished the jersey to the back of a drawer. After all, it was a gift and she couldn't bear to throw it out. Besides she'd occasionally wear it in the summer when she decided that it could do no harm.

The Leafs had ups and downs over the next few years, but they never made it to the Stanley Cup finals. Even if the jersey was bad luck, banishing it didn't suddenly bring good luck. But my mom still wasn't going to risk taking it out again.

Years passed and then during the 2002 playoffs I was a teenager who was just starting to get into hockey. I brought the jersey out, partly because I found that all the boys at school flirted with me when I wore it.

My mother wasn't thrilled, but it had been a lot of years and she decided to let me wear it. The first time I wore it, the Leafs lost, badly. I figured it was a coincidence, but I couldn't quite forget my mother's old conviction that the jersey was cursed. So the next time I wore it, I took it off before the game started, but the Leafs still lost.

My mother forbade me from wearing the jersey again and I was spooked enough by the two losses that I did as she asked. My father thought I was as silly as my mother. "It's just a piece of clothing. There's no way it can influence a hockey game over a hundred kilometres away," he'd point out. But my mother didn't care and I thought she might be onto something. I didn't wear the jersey after that, but soon it didn't look like that decision mattered.

Game Six in the second round against the Ottawa Senators, the Leafs were down three games to two. The game started off badly for the Leafs, with the Senators scoring two goals in the first five minutes. It looked like it was going to be a humiliating end to the playoffs for the Leafs and that the jersey had no part in it at all—it was just silly superstition on my mother's part.

Then, I happened to notice that the jersey was sitting in a pile of laundry in the living room, right in front of the television. I knew I was being silly, but I decided to bring the jersey upstairs. As soon as I left the room, the Leafs scored a goal and the game no longer looked like a lost cause.

The Leafs ended up winning that game and they won the series. They lost in the next round to the Carolina Hurricanes. But we never claimed that banishing the jersey brought good luck, just that the jersey itself was bad luck.

My father was never convinced. And every time he hears the story, my husband rolls his eyes. But my mother and I both firmly believe that her jersey, lovingly given as a present by her non-Leafs fan husband, was cursed. Neither of us has ever worn it since then.

~Michelle McKague-Radic

# 33

# Blindsided by Hockey

*I love those hockey moms. You know what they say the difference*
*between a hockey mom and a pit bull is? Lipstick.*
*~Sarah Palin*

I've never understood hockey. I live in a hockey town in Canada but never watched a game until I was forty years old. Hockey to me was boring, confusing and a waste of time. I had three kids who had never succumbed to its allure, and all were past the age of playing beginner hockey. I had escaped the dreaded status of "Hockey Mom." Most kids started on the ice around three or four, and had already developed skills and a passion for the game by the time they were six or seven. So when my eight-year-old son Simon started talking about playing hockey, I didn't pay much attention.

He was persistent, insisting that he wasn't too old to start playing, and that despite the rest of our family's ambivalence towards hockey, he loved the game. He had barely been on skates, and we didn't even own any hockey equipment.

A summer of playing road hockey had heightened his interest in ice hockey and he was relentless in begging us to let him start.

Reluctantly we signed him up that fall, warning the coach that he had never played at all, and couldn't even skate, much less follow the rules of the game. The coach asked him what number he would like to have on his hockey shirt, and he chose #5. I wondered why that would matter since he would just be quitting anyway! I was sure this was a short-lived passion.

We outfitted him in what seemed like an enormous pile of specialized hockey gear—guards for every part of his body, and took him to his first practice. He was well behind the others, who had been playing hockey for three or four seasons, and who could skate circles around him and handle the puck with ease. Simon just grinned, and clung tightly to his hockey stick to keep him upright.

The other players skated backwards and did sliding skid stops, while to stop, Simon simply fell down to his knees.

I sat in the stands with the other hockey moms, and watched, understanding nothing, especially the growing passion in my son's eyes.

How could he like hockey? He would never be able to get to that puck, much less keep himself on the ice for one trip down the rink.

His persistence and diligence grew along with my apprehension. His first game was disastrous. His teammates skated around him, while he spent most of the time falling down, or hanging desperately onto his stick.

I met him after the game, expecting a humiliated sad little boy, ready to quit, but he was sweaty and exuberant. "Mom, hockey is so much fun!"

"Really?" I sighed. "Fun?"

But that night was a different story. "I'm no good, Mom. I'll never play like the other guys on my team! I can't even skate!" Tears filled Simon's eyes.

"You're right!" I wanted to shout. "Hockey is too hard to play, or to understand." This was my ticket out of the freezing arenas, out of early morning practices and feeling like the underdog with the hockey moms.

But I bit my tongue and smiled. "Simon, we're proud of you. I know you can play hockey like the others, if you work hard. You can't give up now." I pulled the NHL hockey blanket around him as I said good night.

"Thanks, Mom."

I guess we were going to continue with hockey after all.

And so it went. I learned about early Saturday morning practices, where parents kept their eyes open with extra-large Tim Hortons coffee. I learned about hunting for hockey arenas in tiny towns, about how incredibly smelly hockey equipment gets, and the ever-growing passion my son had for the game.

For the first time in my life I was going to hockey games, and learning basic hockey facts—like there are three periods and that it was especially important to remember that the goalies changed sides for each period.

A few months after he started playing hockey, Simon, his team, and thousands of local hockey fans were excitedly awaiting the arrival of the Atlanta Thrashers team, who were coming to our small town to practice. A contest was held, and tickets were drawn for a lucky few who would get to sit and eat lunch with the Thrashers.

When I got the call that Simon had won a coveted spot with the Thrashers, I was less than impressed, but he couldn't contain his excitement.

As the day arrived, he was beside himself with anticipation. In awe, he watched the Thrashers practice, along with a packed-full arena of enthusiastic fans.

The small group of winners was led into the lunchroom, where a feast sat on tables ready for the players to enjoy. The Thrashers entered, talking and joking loudly, paying no attention to the group of pint-sized hockey players, standing wide-eyed watching them. They loaded their plates, sat and ate, seemingly unaware that they were hosting a group of kids who had anticipated their meal with them. The kids stood, shattered that they were being ignored, and that their adventure wasn't happening.

One more player entered the room, a bit later than the others. He saw the kids standing by the door and bent down to shake their hands. He invited them to join him, and they eagerly followed him, each one jockeying to be the one sitting closest to him. They all sat at one big table—one larger than life hockey player, and six eager young hockey fans. He talked to them about the game, asked them about their teams, and told them what it was like to be a National League Hockey player.

At the end of the meal, Colby Armstrong had made a half-dozen devoted fans for life.

Now Simon was absolutely hooked, while I sat and watched his games, wishing for a *Hockey for Dummies* book. The months went on, game after game, and he was getting better. He learned how to stop without falling, and actually scored his first goal.

At the playoffs, his team won the first place trophy in their division. Canada had just won the gold in the Olympic hockey game, and I am sure that the cheering of the parents in that arena rivaled the national pride when Canada won.

Simon was the first player to exuberantly skate around the rink at the end of the game, the trophy high in the air. A few days later, at the hockey banquet for all the teams, Simon went home with the "Most Improved Player" award.

He is now in his third year of playing hockey, plays right wing, and is the highest goal scorer on his team. Last week he got a hat trick. (I just learned that that refers to scoring three goals in one game.) I still don't understand hockey, but I like it! Don't ask me about offside or penalty shots or blue lines. I won't know what you're talking about. But you can find me every weekend sitting on the edge of my seat, cheering on my favorite hockey player—#5!

~Lori Zenker

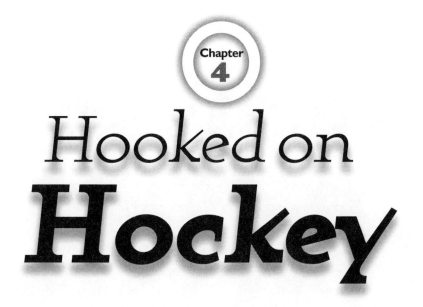

# Chapter 4

# Hooked on Hockey

# Heroes Among Us

# 34

# Five Minutes with Bobby Orr

*It's nice to be important, but it's more important to be nice.*
*~Author Unknown*

To hockey fans, Bobby Orr is a legend. To our family, he's a gentleman.

The Sports Museum of New England, founded in Cambridge, Massachusetts and now located in Boston's iconic "Gahden," home of the Bruins and Celtics, has always held impressive attractions, including sports artist Armand LaMontagne's life-sized wooden sculptures of some of Boston's greatest athletes. Bobby Orr is one of those LaMontagne immortalized in basswood.

My sister-in-law Denise worked for the company that commissioned the Sports Museum Orr sculpture, and to celebrate the work's completion the firm hosted an unveiling there for its employees at a hotel ballroom. Retired Bruins defenseman Bobby Orr would be on hand to pose for pictures beside his wooden look-alike. As her guest, Denise brought her mom Bertie, a huge fan of the Bruins in general and Bobby Orr in particular.

My mother-in-law had been diagnosed with multiple sclerosis years earlier and by the time of the sports museum gala she was largely confined to a wheelchair. Neither MS nor the chair stopped Bertie from living with grace and gusto, and she dressed to the nines, complete with earrings and pearls, for the evening with Bobby Orr.

When Denise and Bertie arrived, a long line already stretched from the hockey great and his chiseled likeness. It would be a while, it appeared, before they'd be able to shake Orr's hand. Then Bobby looked up and saw them. Excusing himself, he walked to the back of the line, introduced himself to Bertie and asked permission to take her for a spin.

As people watched, Orr wheeled a smiling, delighted Bertie through the venue and to the statue. For a full five minutes—or at least what felt to Bertie like five amazing minutes—he focused solely on her. They talked, laughed and admired the artist's work. Bobby Orr conducted a private showing in a crowded room, just for Bertie.

A few years after Bertie died my husband Mike attended a business dinner that included a charity fundraising auction. Mike zeroed in on one item: an 8x10 color photo of a young Boston Bruins' #4 in action on the ice, autographed, "Best of Luck, Bobby Orr."

Mike put in bid after bid, but another man, in the interest of raising as much as possible for the charity, kept outbidding him. Finally, when the man's bid reached a level bordering on too rich for Mike's wallet, Mike approached the man and told him about his mom's evening with the gracious former Bruin.

"That's an incredible story," said the bidder. "You can have the picture. And not only that, but I'm going to buy it for you!"

It hangs on our wall today, and when we look at it, we see more than a hockey player. We see a caring human being who brought joy to another through a simple act of kindness. And we also remember that kind man at the auction who carried on in the same tradition.

~Lori Hein

# One of the Guys

*You can motivate players better with kind words than you can with a whip.*
~Bud Wilkinson

I was desperate. My seven-year-old son Theo really didn't want to go to hockey, and I had been hearing this mantra for days. I explained, yet again, that he had played last year and he had loved, loved, loved it. But, of course, he had no memory of that, and now this year... he didn't want to play.

For days I heard: "I AM NOT GOING TO HOCKEY, MOM!"

No amount of reasoning worked. No amount of explaining, "transitions are hard" "this has happened before" or "trust me, you'll have a good time" worked with him.

In fact, in this particular instance, I was so frustrated I considered doing what my grandfather would have done. He would have screamed at the top of his lungs: "God dammit Theo! Get out on that freakin' ice or I'll whip your butt till it's blue, you ungrateful little brat! You have no idea how lucky you are...."

But, alas, if I did that, social services would take my children away.

Now, if I actually thought what Theo was saying was true, I wouldn't force him to go. But this had happened with every sport, every season.

No, he didn't want to play soccer, but after the first practice, if you asked him what favorite sport was, he'd say: "Soccer!" The same thing happened with flag football, and hockey the year before.

That's just what he did. He screamed and fussed and cried and revolted, but after ten minutes of actually doing it—he loved it. Flat out loved it, and then looked forward to it every week. Then my kid was happy, outside, with friends, and getting exercise. And with every new sport season I got a few new gray hairs to commemorate its passing.

Now it was November. It was hockey time and Theo didn't want to go. As an added bonus this time around, he had missed the first week because he was sick, and now he really didn't want to go.

"All my friends are already better than I am! They've had more practice!"

In my despair, I did what I normally did—I called a friend. This time it was Maria, a dear friend from Argentina who lives in our town, the mother of one of Theo's best friends, who was also on the hockey team.

I explained my predicament and asked if she could swing by our house, grab Theo, who would be all ready for hockey, and take him to a "play date on the ice."

Theo was much less apt to squawk at another mother, of course.

I reassured her that I would arrive ten minutes after hockey started, it would just be easier for him—and, more importantly, me—to make this dreaded initial transition.

Have I mentioned she is a dear, dear friend?

All went as planned and I arrived ten minutes after practice began. I scanned the ice and there was no Theo. Bad thoughts darted through my head until I saw him on the bench getting his skates tightened by a coach.

He saw me and waved, and gave me a thumb's up.

I surveyed the rink to find Maria to thank her and ask how it went. She gave me a second-by-second report. (What else are we supposed to do on the sidelines?)

She said that she could tell Theo was nervous, but he hung in there until right after she had tied his skates. But then, as she tied her own son's skates she noticed that Theo was struggling to hold back tears. Suddenly, Theo couldn't control it any longer and spouted, "Mrs. A., I don't want to play hockey!" and the tears fell.

She looked up from her son's skates again and saw a man standing nearby in hockey attire.

"Are you a coach?" she pleaded.

"Ah, yeah, I am one of them," he replied.

She pointed to my Theo and said, "Can you help him please?"

Don't you love how I transfer my desperation onto my friends?

The coach swooped in and, seeing "Theo" written in black permanent marker on the top of his helmet, said, "Hey Theo! How ya doing? Will you come out on the ice with me? Do you like hockey?"

Theo wiped his tears and followed the coach.

As I listened to Maria tell the story, Theo was skating happily on the ice. Over the next hour I saw Theo fist-bumping the helpful coach, in his own little unknowing way, grateful to the person who took him from panic to pleasure with a warm welcoming arm.

As I stood listening to this recap and watching Theo, I, too, felt grateful to Maria and to that coach. I had never seen him before.

Just then another coach, who I did know, walked past us to get on the ice.

As he headed out he said, "Theo doing okay, Jen?"

"Yes, but it was a close one!" I replied.

"No one's better than the master," he replied. Maria and I stood dumbfounded, and he noticed. "You know that's Mark Messier, right?"

Of course, we didn't. Being from Argentina, Maria had no idea who he was. Being so old, gray, and blind, I couldn't see who it was since he was so far away, and I was looking through thick plexiglass. But how cool was that?

After hockey I asked Theo if he had fun. He replied, "It was awesome, Mom! Hockey's awesome!"

"And what did you think of the coach who helped you out?"

"He was really nice," he said, very blasé.

"His name is Mark Messier, and he is one of the greatest hockey players in the whole world, Theo."

He shrugged his shoulders. "Cool. But, Mom, I really like hockey."

I shook my head. "Of course, you do Theo," I said.

~Jennifer Quasha

# Meeting the Gods with My Dad

*Generosity lies less in giving much than in giving at the right moment.*
~Jean de la Bruyère

When I was a little boy, about nine, I was diagnosed with pes planus. Or for those of you who don't speak fluent Latin… flat feet. I would have to go to a specialist. My dad, William James Davidson, took it upon himself to take care of the situation. He had a doctor friend, a specialist, and we set up an appointment.

On a crisp winter morning we jumped into the car and headed into Montreal from our farm in Châteauguay. We headed up Atwater Street toward the children's hospital. I knew where it was because I'd been there to have my tonsils out, which for a little kid is really traumatic until after the operation when you are offered all the ice cream you can eat.

But I digress.

So there we were, heading to the hospital. Suddenly I realized my dad had driven right by it and was parking the car in front of the most important building in all the world. A building that represented everything that was good and true to a little kid in Quebec. Le Forum de Montréal, home of the greatest hockey team in my universe. Les Canadiens!

We walked in and Dad headed straight to the team's locker room.

I couldn't believe he actually knew where to go. He opened a door and I walked into the office of the team's physiotherapist, Bill Head.

My dad actually knew the team's physiotherapist? They actually KNEW each other? I was dumbstruck!

Dr. Head had me take off my shoes and hop up on his examination table… the same table that the Montreal players sat on. My friends were going to be so jealous.

He began his examination. I had to concentrate on the instructions he was giving me, so I wasn't aware that two other people had joined us until Dad, who was perfectly bilingual, started rattling away in French. All very jovial and sprinkled with lots of interesting words that he would never say in English and that I wasn't even supposed to know.

Dad excused me from the doctor and said, "Son, say hello to a couple of my old friends." I turned to see who he was talking to and looked straight into the eyes of Jean Béliveau, who stuck out his hand and shook mine, like I was somebody important. Then he turned and said, "You probably know this guy, eh," and there he was, the player I wanted to be every time we played hockey—Bernie "Boom Boom" Geoffrion. The world's greatest right winger. The hardest slap shot in the league!

It was like being on Mount Olympus and meeting the gods. My dad just stood back and took it all in.

Boom Boom and Jean, my two new best friends, got into a discussion with Dr. Head and everybody was really interested in my feet and how to fix my condition.

Just about the time that I thought nothing was better than the moment I was living, there was another flurry of French and my dad said, "Maurice ceci est mon fils. Bruce say hello to Mr. Richard." I looked up and there he was, the god Zeus, the Greatest Hockey Player in the World, Maurice "The Rocket" Richard. My nine-year-old heart felt like it stopped beating!

After that I don't remember exactly what happened because my tiny nine-year-old brain seemed to explode. I do have an image burned in my mind of Gentleman Jean, Boom Boom and The Rocket all hunkered down on the floor in front of me talking flat feet with Dr. Head like it was the most important thing in the world. Fixing the problem was all about being able to pick up marbles with your toes, they said. They assured me that they all did it every day to keep from getting flat feet.

Then, to drive the message home, Boom Boom took off his shoes and socks, and proceeded to demonstrate the intricacies of Elite Athlete Marble Picking.

When the appointment ended, I left with a list of foot exercises that I had to do each day to strengthen my feet, along with a hockey stick that belonged to Boom Boom and was signed by everybody, and an official Canadiens puck.

I also left with a newfound respect for my dad. He wasn't just a salesman for Dominion Glass. He knew the Hockey Gods and more importantly... they knew him.

Even as I write this I can remember the drive home. Me babbling about all the exciting things that happened to me that day. How I was going to pick up marbles every day until I was as good as Boom Boom. And Dad nodding and smiling and smiling and smiling.

Years later my mother told me that Dad had said the day he introduced me to The Hockey Gods was one of the best memories in his life. It was one of mine too!

I still have flat feet.

~Bruce Davidsen

# Super Mario

*How far you go in life depends on your being tender with the young, compassionate with the aged, sympathetic with the striving and tolerant of the weak and strong. Because someday in your life you will have been all of these.*
~George Washington Carver

It was a sports fan's dream—meeting legends from every sport imaginable. It was February 1995. I was a junior in college and had just driven six hours south to the Super Show in Atlanta, a sporting goods expo for thousands of retail store managers, buyers, companies, and their celebrity athlete spokespeople.

So there we were, a friend and I, two college kids trying to fit in with thousands of corporate bigwigs from Nike, Reebok, Adidas, Champion, and just about every sporting goods company conceivable. They each had a huge display that featured visits from their spokespeople. The purpose of the show was for retailers to make purchases and hold corporate meetings, but we planned our days around the "stars" we wanted to meet—boxers Evander Holyfield and Muhammad Ali, little-known rookie baseball player Carlos Delgado, Hall of Fame footballer Paul Warfield, boxing promoter Don King, tennis star Chris Evert, Olympic gymnast Mary Lou Retton, baseball strikeout master Nolan Ryan, and many more. One interaction had a lasting impact on us.

After waiting in by far the longest line of the weekend, it was time to meet one of the best hockey players of all time, Mario Lemieux. I had grown up resenting this guy—not personally, of course, but as a fan. I'd get so frustrated because no matter how little or how much he did during a game, he found a way to beat my beloved Washington Capitals. He was the Lebron James of hockey—you hated to play against him, but you'd love him on your team. To say I was going through the motions just to get another autograph from an overpaid celebrity was an understatement. Sure, he was good, but I was still bitter at the suffering he caused Capitals fans.

But then I remembered that Lemieux was taking a leave of absence from the 1994-95 National Hockey League season after receiving radiation to treat Hodgkin's disease, a form of cancer. He was also recovering from his second back surgery in three years, so the time away served multiple purposes. Nobody in line for his autograph seemed to care about his personal struggles though.

Mario was like a robot—shaking hands, posing for pictures, signing posters... shake, smile, sign... shake, smile, sign.... People weren't taking time to carry on a conversation—either because others were rushing them or because they were in a hurry to meet other athletes. As I got closer, I noticed he was hardly saying a word as he continuously did whatever was demanded by fans—sign this, sign that, pose with this person, etc., never once showing an ounce of frustration.

As I approached one of the greatest players of all time, he began signing a poster without being prompted. I quietly asked him, "How ya feelin'?" He paused in mid-signature, looked up at me, nodded his head in what seemed like disbelief, and replied, "Good... thank you for asking." Those five words changed the way I viewed him. He had a grateful look in his eyes and genuinely appreciated me asking. I took the poster, shook his hand, thanked him and wished him well with his recovery, and walked away with nothing but shame.

Here was a guy who was battling much more than I could imagine. He eventually returned to action and played several more years, yet all we, as fans, were interested in was getting another autograph or saying we met someone famous. He stood on a pedestal, as many celebrities do, with his life sprawled in newspapers and magazines and the Internet. We often forget that our idols are human, too.

He retired in 2006 with a heart ailment after seventeen seasons, all with the Pittsburgh Penguins. During his career he won rookie of the year, six scoring titles, three league MVP awards, and two Stanley Cups—both times winning the playoff MVP. He played in thirteen All-Star games, earning All-Star Game MVP three times. He led Team Canada to gold medals at the 1987 Canada Cup and in the 2002 Winter Olympics and 2004 World Cup of Hockey where he served as team captain. So you can see how he earned the nickname Super Mario on the ice.

To me, though, he's Super Mario for what he accomplished off the ice.

~Jim Bove

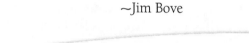

# 38

# Little Devil

*He didn't tell me how to live; he lived,*
*and let me watch him do it.*
~Clarence Budington Kelland

"You ready, bud?" my dad asked, as we glided out onto the ice after one of his big games. Even as a seventh grader now, I can still picture that moment, all those years ago, when I toddled onto the ice rink of the Continental Airlines stadium, home of the New Jersey Devils at the time. With pride, I wore my dad's name and number on the back of my little red hockey jersey. "Representing #3, defenseman, Ken Daneyko!" The dramatic voice of the announcer echoed as the crowd responded with an exuberant roar. They chanted, "Dano! Dano! Dano!" and when the crowd saw me and Dad, hand in hand, they let out a genuine "Awww!" I felt like a superstar, and from that point on, I've always craved that sense of admiration. But with that came expectations.

Since I entered this world, most people have assumed that I would be the next Ken Daneyko, famous hockey star. But watching my sister Taylor and me doing splits and dancing to Britney Spears' "Oops! I Did it Again" and 'NSync's "Bye Bye Bye," my family soon realized that hockey wasn't what I was destined to pursue.

Despite the different path I began to follow, my dad's team-mates were like a second family to me. At least a couple of times a week, the hockey wives and their "little devils" would eat dinner together at my dad's old restaurant, Mezzanotte. I also remember hanging out in the Devils locker room before and after games. Patrik Elias, Scott Gomez, Marty Brodeur, and the other players nicknamed me "Tank" because I had always been big for my age. They also gave me the nickname "Mini Me" because, compared to my dad, I appeared to be a pint-size clone of him. At one point we even had the same missing teeth, just not for the same reason.

I can recall one time, Scott Stevens, hockey legend and one of my dad's best friends, gently placed his large hand on my shoulder and asked that question children get asked all the time, half-expecting to already know the answer. "So what do you want to be when you grow up?" I belted out theatrically, "I want to be the next hunka hunka Elvis Presley!" As I was shaking my pelvis in circles, all the hockey players looked at my dad, not knowing how to respond. Dad chuckled and ruffled my hair and said, "Playing hockey is just not his passion. He loves to sing, he loves to dance, and he loves to act." The players reacted with a look on their faces that questioned, Seriously? Are you okay with that? Dad said proudly, "Of course, I'll support him in anything he chooses to do."

By the time I entered middle school, the expectations still followed me throughout my days. As the new kid in sixth grade, I was constantly being asked a variety of questions from my classmates. "Isn't your dad Ken Daneyko?" "Can you get me an autograph?" "Can you get me a jersey?" "Can you get me tickets to a game?" Surprisingly though, the easiest question to answer was, "Do you play hockey?"

"No, I go to all of the games, and I love watching my dad play, but it's just not my thing." The other kids gave me that same look I've always gotten, but I can handle it. I inherited that confidence from my dad. Although I have an eclectic personality, I really know my dad meant it when he said he supports me in anything I choose to do. And I thank the Lord every day to have a father like him. You see, my dad and I are both performers, just in different arenas. Although I wasn't born to live my life on the ice, my name is Shane Daneyko, and I'm proud to be me.

~Shane Kenneth Daneyko, age 13

# 39

# Hockey Heroes Off the Ice

*It takes generosity to discover the whole through others. If you realize you are only a violin, you can open yourself up to the world by playing your role in the concert.*

*~Jacques-Yves Cousteau*

Though I lived in Buffalo, one of the most hockey-crazed cities in America, I wasn't much of a fan of the game. Sure, I would watch occasionally, following it enough to have the obligatory water-cooler conversation at the office, but I was a casual fan at best.

All that changed the day I met D.J.

My six-year-old daughter had been sick for a few months, with doctors unable to diagnose what ailed her. They sent us to a specialist for testing at the local children's hospital. I was a nervous wreck. How would I stay strong? How could I put on a brave face when I was terrified of the process? As it turned out, I didn't have to.

Once we arrived at the hospital we were ushered into a waiting room and it was there that we met D.J. Based on his stature, I pegged him for nine or ten years old. Later, I would find out that a rare genetic disease had stopped his growth and he was almost fourteen.

Almost immediately, D.J. came over and began to talk to us. He talked about the hospital. He talked about the medical procedures Zoey was about to have. He explained to her what the hospital room was like and he told her not to worry.

D.J. shared his story too. Among the many medical problems he has experienced in his young life, he had endured a kidney transplant the year before. He raised his shirt to show off the tubes protruding from his rib cage.

After a year of working well, his body was now rejecting his new kidney. There were problems with his liver too and things did not look good. That last part we never heard from D.J., but rather from his mom. He was too busy smiling, laughing and telling us, with absolute confidence, that the doctors would figure it out and fix him up.

Here I was an absolute wreck, and this boy, who was taking dozen of pills every day to stay alive, who was living a life of absolute uncertainty, couldn't stop smiling. It was contagious, it was inspirational, and it was just what we needed.

At one point in the conversation, talk turned to hockey. D.J. was a diehard Sabres fan and he lit up as he talked about his favorite players. He had three — Patrick Kaleta, because "he is a fighter like me," he said; Nathan Gerbe, because "we are both so small," he joked; and Jhonas Enroth, the team's back-up goaltender at the time.

We talked hockey for a bit, me bluffing my way through with the little bit of knowledge I had, and then a nurse arrived at the door, announcing it was time for D.J. to go.

Forty-five minutes later, D.J. and his family popped back into the room. His visit was done, but they wanted to say goodbye to Zoey, to show her that he was okay and she would be too. It was one of the most powerful experiences I have ever been part of, watching those two children sharing that moment.

We eventually saw the specialist and were discharged from the hospital, but I couldn't get D.J. out of my head. I felt like I wanted to do something for him to show my appreciation for everything he had unknowingly done for me.

Through my job, I knew a woman who was an attorney, but also served on the board of directors for Sabres forward Patrick Kaleta's HITS Foundation. I thought if I called in a favor, maybe she could get D.J.'s favorite player to sign a photo I could give to him, a token of my appreciation and admiration of him.

Audrey said she would check in with Patrick, and was sure she could get a signed photo. Little did we know what would really transpire.

I got a call from her later that week. She told me that she had shared D.J.'s story with Patrick, and he was so moved he wanted to meet D.J. personally. I was shocked.

We worked out the details and a few days later, D.J., his mom, dad, and an uncle met me downtown. D.J. had no idea why he was coming. As we chatted in a conference room, Audrey knocked and called me into the hall. Patrick was there and it was time for D.J. to meet one of his heroes. But there was more. Not only did Patrick Kaleta take time out of his schedule to visit, he brought Nathan Gerbe, one of D.J.'s other favorite players, with him!

As we walked back into the conference room and D.J. looked up, it was a moment I will never forget. The look on his face was magical. Patrick and Nathan sat with him and once the shock wore off, the three began talking hockey. Patrick brought him a Sabres jersey, hats, and photos, and signed everything. It was incredible to watch while these two professional athletes stepped out of their lives and gave so selflessly to this young boy. Watching D.J., it was clear that for those few minutes his health was the last thing on his mind. Sure, he was just as sick as the day before, but thanks to these two hockey players, he was given a brief respite from the challenges he faced.

But Kaleta wasn't done. As they prepared to leave, he invited D.J. to be his guest in the locker room after the Sabres' next home game. None of us in the room knew what to say, but the smile on D.J.'s face said it all.

Though the Sabres lost the game that night, Patrick Kaleta scored a goal early in the second period. Instead of skating off to the bench, he paused, collected the puck and saved it. Despite losing a hard-fought battle, not only did he bring D.J. and his family into the locker room, but he presented him with that puck, posed for pictures and introduced him to U.S. Olympic goaltender and teammate Ryan Miller and D.J.'s other favorite player Jhonas Enroth.

D.J. left the arena that night with both Miller's and Enroth's signed goalie sticks, as well as sticks from a half dozen other players. As he continued to fight for his life battling a disease that at times appeared to be winning, for one afternoon in that conference room and later for one night in a National Hockey League locker room, D.J. forgot about it all and was just a thirteen-year-old hockey fan living out his dream.

As I read about athletes getting arrested, refusing to sign autographs, and making outrageous contract demands, I think of Patrick Kaleta and what he did for a young man he had never met. His willingness to use his celebrity, to take his talent on the ice and use it to touch the life of a boy in need was awe-inspiring.

I may not have been much of a hockey fan before that season, but seeing the character and quality of these athletes, and what they were willing to do to help a child, sold me.

~Matt Chandler

# Breaking the Ice

*A smile is a powerful weapon; you can even break ice with it.*
*~Author Unknown*

"Can you go into the Calgary Flames dressing room and do a post-game story?" I stared at the phone and cringed because I had been dreading this call for months.

It was make it or break it time. So I did what any enterprising young reporter would do; I lied through my teeth.

"Sure, no problem," I told my assignment editor. "I can do that."

I started shaking in the second period and by the end of the game I was filled with such terror I thought I was going to pass out. The Flames did their part by winning that night, but by the time I met up with my cameraman outside the dressing room door I was a trembling, sweating mess. Being the lone woman in the group I stood out like a sore thumb and more than a few smirks and eye rolls were tossed my way by all the male reporters waiting to get into the dressing room.

The doors swung open and we charged through like a massive cattle drive heading for the barn. Caught up in the wave, I kept my eyes firmly glued to the red rug on the floor. Not daring to look up, I followed the microphone cable that was attached to my camera and it led me to a pair of naked feet. Looking up quickly, I found myself interviewing Jim Peplinski. Once the scrum was over the herd was off again and the microphone cable led me over to another pair of feet. This time as I glanced up, I looked into the bemused eyes of Lanny

McDonald, whose trademark mustache was twitching as he looked at the stressed out woman with the shaking microphone. Soon the herd departed again and glancing wildly around the room I noticed goaltender Mike Vernon in the corner. After collecting a few more good clips I ran out the door. We shot a fast standup extra for the story at ice level and then drove the videotape to the airport to make the last flight to Toronto. My first hockey post-game report was winging its way to TSN and my job prospects were flying along with it.

The mid to late eighties were glory years for hockey in Alberta. Calgary was beginning to make a serious run for the Cup but the spotlight was shining on the Edmonton Oilers. When Gretzky and the boys came to town the Calgary Saddledome exploded like a three ring circus. Everyone wanted to talk to the Great One and heaven help you if you ever missed his pre-game press conference.

But one day, TSN didn't need any extra Gretzky clips. They wanted Mark Messier, the tough guy everyone called The Moose. In the early days of his career Messier was a man of few words and let his fierce, physical play on the ice do the talking. He was 205 pounds of muscle, aggression and to put it bluntly, he scared the living daylights out his opponents—and me. Whenever the media wanted to talk to Messier we were always told he was in the trainer's room. A few of us would try waiting for him but one by one the reporters would disappear and then finally give up all together.

On this night, TSN was willing to wait. My cameraman Brad sat down near an empty player's stall and I hid out in the stick room. One hour passed and no Mark Messier. The team bus left. Messier was still with the trainer. We weren't leaving and neither was he. Finally the weary PR guy came up and yelled, "Get your camera ready—Mark's coming out!" I ran towards Brad and grabbed the microphone. With my eyes fixed on the floor I could hear Messier approaching and you could tell right away that he wasn't happy. The feet were getting closer and I started to panic, praying that Brad would get the camera going before The Moose exploded into the room. As Brad fiddled with the camera and fumbled in his bag for a white balance card, the large pair of irate feet arrived in front of us.

"We'll be right with you Mark."

"Let's just get this over with!" Messier barked.

Finally after what seemed like an eternity we got the camera rolling and I snapped my eyes up from the floor to stare at the seething face of Mark Messier. He was clearly not impressed and I swear I could see steam coming out of his ears. But something had caught my eye and I don't know if it was from nervousness, tension or exhaustion but as I looked into Mark's eyes I suddenly burst into laughter. Not just little snickers but huge embarrassing gasps and guffaws. Now it was obvious Mark was angry. My cameraman looked at me like I was mad, and the PR guy just about had a nervous breakdown.

"What's so funny?" Mark asked through clenched teeth.

I settled down a bit and gasped, "I'm sorry Mark but...."

I pointed down towards his kneecaps. One of the toughest guys in the NHL, the man known as The Moose, was wearing Frosty the Snowman boxer shorts. Mark glanced down at the cartoon figures dancing across his shorts and I watched the sneer change to a smile as he started to chuckle.

"Yep, they're something, aren't they?" he said proudly.

Now everyone was laughing, even Mark. I apologized, pulled myself together and did the interview.

A few weeks later, the Oilers were back in town again. We had just finished our pre-game interviews with the Flames and all the media had gone out to the stands to watch Edmonton's morning skate. One by one the players came out on the ice, stretching and doing slow laps. Messier arrived and began to skate. As he glided by he looked up in the stands, nodded his head and said, "Hi Teresa." My cameraman gasped and all the male reporters sitting near me were in shock. One of the top players in the NHL had acknowledged a rookie female sports reporter. With one simple gesture, I was now part of "the club."

Years later, I was sent to New York to follow one of the Rangers' playoff series. Over time my confidence had grown and I wasn't such a novelty anymore. But the New York media were a tough bunch and this group was acting like a pack of jerks. Mark Messier was now the captain of the Rangers and my cameraman and I waited patiently beside his stall. Finally he burst through the door and strode up to the assembled media. With elbows flying, the pack of New York media hounds physically shoved us to the back of the scrum. Winded and shocked, I pushed back into the fray trying to get my microphone near Mark. As he began answering the first question his eyes scanned the assembled media. To my surprise, he suddenly stopped and yelled, "Hey, Teresa. Get up here!"

His arm shot out through the New York journalists, parting the way like Moses and the Red Sea, allowing my cameraman and me to walk right up to the front. All the reporters had stopped taking notes and were now standing with their mouths open.

"Who is *she*?" I heard one of them mutter.

Satisfied he had things the way he wanted them, Mark looked back at all the reporters and said with a smirk, "Okay, we can start again. Teresa, did you have a question?"

I will always remember the kindness of Mark Messier as I struggled to make my mark as a sports reporter. There were so many times when I questioned my sanity and willpower to keep going. But with a simple gesture, one of the toughest guys ever to lace up a pair of skates validated what I was doing and served notice to the male dominated world of sports that women could do the job and be accepted for their knowledge and skills.

Looking back on fourteen phenomenal years at TSN I still have to laugh. Who knew it would be a pair of Frosty the Snowman boxer shorts that would break the ice?

~Teresa Kruze

# The Day Fate Was an Islanders Fan

*Luck is when opportunity knocks and you answer.*
*~Author Unknown*

When you are a fourteen-year-old boy, there isn't a whole lot in life that is truly important. Usually it is doing well in school, or hanging out with friends. But for this fourteen-year-old, there really was nothing more important than ice hockey and especially being a huge New York Islanders fan.

I had started playing hockey when I was eight. Every day, in the schoolyard outside my house, a group of much older kids (maybe ten or eleven years old) would play roller hockey and I always wanted to play. I would take my roller skates and stick and just hit a puck against the wall while these older kids battled with each other for schoolyard supremacy, and I would watch waiting to join in.

Soon I got my chance to join the afternoon battle and, after a few months, schoolyard shinny turned into organized roller hockey, which in turn blossomed into my true passion of playing on ice. I loved playing ice hockey more than anything and as kid growing up on Long Island, who better to be a fan of than the New York Islanders?

I began following the Islanders just as the championship teams of the 1980s started to wind down. The big star of the day was Pat LaFontaine, who despite playing for the Isles for only two years after I started following the team remains my favorite player to this day.

Other players such as Bryan Trottier, Brent Sutter, and Derek King were the players I grew up watching with awe. These weren't just twenty-somethings who played a sport. To me they were heroes.

I played ice hockey by day, and watched Islanders games at night. I collected hockey cards by the bucket full. I even attended hockey camps in the summertime hosted by Derek King and Brian Mullen (who, although a hated Ranger, would eventually become a cherished Islander).

As I played over the years and truly became a student of the game, it was time that I took a trip to the Mecca of the hockey world and visit the Hockey Hall of Fame in Toronto, Canada. My parents arranged for us to take a long weekend up there in October of 1994. I was so excited. As the days ticked by, I couldn't wait.

As we boarded our plane at LaGuardia Airport I was full of anticipation. The weekend wasn't going to be 100 percent hockey stuff but that was okay. I was willing to do boring adult stuff with my parents as long as I got my time at the Hall of Fame. I was really looking forward to seeing Denis Potvin, Mike Bossy, Billy Smith, and others who had been enshrined forever in those hallowed halls. It was going to be great. It turned out it would be better than I could have ever imagined.

As mentioned previously, one of my favorite things to do was collect hockey cards. I had binders stuffed to the gills with my favorite players from all of the teams in the NHL. But there was always one binder that meant the most to me, and that was my New York Islanders hockey card collection. Just by chance, I took it with me on our trip to Toronto. It gave me something to do and I was always on the lookout for a card shop so I could add to my collection.

While in Toronto, it just so happened that the Islanders were going to be playing the Maple Leafs at Maple Leaf Gardens the day we were scheduled to leave. We weren't going to the game but I remember begging my parents to swing by the Gardens, which was not far from our hotel, to see if maybe we could catch a glimpse of the players as they were going to or from their pre-game skate. Unfortunately, they weren't there when we stopped by but I'll never forget thinking how cool it would have been to have not only visited the Hockey Hall of Fame, but to have also met my heroes all in the same weekend. A kid can dream, right?

The weekend was a hit. The Hall of Fame lived up to its expectations and I had an amazing time. On that final day, we went back to the hotel to pack up, go out for lunch and then grab an evening flight back to Long Island. As we waited in the hotel lobby for a taxi, I could have sworn I saw a guy that looked just like Alexander Semak (a forward for the Islanders at the time) walk through the lobby. No, it couldn't be. As this dapper individual stood in the lobby, I took another glance. It was him! What was he doing here? It hit me when I saw Tommy Salo walk out into the lobby of the hotel. The Islanders were staying in my hotel! At first I wasn't sure what to do. Could I ask for their autographs here? Why not? I was a hotel guest, not a random fan chasing them down the street (even if it seemed like it). Well, our plans for the afternoon had changed. I ran up to the room, grabbed my binder, sprinted down to the lobby and amazingly managed to meet almost the entire team as they made their way to the rink for that evening's game.

I met and got autographs from almost everyone, including Kirk Muller, Brent Severyn, Mathieu Schneider, Tommy Salo, Alexander Semak, Derek King, and rookie stars like Brett Lindros, Todd Bertuzzi, and Bryan McCabe! Lindros, Bertuzzi, and McCabe were kind enough to take pictures with me, which I still have sixteen years later. My entire Islanders card collection returned to New York with names written in indistinguishable scribble on them, but to me it was the most cherished thing in my life.

What is amazing to me all these years later is that when I glance at the pictures from that day, I see a bunch of kids together. Bertuzzi, McCabe, and Lindros were all of nineteen years old at the time, with just five years on me. But to me they were NHL hockey players! They were Gods of the Ice! At that age, five years is a huge age difference. But when think about it today, they probably pictured themselves when they were younger, which would explain why they were so welcoming when I asked for autographs and pictures.

That whole weekend was an incredible experience and one that I will never forget. But that last day was the true cherry on top. To meet my heroes in a setting where it was essentially just me getting to meet them was unbelievable. It was the most amazing thing. Not only did we happen to be in the same hotel, but sitting in the lobby right as they were leaving. We could have been anywhere that afternoon! It was as if fate was an Islanders fan that day.

~Justin Schlechter

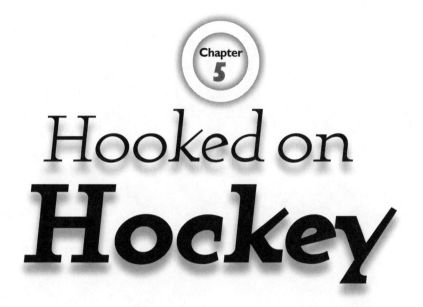

Chapter
**5**

# Hooked on Hockey

## Family Ties

# 42

# Hockey Family

*I would thank you from the bottom of my heart,*
*but for you my heart has no bottom.*
*~Author Unknown*

I first experienced hockey on my grandparents' farm in Cornwall, Ontario. My mother grew up there and had four brothers, all who played hockey. Three of them were drafted into NCAA and two went into the NHL. One went into coaching and was the coach for the Anaheim Ducks when they won the Stanley Cup in 2007 and currently coaches the Vancouver Canucks. Let's just say… there was a lot of hockey going on around me.

My extended family would gather at the farm on weekends and every Christmas. A big group would trudge through the snow with shovels and skates and spend the day at one of the ponds, clearing off the snow and playing hockey all day long, using boots for goal posts. When I was two years old, I was already pretty big for my age and the story goes that I was so obsessed with puck handling I didn't even want to learn to skate. One afternoon my mother had to carry me around under her arm for hours while I held a hockey stick five times too big for me because I was so obsessed… and later she had the back spasms to prove it. There's no better form of hockey than pond hockey—it's completely pure and a ton of fun. I don't think it gets any better than that.

The fact that I was able to become a professional hockey player had and has everything to do with family. Toronto is almost like a hockey factory, where some families and kids can even afford personal coaches. I was from much farther north in Haliburton, Ontario—a great town, but far from the bigger cities—not many of the players that I meet in the NHL come from such rural backgrounds. Learning serious hockey meant that on many, many days one of my parents might have to drive me an hour and a half or even two hours just so that I could go to a one-hour practice. Without my family, I don't believe I could ever have achieved the level of play that is required in the NHL.

Besides having a loving mother willing to carry or drive me around all day, and a lot of supporting, dedicated hockey uncles, aunts and cousins, there was my dad. He has been the big influence on my hockey career.

His dedication to me really learning and excelling at the game knew no boundaries. One winter day when I was about ten I was playing ball hockey on the driveway and I found a small patch of ice. Excitedly, I went to my dad and asked him if we could make it into a rink. Even though it was mid-January and half the winter was already gone, he said okay and went straight to work. The rink was really small, maybe only a 20 by 20 foot square, but it was everything to me. And although he had to get up early for work he would get up every hour, all night sometimes, just to build up the ice, even when it was twenty or thirty below outside.

I played every chance I got, day after day. Sometimes I would play with several younger kids in the neighborhood, mostly friends of my sister. It was one against three or four or sometimes even five, and though they were not as good as I was, it still trained me to think and react quickly and decisively, especially seeing as it was on such a small rink. It forced me to get really good on my edges and with stick handling. It was around then that I was working with a trainer from Oshawa and he and my dad would collaborate on the drills so that we could work on them later at home. In one of the drills that I vividly remember, my dad would loop a huge rubber band around my waist, get into a snowplow position on his skates and create resistance while I would try to take off. We would do this over and over until I would end up on my hands and knees, panting for air. I believe it was because of this drill that I have such explosive leg power on the ice.

I was always focused on hockey. My earliest memories are of watching Hockey Night in Canada when I was maybe three years old. My parents have pictures of me watching the game in our living room, decked out in my goalie gear, moving wildly all over the place, playing carpet hockey with my dad. And this all was happening right underneath my mom's china cabinet. It was my dad who did the shooting, so he took all the risk! When I think of everything that my parents did for me it makes me realize how important their sacrifice of both time and money was to my success. I never missed practices, no matter what the weather. I was always driven the seventy-five minute drive to the rink.

When I was around nine, I was good enough to be playing alongside eleven-year-olds, but the local hockey organization wouldn't allow it. My dad, forever at my side, worked and worked with the organization until he found a way for me to "play up."

That was such an important step in my development. You get better fast when you are playing with people that are more experienced and accomplished than you. It was intimidating, for sure, to play with older bigger kids, and I was scared. But sometimes, being scared is the best thing. It made me push even harder, to listen, to learn, to do my best, every second of the games and practices. The team took me in as their little brother that year and I learned so much. It developed me for the pressure. If you have people to rely on, you don't improve as much. I also learned an important lesson — that it is also important to lose before you win. You learn more in adversity than you do in succeeding.

When I was twelve, maybe even thirteen years old, my bedroom was in the middle of the house upstairs, and on my way to and from the bathroom, if I stopped at the top of the stairs, I could sometimes hear what was being discussed down in the living room. One night I heard my parents talking about me and about how much I loved hockey. I remember my mother saying, "He truly believes he's going to make it, doesn't he?" And my dad replied, "Yeah, he does."

After that I went back to bed and I remember thinking that it was a little weird because my parents were kind of questioning me… but I realized that they were also saying that what I had was different from a lot of other kids. They were identifying my belief in myself and my dedication and the fact that they didn't know any other kids that were like that. I lay there in bed, wide awake, thinking, "Am I crazy to believe that I have what it takes?" And then I thought, "Yeah, I am different and maybe I am also crazy, but I do believe that this is going to work out for me and I'm going to do this for the rest of my life."

And it was true. I was different. Growing up, there just was no one who thought about hockey as much as I did. The minute I got home from school every day, out on the ice I'd go, still fantasizing about my future. And when I was at school I would often find myself daydreaming about hockey. I had my favorite players' names written on the outside of my binder, and had them all ranked as well. I would sketch little logos of my favorite team, the Colorado Avalanche, which is the team I was drafted to in 2009, when I was eighteen — third pick of the draft. When I slipped on the Av's jersey they handed me with my name on it that day, I kept looking down at the logo, thinking that was what I used to draw on my books in school, and now here I was. Talk about a dream come true.

My friends back home tell me that they all always knew I was going to make it… even some of the friends that had never actually seen me play.

I was the only kid from my town that played at the level I did and for me, social life was nonexistent, but I didn't mind — that was fine because I had little interest in doing anything else. And I have to say, it is special to be a professional hockey player from Canada, because unlike many other countries, the States for instance, it is the main sport. So, it feels amazing when you play knowing that the whole country is behind you and the game.

When I look back over my childhood and my career, I owe so much to my family, to all of the ones who loved and supported me from the little guy with a dream to the NHL player who gets to live that dream. But I owe the most to my parents, Chris and Vince

Duchene—I truly would not be where I am, doing what I love, were it not for them and everything they did for me.

When I heard my name called that day in Montreal, that moment when my whole life changed, when I was drafted to Colorado, I looked in my parents' eyes and said, "We did it." And I truly meant it.

Thanks Mom and Dad. I couldn't have done it without you.

~Matt Duchene

43

# Frozen Tales

*Every man's memory is his private literature.*
*~Aldous Huxley*

As a young hockey fan, nothing was more exciting than the time my father scored tickets to see my favorite team play. That it was a big Stanley Cup playoff game between the Leafs and the Rangers made it even more exciting, and the night became a memory with my dad I will never forget.

We left the house as the snow came down over the darkening city, and I'd certainly done my preparation. The night before, my mother got me heavy posterboard and watched as I prepared a sign, hoping my mom and sister would see me on television. The sign read: "THE RANGERS ARE LOST IN A FOREST OF LEAFS," which I thought up myself and considered quite a clever pun. Apparently other people agreed, as the camera showed my sign and me on three separate occasions. My sign was even mentioned in the newspapers the next day! Needless to say, there was a lot of shouting and screaming coming from our TV room that night as they watched little old me on Hockey Night In Canada.

From Maple Leaf Gardens to the small rink in the park across from our house, the winters in Canada were all about hockey for most of my friends. When I was a kid playing minor hockey, we sometimes had to practice on outdoor rinks. Man, they could be cold, but, I have to say the indoor rinks weren't much warmer. All the parents in the stands would shuffle their feet and rub their hands to keep warm. I can still vividly recall the crisp, icy smell of the air in those hometown arenas. It was the smell of a game we all loved to play.

For some reason, I was always the slowest player to get my gear on, the last one out of the dressing room before and after the game. But I didn't care... maybe I just loved the anticipation of that first step and glide onto the ice. Sometimes the Zamboni would be out of commission and all the players would have to skate huge metal shovels around for fifteen minutes or so to clear the snow off the ice before we could play or practice. Your ankles and arms could get pretty exhausted, but it turned out to be good for improving your skating.

I never scored many goals as a defenseman my whole career, and I never forgot my first one. A total fluke. I was coming out from behind my own net, took a swipe and iced the puck on a penalty kill. The puck hit a rut at the far blue line, bounced up on its edge, rolled slowly towards the net and somehow miraculously went right between the opposing goalie's legs. I'll never forget the joyful "Hurray" that came from my dad in the wooden bleachers.

We lived in the fairly large town of London, Ontario. But for a few years, most of our games were played out of town in a tin can of an arena in Glencoe, Ontario, over an hour's drive from our house. My family drove to most games, carrying three or four other players with us in the car. One time, I realized halfway there that I'd forgotten my skates! Pops turned around, went back to our house, and then raced us to the arena. As time was getting tight, he suggested we put on our equipment in the car. Arms, legs, jerseys, pads, socks and skates were flying everywhere and anywhere, and we were all freaking out that we were going to miss our game. When we finally got there and quickly tiptoed across the snow-dusted gravel parking lot into the arena, we discovered that the game before us had been delayed. So we skated right out onto the ice just before the puck dropped. I think the adrenalin worked in our favour... we were on fire that game and won 7 to zip!

The other thing that sticks in my mind about those days in the frigid rinks was how our feet would slowly freeze up during the game. By the end, when we were back in the dressing room, all the fathers would be invited in to rub their sons' feet to try and get some of the feeling back in those "popsicle toes."

Later, when I had the great fortune of having a son of my own, he didn't go out for organized hockey but we still loved the game together. Table hockey with the cat on a chair watching, hand hockey on the front room rug in between periods of watching Hockey Night in Canada, and even making a fake Stanley Cup out of cardboard and tinfoil and singing the national anthem before playing hockey in the driveway for hours.

But I think my fondest memories are of the two of us playing outside on a frozen pond near my parents' house. We'd trudge through the snow with our skates hanging from tied laces around our shoulders and carrying shovels... just in case. Sometimes clearing off a space big enough to play would take us well over an hour... but the thrill of being able to teach my son how to shoot and pass a puck in every way possible and make up dazzling plays, usually against imaginary opponents, was a true winter joy I will cherish forever.

~Chris Robinson

44

# Someday Finally Came

*You don't raise heroes, you raise sons. And if you treat them like sons,*
*they'll turn out to be heroes, even if it's just in your own eyes.*
*~Walter M. Schirra, Sr.*

My husband, Ron, just crossed something off his bucket list. Forty-five years ago, Ron's dad took him to his first hockey game at the Chicago Stadium. Back then there were only the original six hockey teams. The game was the Blackhawks versus the Red Wings. At that time, Ron's family could not afford seats at the game. The best his dad could afford was standing room only, in the nosebleed section. He bought the tickets for one dollar each. Ron remembers the feeling of excitement just being there with his dad, in the midst of all those other hockey fans. The standing crowd was four people deep. They were so high up that Ron said when got a glimpse of the players they looked like ants on the ice. Even so, Ron says that night at the Stadium was one of his best memories of being with his dad.

Ron always thought that he would reciprocate and take his dad to a game. But sometimes life happens and we don't get the opportunity to make good on our promises, even when those promises are to ourselves.

After Ron and I got married, we got a call that his dad had a terrible accident at work. Ron's dad worked in construction. When we arrived at the hospital, the doctors told us that Dad was going in for surgery. The doctors feared that he might lose his leg. Luckily, his leg was spared. The doctor built a cage, held by pins that pierced through his leg, that he wore for a year. The technology that held his leg together was new and we often joked that he was the bionic man. Eventually Dad went back to his construction job, but the cold winter in Chicago bothered his leg immensely. So over thirty years ago, Mom and Dad moved to Florida until just this September, when they moved back home to be close to us.

As Christmas approached, Ron wanted to get Dad something very special. He remembered his promise to take his father to a hockey game; he wanted to recreate one of his favorite father and son memories. When Dad opened his Christmas gift, there were tears of joy in his eyes, which matched the ones in Ron's.

The game night arrived. Ron and Dad were both excited about once again seeing the Blackhawks versus the Red Wings, this time at the United Center.

At the beginning of the game, they showed Red Hawks highlights for four minutes. When it was over the attendants rolled out a red carpet, two veterans walked out—one from World War II and one from the Iraq War and stood on center ice. Then Jim Cornelison, the national anthem singer, walked out. The lights dimmed and they shined a spotlight on the three men as well as on the American Flag. The veterans saluted while Cornelison sang the national anthem. Ron and Dad were proud and emotional, as I am sure many people in the crowd were.

In the United Center, there are four large screens on the scoreboard showing the score, replays of the game and fan participation. Throughout the game, the video screens showed highlights of games played in the past as well. Ron and Dad saw the game they were at forty-three years earlier as the screen continued to combine showing the old with the new!

Their favorite part of the evening was during one of the crowd scans, the camera showed Stan Mikita in a luxury suite with his grandsons, and Bobby Hull with his family in another luxury suite.

Ron looked over to his dad and asked him if he knew who that was up on the screen. Dad said, "Yes, of course, the Golden Jet."

Times had changed. Ron and Dad now sat in great seats on the main level. The tickets cost more than a dollar, but the feeling was the same. This lucky father and son enjoyed simply being at the game together. And what more do you need than that?

~Julienne Mascitti-Lentz

# 45

# The Zamboni

*My other car is a Zamboni.*
*~Hockey Saying*

**B**y the middle of December the small pond in back of our home was starting to freeze, the first fragile layers of thin ice crusting on its surface. As soon as we saw those, my brother and I kept a constant vigil. We walked down to the water's edge each day after school, putting progressively more and more weight onto the ice until one of us—the braver, usually my brother—was able to tiptoe out a few feet, one arm grabbing tightly to a rope. Once there, he would jump up and down, pounding his boots into the ice, testing it.

"It's a few inches, at least," he turned to me and said a week after the vigil had started. "Come out."

I let the rope down and picked up my hockey stick, holding it horizontally so I formed a giant "T." Should I go through, the stick would hopefully bar me from going completely under. Inching onto the ice, I stood next to my brother and then both of us jumped up and down, shuffling closer to the middle of the pond. The ice creaked beneath us and we stopped, waiting to go through, hockey sticks ready. But the ice was quiet, easily four to six inches thick.

"Tomorrow," I announced. "It'll be perfect tomorrow."

Rain can do one of two things to a backyard hockey rink. It can either make it the sweetest, smoothest surface you have ever glided across, or it can turn it into those bone-jarring rumble strips on the side of major highways. Bam-bam-bam-bam-bam-bam. More often it is the latter, especially early in the season when the weather shifts between freezing and melting during an afternoon. On Saturday morning we discovered that was what had happened to our ice. Millions of ice pebbles scarred the surface. Undeterred, we strapped on skates, threw down a puck and tried to make the most of it.

Shortly after christening this year's season, my brother skated over to me. "Th-th-th-th-th-is... s-s-s-s-s-t-t-t-inks," he said, bouncing to a rest beside me.

"Yes, it does," I agreed. "Let's go see Dad."

Our father has a gift for figuring out solutions to such problems, rigging up impossibly complex contraptions that sputter and smoke and break numerous environmental laws. Creating the perfect ice rink was one of his favorite projects. One year, we ran a series of hoses onto the ice to flood a new inch of water on top of the bad one. The hoses froze, the ice clumped in awkward waves, and the rink was useless until it melted and refroze a week later. Another year, we took an axe to a corner of the pond and chopped through to the liquid beneath. We then set a sump pump into it with a hose running out to the middle of the pond. The theory again was to flood the old surface and create "glass" to skate on. At the rate the pump worked, it would have taken us the entire winter. As it was, after a few hours, the hose froze, the ice clumped in awkward waves, and the rink was useless until it melted and refroze a week later. This year, however, he tried something totally different. Revolutionary.

The homemade, portable Zamboni machine.

Taking an old feed trough from the back yard, my father instructed us, once we dragged it down to the ice, to fill it with wood—twigs, branches, logs, anything. He then tied a rope to a hole at one end of it and with the help of some lighter fluid and a match, set the whole contraption alight. My brother and I stared, perplexed. Half the enjoyment for my father, I think, came in explaining how his contraptions were supposed to work.

"Once the fire really gets going, the metal will get really hot," he said. "Hot enough to melt ice. Then we just drag it around and it will act like an iron, smoothing down the rough spots." As always, my brother and I smiled. His plan did sound good.

Half an hour later, a suitable time as any, my father picked up the free end of the rope, latched it over his shoulder, turned about and leaned forward.

The Zamboni didn't move.

He tried again.

It still didn't budge.

"It's too heavy," he announced. "We need to take some of the wood out."

My brother and I looked at each other and then at the wood. It was on fire, right?

Dad grunted. "Fine. I'll do it." Deftly pinching unlit pieces, he emptied half the wood out and picked up the rope again. By now, hours had passed since we first stepped onto the ice.

"Here we go," he said and hefted once more.

The Zamboni jerked to life. Dad set forth across the pond.

More so than any image I carry with me from a decade of skating on ponds with friends and family, I can picture perfectly Dad trudging away from the two of us, his thick mountain-man jacket on, a ratty pair of blue jeans, tan boots and a red Folgers Coffee hat on his head. Behind him, like some poor, mistreated pet, stumbled the gray trough, tiny embers shooting over its lip onto the ice.

He walked slowly, so as to give the Zamboni extra time to do its ironing. After about twenty yards, still moving forward, he said to us over his shoulder, "Well?"

I'd like to say that there before us was blazed a path of glassy ice, as neatly done as any giant machine in a professional rink... and that over the next few hours he patiently walked line after line, like mowing a lawn, until the entire pond was the sweetest, most perfect surface ever created in a back yard. I'd like to say that. Sadly, it was impossible to tell where exactly the Zamboni had traveled. The bumps and grooves caused by the rain were still there, though they might have glistened a bit more, as if sweating.

"Well?" he said again.

"Nothing," I answered.

For many people this might have been the sign to end the project—drag the trough off the ice, put the fire out, and wait for the pond to melt and refreeze in a week. That was what my brother and I thought. But not our father. As we scooted off the ice and returned to the kitchen for hot chocolate, he kept going, patiently walking line after line. He stayed out there for another hour, perhaps two, while we watched occasionally through the sliding glass door. Eventually, as afternoon turned into early evening and the temperature got colder and no one was checking up on him anymore, he dumped the trough into the snow on the bank and clambered through the back yard into the basement. The pond would have to wait for warmer weather.

There's a lesson in the Zamboni about fatherhood, I think: that it is not about being perfect in your actions but perfect in your intent. Love is not smooth as glass, but bumpy as pebbled ice with ridges, and holes, and places to fall down. Sometimes no one will be watching you walk line after line, but they'll remember that you were out there and they'll smile, the sweetest, smoothest, warmest smile you've ever seen.

Perhaps the Zamboni really did work.

~Michael Sullivan

# 46

# Our Last Game

*Having a place to go — is a home.*
*Having someone to love — is a family.*
*Having both — is a blessing.*
*~Donna Hedges*

Our family loves hockey... and we are huge fans of the Toronto Maple Leafs. We have watched them on television since I was a little kid. But the most exciting part of hockey for my family was travelling from our home in the country to Toronto to watch them play live at Maple Leaf Gardens!

My mom's dad died when she was a teenager. My grandpa had season tickets to the Gardens. The tickets were given to my grandma and eventually they were passed on to my mom. Four seats. First Row Green, centre ice. Perfect. My dad, mom, twin sister and I used to go to the Gardens and cheer ourselves hoarse. We would drive from our home in Georgetown into the big city and excitement would build as we travelled along Highway 401. We would guess the score and see who would be the closest, as the anticipation built up for the game.

My younger sister Aynsley was born in 1978. Now our family had grown to five. As she grew up, she also began to watch hockey and travel to Toronto to Maple Leaf Gardens. Because there were only four seats, many times my mom would stay home as the four of us — my dad, two sisters and I — went to see the Leafs. We always wished it could have been the five of us going together.

Sadly, the Maple Leaf Gardens announced they were closing their doors and the last game would be on February 13, 1999. The Leafs would host the Chicago Blackhawks for the last historic game in the Gardens.

A very special thing happened that night for our family of five. We all wanted to go to the last game so we decided that the best thing to do would be to have all five of us travel to the game. We would rotate ourselves through the three periods of play—that way we would all have a turn to see the Leafs play their last game in the Gardens. My sister Susan volunteered to be the first to sit out for part of the first period. Then I was set to change places with her so that she could see the game too.

As we all arrived at the Gardens that night, Susan made her way to a spot near the entry gate as the four of us went up to our seats in the Green section. After the national anthems played, I was overcome with a feeling that my sister should be sitting up there and I left my seat to go and change places with her earlier than planned. As I walked downstairs, heading towards the gate, a Maple Leaf Gardens ticket collector asked me where I was going. I explained that I was going to let my sister watch the game. He asked to see my ticket. "So you have a ticket?" he asked. "Yes I do," was my reply. I walked a little farther and saw Susan waiting there, wondering why I had come down so early. I handed her my ticket and said, "You are missing out. Go up and we'll change places later on." The same ticket collector had followed me and listened to what I said. With a twinkle in his eye he then asked Susan, "So you have a ticket too?" Now, he had clearly seen me give my ticket to Susan. He smiled at us. Susan said, "Yes." After a moment's pause, the ticket collector said, "Well as far as I can see, you both have a ticket, so what are you waiting for? In you two go!" gesturing us into the rink by waving his arms. And in we went!

This man's kindness, understanding and willingness to overlook the "rules" for this special night are something I will never forget.

"Thank you" is all we could think of saying at the time, and we shouted it to him as we ran up the wooden stairs. As it happened, our seats were located right beside the stairs at centre ice. As Susan and I smiled and joyfully descended the stairs, my parents saw the two of us coming to watch the game together and were speechless. Excitedly, we told them about the amazing gift we had just experienced. My dad moved over to sit on the edge of the stair, so that the five of us could sit and watch the game in a row, all together. We were so happy and felt so lucky. The last game at the historic Gardens and the first game we all watched our beloved Leafs together as a family!

I often have thought so fondly about the man who allowed us both in that night. It might have seemed like a little thing to him, easily forgotten, but it made a huge difference to us, and when I think of that night, I still remember what he did for our family.

If he is reading this story now, I want him to know how grateful I am.

~Leigh Anne Saxe

# 47

# Back to School, Back to Hockey

*If you can't laugh at yourself, then how can you laugh at anybody else?*
*I think people see the human side of you when you do that.*
~Payne Stewart

**B**ack to school means back to hockey if you are a hockey mom. Everything comes at once! Some moms welcome this, but I always found it a little sad, or at least the anticipation of it a little sad. Once it was upon me, I was way too busy to feel anything.

One particular back to school and back to hockey week stands out in my mind. All three boys were in the midst of tryouts, as was their father, who was coaching each of them in some capacity. The girls were full bore into the social relationships that the start of a new school year brings, and I was trying yet again to turn over a new leaf and be organized this time round.

We were in the midst of the morning rush, which meant getting five kids to the bus on time, with backpacks and lunches in tow. My husband, retired NHL hockey player, Ryan Walter helped me pack lunches in the kitchen while the kids ate breakfast. Ryan is fast on his feet and quick with his hands… he had ten slices of bread laid out and was slapping mustard and mayo around like nobody's business. I was rounding out the lunches with fruit, snacks and beverages. This year I had decided to forego juice boxes that were never big enough for our growing hockey players, and replace them with the cans of iced tea I had chilling in the fridge. I was so organized!

We had officially ended summer on Labor Day weekend by hosting a barbecue for Ryan's employees and their families. The weather had been great, kids swam and played ball hockey, we provided the food, and the guests brought their own beverages. It was our last hurrah before the school and hockey schedules would rule our lives for the next nine months.

Well, the kids and their lunches made the bus, and I hurried off to a Creative Planning Team meeting at our church. When I arrived home, Ryan told me he had received a call from the principal. That is never a good thing during the first week of school, but Ryan had a smile on his face, so I wasn't too worried. That was not about to last, however.

It seemed that our elementary school's principal, Henry, had called to asked Ryan who had packed the lunches that morning. Ryan answered that we both did. Then Henry proceeded to say that our youngest son, Joey, had taken a big swig from his drink in his grade six class, spat it out and said, "This tastes terrible!" What I thought had been a can of iced tea, sitting sideways in our refrigerator door, evidently was instead a leftover beverage from the weekend barbecue. It turns out that I had sent our son to Langley Christian School with a Coors Light in his lunch!

I decided right there and then that no way could I ever show my face at that school again. I was devastated. I was the worst mother ever, hockey or not. While I had been at a meeting with our worship pastor, who just happens to be our principal's son, the principal and every teacher at our school had been laughing hysterically in the staff room. I somehow failed to see the humor.

Time does heal, though. I lifted my head and went to that first chapel at the school, and lived to tell the tale. I made it through tryouts. The kids had fun seasons. Now here I am telling you about one of the most humiliating moments of my life. Being a hockey mom is so not about being perfect and I am stunning evidence of that fact. So, please don't feel overwhelmed by back to school or back to hockey or back to dance or back to work. Do your best, and forgive yourself if you mess up, because let's face it, no way will you ever mess up as badly as I did! The important thing is to have your heart in the right place and to refuse to miss out on any part of your children's lives, even when it is difficult or embarrassing, because, trust me, one day you will laugh about it.

~Jennifer Walter

# 48

# Will There Be Hockey in Heaven?

*Why are men reluctant to become fathers?*
*They aren't through being children.*
*~Cindy Garner*

My blank stare must have encouraged him because he asked another question. "You like the Toronto Maple Leafs don't you?"

There was no doubt as to how I should answer this question. "Sure," I said.

"In that case, I'll let you marry my daughter." He followed up with, "If you decide to elope I'll give you three hundred dollars. Then I won't have to pay for a wedding." After a brief pause he added, "You wouldn't have to use a ladder either. Her room is on the first floor." It took a while for me to realize he was kidding—except for the Maple Leaf part.

I'd known Randy for less than an hour, and Bonnie and I weren't even formally dating, but that was my introduction to my future father-in-law. His obsession with hockey—of the Maple Leafs variety—is only second to his love for God and his family.

As far as Randy is concerned, every night is Hockey Night in Canada. My first encounter with him on a real hockey night happened that first time I visited. I kept hearing shouting from the upstairs family room so I went up to see what all the shouting was about. Randy was in front of the television and all dressed up for the occasion: Maple Leafs slipper socks, Maple Leafs sweat pants, Maple Leafs hat, no shirt! He had the balcony door open a bit for winter air ventilation and held a rag in one hand in case he perspired too much during intense action. He was cheering and yelling at the players as if he were sitting at Maple Leaf Gardens at center ice! That's how it was every time there was a hockey game, and if the Leafs weren't playing, he'd pick another team and cheer for them instead, though not nearly as enthusiastically.

I soon discovered that Randy also had T-shirts, sweatshirts, a jacket and a wallet to match. The wallet, though a little threadbare, is proudly displayed when he meets another fan. Seeing someone wearing Maple Leafs gear, he has been known to walk up to total strangers, pull out his blue and white wallet and ask, "Would you like to rub my wallet for luck?" His license plate also reflects his love of the game. It reads 75TO67. He received the plate when he turned seventy-five years old and it commemorates the winning of the Stanley Cup championship in 1967. Though the Leafs have won the cup eleven times, 1967 marks their most recent win. It is the longest running championship drought in NHL history so Randy cherishes this particular series as "precious."

Randy's enthusiasm has not always been appreciated. Once, while attending a game in Buffalo with his friend Skip, he was almost attacked by a group of drunken Buffalo fans for cheering too loudly for Toronto. The Leafs were winning when the men threatened to throw Randy over the wall. Skip, who was a very big man, stood up and glared at the men and they became very quiet. He told them, "This is my friend and he's a Maple Leafs fan. I'm a Buffalo fan. If anyone's going to throw him over the side, it'll be me!" After that, they all got along well and there was no more trouble even though the Leafs won.

It was at another Buffalo versus Toronto game that Randy had a real scare. Just as the game started, he experienced a heart attack. He knew what was happening, but in spite of his fear he refused to leave. He stayed and watched the entire game before seeking treatment. After that, his doctor warned him that he had to be "a little less involved" in hockey games.

The love of hockey was passed on to Randy's son, my brother-in-law Scot, who grew up watching hockey on TV with his dad and playing the game on their backyard rink. Randy worked hard on the rink and it was one of the best in town. Kids, young and old, came from all around the neighborhood to skate on that ice. In fact, it wasn't unusual for one twenty-five-year-old neighbor, Rick, to knock on the door after supper and ask, "Can Scot come out and play hockey?" Scot was seven.

Randy was very particular about his hockey rink. One evening, his next-door neighbor Albert slipped and fell on the ice. Randy rushed over and asked him, "Are you okay?" When Albert replied that he was, Randy said to him, "Then can you move over onto your own lawn? I don't want to get blood on my ice."

When Scot was very young, his heroes were hockey players. One day his father heard him running through the house with a hockey stick yelling, "I'm Bobby Orr, I'm Bobby Orr." His father snatched him up and told him in a very serious voice, "Son, in this house you're Davey Keon." He put Scot down and off he ran yelling, "I'm Davey Keon, I'm Davey Keon."

Years later, when Scot was in college and recruited to play on the school hockey team, Randy and Pauline became hockey parents. Seriously devoted, they were the only parents who never missed a game. On one occasion, Scot, who was the goalie, lost a glove. It slid just out of reach behind the net and the puck was still in play. In his excitement, Scot forgot the loss of equipment as the puck moved down the ice toward the net. When a slap shot sped directly at him, he lifted his bare hand to block the shot and almost broke his wrist. He fell to the ice in pain and the play was stopped. That's when Pauline, his mom, ran down from the stands yelling, "Honey, are you okay? Honey, are you okay?" When she reached the area behind the goal she banged on the glass and shouted, "Show me your hand, son. Show me your hand!"

Finally, the referee skated over to Scot and said, "Son, you'd better show your mom your hand." After that, Scot's teammates never let him live it down. At the slightest bump they'd call out, "Show us your hand, Son." This taunt even made it into the college yearbook.

Randy loves hockey so much that he composed a little ditty to celebrate the game. At the most inappropriate moment and with almost no encouragement he'll burst into song. He did this at Scot's wedding reception. During a time when guests had been invited to share their thoughts about the bridal couple Randy stood and sang:

"Will there be hockey in heaven,
Will there be ice to play?
Will there be hockey in heaven?
It would melt if it was the other way."

I've now been married into this hockey-loving family for almost thirty years. They still surprise me with their devotion to the game. I have a feeling that when Randy finally arrives in heaven, if he finds no hockey, he'll ask the Lord for cold air and buckets of water to build a rink. A really big one!

~John P. Walker

**49**

# When I Think of Summer, I Think of Zambonis

*Just as you have the ability to change your mind, you also have the ability to change the state of your mind. Happiness and joy are states of mind to be enjoyed any time you want.*

*~Author Unknown*

On a recent morning, the temperature was hovering in the high 80s and the sun was blazing overhead. It was a perfect day to head to the local pool to cool off with my four-year-old son Nicholas. Instead, we decided to glide over to our local skating rink. "Let's go watch the Zamboni," Nicholas said after breakfast.

When it comes to spending time with my son, I try to think outside the box. I like to take him on adventures more than play dates. Maybe it's because I'm a dad. I'd rather ride a train or watch a fire engine with him than lounge around a pool.

For his part, Nicholas enjoys anything with wheels. So I called the arena to ask what time the Zamboni was going to cut the ice.

"I have a four-year-old boy who loves to watch the Zamboni," I explained sheepishly. The woman on the line chuckled. "Lemme check," she said. She put me on hold and returned with the time.

At the appointed hour, I strapped Nicholas into his car seat and we drove past the pool to the arena. We walked inside, our sandals slapping the arena floor as we passed a boy wearing his goalie pads and skates after hockey practice. The goalie joined his exhausted teammates sitting around tables in the lobby, inhaling snacks.

The cool air wrapped itself around us like fog on an autumn morning. I immediately forgot about the summer heat. The chilly air filled the arena and we, in our T-shirts and shorts, basked in it as if it were pool water. With the temperature around sixty degrees Fahrenheit, in more ways than one it was one of the coolest places I knew to hang out.

The Zamboni driver, wearing white gloves, a black jacket and a blue baseball cap for warmth, was just backing the forest green and white Zamboni out of the garage to begin his oval route. Nicholas and I clanked up the steps of the metal bleachers and he ran to choose a bench in the sixth row for the best view.

"Sit here, Daddy," he said, patting the bench next to him. "We can see great from here!" We had the bleachers to ourselves. Why hadn't anyone else thought of this?

Nicholas didn't frolic in the water at the rink — the water's frozen. He didn't learn to share and play nicely — he was a mere spectator. But we were together, and we were both having a great time. I get bored silly at the pool. And, quite frankly, a lot of the other parents I've seen there look bored, too, as they fidget with their cell phones.

We sat there entranced by the loud, hypnotic hum of the Zamboni echoing around the arena as its fat rubber tires rolled over the chipped and scratched ice. The machine shaved off the powdery ice shards left by the young hockey players and left behind a shiny, glistening surface, brightened by the reflection of the overhead fluorescent lights. This was the closest we needed to get to water.

Much of the time, my philosophy is as follows: If Nicholas is happy, I'm happy. But the reverse can also be true: If I'm happy, he's happy, and I think that goes a long way in adding value to our time together.

After fifteen minutes, the Zamboni left the ice and was replaced by figure skaters who twirled, jumped and coasted like synchronized swimmers. We watched them for a while.

"I'm feeling a little cold," Nicholas said. "But just a little."

So we left. No use stretching our stay into overtime and inviting illness. Back outside, the humidity drenched us like a thick rain.

Don't get me wrong, Nicholas enjoys the pool. After all, he's four years old. But he also likes it when we discover and explore new and unusual places together, like an ice rink in the middle of summer. I've tried to instill a sense of adventure in him, and when I see him get a thrill from taking a walk—or a train ride—off the beaten path, I feel like I'm doing something right.

When we visit the zoo (conveniently located next to the arena), he doesn't go to visit the animals—too cliché. He wants to ride the miniature train and the carousel. By the same token, we don't go to the rink for the hockey or figure skating. Instead, he finds the entertainment between the main attractions.

He likes to watch the Zambonis in life, and that makes me proud. Maybe next summer I'll sign him up for skating lessons instead of swim lessons.

~Christopher Harder

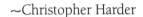

# Ice in Our Veins

*What makes it all worthwhile is we just play for the sheer enjoyment of entertaining people and... make our families and the team we played on and the people watching, proud of what we did.*

*~Bobby Hull*

It was 1917 when seventeen-year-old Elizabeth lost her two front teeth. More surprising than the gap in her smile was the reason for its presence: as goalie for the University of Minnesota's first-ever women's club hockey team, she had been pummeled with pucks to the mouth. This was a time when hockey was a man's sport and equipment meant strap-on skates and a wooden stick. Helmets and facemasks? Inventions of the future, not to be considered by the flinty (albeit toothless) pioneers of the game. Even after facing countless flying pucks—not to mention adversity as one of few females playing the sport—Elizabeth was not deterred from the rink. Her passion and determination were evident when she smiled.

After graduating, Elizabeth married. It wasn't long before a daughter was born. Maybe the passion for hockey was hereditary, tied to a certain chromosome just like the genes for eye color and height. Maybe it wasn't. But Jackie grew up and wanted to play. However, girls' high school sports in the 1940s were limited to pom-poms and pleated skirts; the girls' "playing field" consisted of the confined area of the sidelines. So, with seemingly no other options, Jackie joined her friends on the cheerleading squad. If she couldn't play hockey, she could at least enjoy the front row seats to the high school boys' games that her cheer position afforded her, right?

Yet it turned out the festive pom-poms were less than comforting. Cheering at the games only heightened Jackie's eagerness to try the sport. So, one blustery winter day, equipped with a persuasive speech and her mother's determination, Jackie brazenly asked to join the boys' team. Today, her move might be admired, even celebrated. However, in that pre-Title IX era, the boys reacted to her request with scoffs and raised eyebrows. No girl had ever demanded something so ridiculous, they said. Jackie's response? She quit cheering for them, and convinced all of her friends to do the same.

Time passed, and Jackie married. She gave birth to seven children, including a daughter, Jana. Their family barely scraped by, cramped within the walls of a small house in Minneapolis. As both Jackie and her husband worked, the children were often left to find ways to entertain themselves. Summertime was easy, affording the siblings long days to splash in the community pool or explore the grassy stretches of the neighborhood baseball field. Winters were more difficult. The biting cold corralled most of the siblings into the house, where the girls baked cookies and designed fashion lines while the one, mischievous boy found ways to annoy his sisters. Jana alone braved the outdoors. Night after night, her silhouette could be seen skating fluidly on a self-constructed backyard rink. Shining and confident in her blade-bedecked boots, she swirled round and round, mirroring the pattern of the falling snow.

Again, time went by. In 1972, Title IX was passed, ushering in a new era of women's sports. Meanwhile, Jana enrolled at St. Catherine University where she used her athletic talents in a warmer, liquid version of her childhood backyard rink: the swimming pool. She enjoyed great success there, but eventually graduated, married, and had children of her own. Despite the labors of motherhood, her long-ago passion for skating was not forgotten. It was with enthusiasm and eagerness that she signed up to join a women's hockey league in 1998.

At the same time, Jana's daughter, Alana, was nurturing her own passion for the sport. Learning to skate at a young age, she soon joined Mites teams and eventually graduated to U-10 and U-12 programs. The summer Alana was twelve years old, she dragged a net and slab of dirty plastic out into the grass of her back yard. Fending off mosquitoes and heat, she diligently shot 5,000 pucks over three months. That twelve-year-old was me.

In my family, hockey is much more than just a game. It is a passion, a tradition, and a legacy that has endured generation after generation, from my great-grandmother Elizabeth to my older sister, also a goaltender, and me. It is something that strengthens us — as competitors and as women — and something that unites us. Although I never knew Elizabeth, I am almost certain that she would agree with me when I describe the feeling of carving the ice beneath your feet and experiencing the wintry rush of skating as exhilarating and empowering. My grandmother Jackie, born before her time, helps me understand that putting on a jersey is a privilege — something I am thankful for every day. And my mom? At fifty-five, Jana continues to skate, sometimes playing in games as often as four nights a week. She knows what I mean when I say that there is no other feeling like seeing that goal light burn red, how winning a big game frees your spirit.

Today, I am a member of St. Olaf College's women's varsity hockey team, a Division III program. Those five thousand pucks I shot as a twelve-year-old — and thousands more afterward — have brought me to a level of competition at which I thrive, and to a team that I call my family. However, when I pull on the jersey every Friday and Saturday night, I also remember my true family: the women who inspired me to play the sport that is now my passion. Someday, I hope to pass on this legacy to daughters (and sons) of my own. For now I skate forward with gratitude, mindful of the generations of role models before me with each, exhilarating stride.

~Alana Patrick

# Love and Hockey

*Sports do not build character; they reveal it.*

*~Heywood Brown*

My husband Roger had been content to watch all of his sports on TV: football, baseball, basketball, and his beloved hockey, until 1993 when a hockey team started up right here in Orange County, California. He couldn't resist the fact that the Mighty Ducks of Anaheim would be playing teams from all over the country, even from Canada.

Roger's from Canada, where hockey is king. His dad flooded the back yard in the winter to form a makeshift ice rink, and he played in college until a knee injury sidelined him. Me, I'm clumsy, have two left feet, and couldn't hit my way out of a paper bag. I had no interest in sports.

Roger brought home season tickets and proudly waved them in front of me. "I got us great seats!"

He was happy and I was horrified. Secretly, I didn't think I could ever enjoy these games and wondered how I could weasel out of going.

Opening night arrived. "Dress warmly," Roger said. He explained that the arena was kept very cold to keep the ice from melting. Even if it was eighty degrees outside I needed to dress in a warm coat, boots, mittens and a scarf. We might as well have been in the back yard on a winter day in Canada. I was sweating by the time we drove the thirty miles to the arena and found a parking space. I had my mind made up this was not going to be fun.

Attendants at the door handed each person a bright orange T-shirt with "Mighty Ducks of Anaheim" emblazoned across the front. Roger put his on right away, showing his support of the team. When a hawker selling team wares walked down the aisle, Roger called him over. He picked out two duck calls, paid the man, and then handed me one. Just what I wanted—a duck call. All around us were excited fans, blowing their duck calls loudly, cheering for the newest hockey team with fervor. My husband was the most enthusiastic of them all, high-fiving the other fans when the Ducks made a goal.

During the intermission between the first of three periods, I stood in line for the ladies' room, which took extra time because of the layers of mittens, scarf, and button-down jacket I had to peel away. I returned to our seats, where Roger was engrossed in conversation with a Montreal Canadiens fan. After two more periods of play, we exited the arena. I couldn't wait to get out of those heavy clothes.

"We have another game Tuesday night," Roger said on the way home.

"Do you want to ask someone else to go with you?" I ventured.

"I like having you with me." He pulled to a stop behind another car and waited for traffic to move. Then he looked at me and added, "Sharing this with you is fun."

I didn't say anything. How could I tell him I really wasn't into it?

The next week it was unusually frigid in the arena, and even with my heavy coat I started shivering before the end of the first period.

"Are you cold?" Roger asked.

"I am tonight," I replied and stuck my hands deeper into my gloves.

"Here, take my jacket." He held it out behind me and I wiggled into it.

"Thanks, that's much better," I said.

Over time, I began to notice certain fans at the Pond. In the section to our left sat a father and his middle-aged daughter who always came together. Just the two of them. Further down our row was a family of four. A dad, mom, a preteen daughter and a boy who was around seven. He sat next to me most nights and I'd often hear him whisper under his breath, "Let's go Ducks." When they scored, he was the first one up and out of his seat.

I looked closer. Around me were husbands and wives, fathers and sons, brothers who came as a twosome, a whole cross-section of families and friends who came together in this cold arena to share in the sport of hockey. The Jumbotron flashed images of the fans between the action on the ice. People laughed, mugged for the cameraman, danced in the aisles, ate with enthusiasm and supported their team.

Just then a frantic push down the ice resulted in a goal for the Ducks and the crowd roared. The father and daughter rose to their feet and she high-fived her dad. His huge smile when his palm met hers told me this was more than hockey for them. Suddenly, it felt like I'd been missing out on something. Something important.

The next time the Ducks scored I jumped up, stuck out my hand, and high-fived first my husband and then the little guy on my left. They were surprised at my enthusiasm, and so was I.

I put my orange Ducks shirt on over my heavy coat the next time we went to a game and wore it proudly into the arena, my duck call nestled deep in one of the pockets. When the audience disagreed with a referee's decision and blew their duck calls, I blew mine right along with them. On the walk out to the car I commented, "That penalty in the third period cost the Ducks the game." Roger looked over at me and I continued. "The other team won because they scored on the power play."

He smiled and reached for my hand. "Wait until you see some of the really cool things in hockey, like a hat trick."

I smiled up at him and added, "Or even a shoot out?" We reached the car and got in for the drive home, my thoughts on the great time we had.

The next summer an ad came up on television about buying hockey tickets. "Let's renew our season seats again this year," I said to Roger. "I'll write out the check and you can take it with you to the box office."

"I thought you didn't like sports," he said.

"I like being with you," I replied. Sports are much more than players on ice or a field or a diamond. I don't have to understand or even love sports as much as my husband, but I love doing things together.

I was finally in the game.

~B.J. Taylor

# C'mon, Boys

*When you look at your life,*
*the greatest happinesses are family happinesses.*
*~Joyce Brothers*

I rush through the doors of our small-town arena, spilling a bit of coffee from my travel mug as I wave at a fellow hockey mom in the concession. Squeezing my daughter's hand excitedly, we climb the stairs to the spectator seating and my eyes sift through a sea of black and yellow jerseys on the ice. My son, #8, gives me a wave with his glove. I wave back, and then nod at my older son, running the warm-up music from the sound booth. I see my husband on the bench, conferring with the other coaches. Finally, I spot my dad in his usual aisle seat on the top row. I slide in beside him, pulling my daughter onto my lap, just in time for the puck to drop. I hear Dad whisper eagerly, "C'mon, boys," and I grin at the familiarity of that phrase.

Hearing Dad cheer at a minor hockey game takes me back to May of 1984. The Edmonton Oilers were set to potentially secure their first Stanley Cup win, playing Game Five at home, against the New York Islanders. Dad had been an Oilers season ticket holder since the team was in the WHL, and he loved nothing better than taking Mom or one of us kids on the forty-minute trip into the city to a game. Three years earlier, our family's passion for the game had been taken to an all-time high, when my cousin, Grant Fuhr, was drafted to the Oilers.

Dad was somewhat torn about who to take to the upcoming

game. We gathered around the kitchen table to sort it out, and he held out his fist with three straws. My brother Russ drew first, while Mom watched excitedly from the kitchen. My brother Stu drew next, and his straw was slightly shorter, so he knew he wasn't going anywhere. I drew next, and it took a few moments to register that, indeed, I had the longest straw. Envy enveloped my brothers as they began to make offers on the ticket. "C'mon, Bev… I'll give you fifty bucks," Russ pleaded. "Whoa… I'll give you $100," Stu eagerly offered. At fourteen years old, I firmly knew that if my brothers were willing to pay those prices for the ticket, it was going to be an event worth going to myself. I refused and smugly looked at my straw.

The night of the game was unforgettable, yet it started out like any other Oiler game outing with Dad. He is fanatical about being on time, so as always, we were among the first to walk into the Coliseum, hand in hand, as the doors opened. Our tradition was simple and we didn't deviate from it that night: we got our souvenir program, made our way downstairs, and lined up for our traditional hot dog and peanut-covered ice cream treat. Next was our trek up to Section 33, Row 26, Seats 3 and 4. Dad knew everyone in the vicinity, and I enjoyed listening to him make small talk.

On this night, the Coliseum buzzed with a new level of excitement. We joined 17,501 other fans, waving orange and blue banners in a frenzy as the lights dimmed. A lady in our row pulled sparkler candles out of her purse, and we all proudly lifted them as the anthem was sung and the puck was dropped.

Truthfully, I can't tell you the details of that game. I can't tell you who scored, or if there was a great game-changing play. I remember that my cousin wasn't in net that night, but I can't remember the details about why. What I can tell you is that when the Oilers played out the final minutes of the third period, and the evident win was solid in the roaring fans' minds, I stopped screaming at the top of my lungs, and looked up at my dad. He was quietly standing tall, and there was a single tear slowly falling down his cheek. At that instant, I fully appreciated his passion for this game in a way that I had never before. I thought of all of the times that I, as a typical teenager, had rolled my eyes at his yelling at Hockey Night in Canada on TV, or my angry mutters at the fight over the sport pages of the *Edmonton Journal*. Suddenly they all made sense as I saw the look of pure pride on my dad's face as he whispered to himself, "C'mon, boys."

His lifelong love affair with hockey was rolled into those two words; I etched that moment into my memory.

Dad is now seventy-two, and rarely goes to an Oilers game. The stairs are tough on his knees, and he doesn't appreciate the commercialization—and rising ticket prices. He believes that an NHL game should be an affordable family activity; that a dad should be able to take his daughter to a game and not "break the bank." So instead, he has chosen to be a regular fan at his grandsons' minor hockey games at the Glenn Hall Centennial Arena in Stony Plain, Alberta. Our hometown venue is small, and Dad will point out that you can't beat the (free) ticket price. Of course, he still knows most of the people who sit around us at a home game. But, best of all, he still cheers, "C'mon, boys!" with the same great passion for the game.

~Beverly A. Suntjens

# Part of the Team

*Teamwork is the fuel that allows common people to*
*attain uncommon results.*
*~Author Unknown*

In 2003, my family decided to move from our home in Los Angeles to Toronto, Canada. My parents were both originally from the East Coast (Ontario and New York) and they really missed their parents and siblings, not to mention the seasons. They also wanted to move my sister and me out of L.A., which was just not as family-oriented a culture as they wanted. I was not sure about it. I knew I would miss my friends and the warm weather and year-round sunshine, not to mention the pure fun that it was living in the Hollywood Hills. I didn't know how I would like Toronto but it turned out that I did really take to it once we got settled in. And one of the things I loved most turned out to be hockey.

Before we moved, I had only been on skates once in my life, at a classmate's birthday party. I remember really liking the sensation of gliding around the ice, but that was about it. Once we were in Toronto I asked my parents if I could join the local house league to see how I liked it. I remember the night my dad took me out to get my equipment. Man, there was a lot to buy—skates, shoulder pads, shin and elbow pads, pants, helmet, stick, etc. And it took a while to put it all on too, but I was excited to try it out.

We had thought that the first evening was going to be a practice. When we got to the arena we found out that there aren't any practices in house-league hockey. So, the very first time I played I found myself right in the middle of a game! Crazy. But I was open and willing to try.

I'd always been pretty athletic. In Los Angeles I played baseball, football, tennis, lots of kickball at school, golf… you name it. But hockey was different. I was trying to play this brand new game, balancing on super-slippery ice, while teetering atop a thin metal blade. Holding the stick was new too, although it did give me something to lean on. Anyway, my hockey coach sent me out on my first "shift" and the very first thing I did was fall flat on my back. I got up quickly, took a couple of strides on my skates and about two seconds later fell again. I fell so much that game I actually got a penalty because I kept running into the referee, even knocking him over a couple of times.

I must have fallen about a hundred times during that game… but I also started to figure out the game and actually got involved in quite a few plays. I didn't get a goal, but I did take a couple of shots. When I came off the ice my mom and dad were right there with concerned looks on their faces. To their surprise, I yelled, "I love it! I think I've found my game!" Everyone laughed, but I meant it.

After that night, I was hooked. I immersed myself in the sport, watching all the NHL games on TV that year, rooting for the Leafs, of course and watching Sports Centre every morning before school. I became a fanatic! The thing that made me improve the most, I think, was the fact that the neighborhood where we lived had so many kids. There was a game of road hockey going on pretty much every day after school. We got a hockey net and the kids across the street had one too. We'd put them out on the street and within minutes, we would have a pick up game going. This would last until my mom would have to call me repeatedly to come in for dinner.

The following year, when I was eleven years old, I tried out for the more advanced, "select" team. I never thought I would make the team… but the coach took me. He was a great coach, a mentor to me and he is still one of our family's really good friends.

And that brings me to one of the best things about hockey — the friendships.

I made some really good friends through my hockey teams. And my parents made great friends too. My family and I were all new to the area, and the parents of my team, the Leaside Flames really welcomed us all into the group. Even my little sister, Julia, who got dragged along to most of games and practices — I think she really only liked the hot chocolate — made new friends.

There were always a few other sisters at the games and they all would run around the arena, going up and down the bleachers, and cheering loudly for us whenever we needed it. It was like we all had an instant social life — traveling to tournaments, sleepovers, fundraisers, carpooling, and that really made us fall in love with Canada!

The other thing I love to do is sing and when I was twelve I joined a children's opera company. I got a solo in this big professional production of La Boheme. With hockey and the show and school my schedule got so crazy. One night, after performing in front of five thousand people I had to change into my hockey gear in the car as my dad rushed me to a game. I ran into the dressing room minutes before the whistle blew and right away all the guys started laughing like mad. I had forgotten to take off the heavy stage make-up they made us wear. It took a while to live that one down! And this last year I was fortunate enough to make it to the semi-finals of *Canada's Got Talent*. Not only did all my hockey friends support me in that journey, I also de-stressed from the pressure of the performances and rehearsals by playing hockey whenever I could. There's nothing better than getting complete drenched in sweat, playing a sport that completely consumes you, to really help a guy chill out.

I just graduated from high school and my school team won the city regional championships. I got to score the winning goal, which was a real thrill. And I go to a performing arts high school too… not bad for a bunch of actor/singer/artist/musicians.

I am off to Queen's University in Kingston, Ontario in the fall and I plan on trying out for the team, and if I don't make it they have a great intramural program too. I look forward to getting to know a whole new hockey family.

Bring it on!

~Jack Ettlinger

# Hooked on Hockey

## Global Games

# The Rink Rat

*Act as if what you do makes a difference. It does.*
~William James

In life, you never know who you will impact just by being yourself. Looking back there were so many people that helped me throughout my childhood and my journey and career in women's professional hockey. I was so fortunate to have a loving, dedicated family and incredible teammates and coaches. They all encouraged me and helped me to achieve my dreams of playing world class hockey. I had the honour of helping the Canadian Women's National Team win seven gold medals in World Cups. I also was a proud member of Team Canada when women's hockey was first introduced as an Olympic medal sport, in 1998, in Nagano, Japan. And I was on the team when we brought home Olympic Gold in Salt Lake City in 2002, in Torino in 2006 and in Vancouver in 2010! Those years were so amazing for me—talk about a wild ride! And it makes me very proud to think of all the other kids and athletes that I have had the honor of coaching and training. But there is one story in particular that stands out in my mind. A person who touched my heart... as I apparently touched hers.

In 2003, after the Salt Lake Olympics, I made decision that would change my life, and change the life of a young girl in the process. After the Salt Lake Olympics I wanted to challenge myself even further, I had this idea to play pro men's hockey and see if I could not only hold my own, but also excel. And so that is what I did. I was invited to go overseas to play professional hockey in Finland. I wanted to push myself out of my comfort zone, and played for the Finnish team called the Salamat, which means Lightning in Finnish.

When I arrived in Finland, in a town about twenty kilometers outside of Helsinki, I met a wonderful family called the Nillsons. They were managers of the rink we practiced on and they generously took me under their wing. Camilla Nillson would prepare a delicious hot lunch for the players after practise—she was like the team mom. They had three children and the youngest, Matilda, was about six years old. This little girl loved hockey and she spent a lot of time at the rink, seeing as both of her parents were working there all day.

One day Matilda came into my dressing room—I had one to myself being the only woman on the team. This cute little girl with long blond hair, almost like a little doll, just wandered in and sat down and stared at me because she didn't speak any English. We instantly became great friends though; we would communicate by doing drills together or by watching hockey games together and she would come to all my games and cheer for me and wear my jersey. She really loved being together, and I loved it too. I spent a lot of time with the Nillson family, especially in my second season, where I even lived with them for a while. Matilda became my shadow.

During practices she would always be coming out onto the rink. Whenever play would stop, even when the professional team was practicing, say when they stopped to hear what the next drill would be, out she would come and skate around. She was so happy on the ice.

The night I left Finland, Camilla, Matilda's mom, came to me and said, "I know Mathilda loves hockey, but I wasn't sure if I should keep her in the game because I've always thought it wasn't really a 'girl' thing to do. Now that I see you and that you still can be feminine and still be a woman, I think I'll let Matilda continue to play."

And she did.

And now it's 2012, Matilda is almost sixteen and she is one of the best players in Finland. I have mentored her over the years. She has flown to meet me at several camps I participate in, in various cities in Europe and we still speak quite often by Skype or phone. This summer she will be attending and helping out the International Ice Hockey Federation Under 18, Nation Performance camp in Finland that I am happy to be participating in hosting.

She is on her way to her dreams, to the Olympics, I hope... and I am so proud of her.

Like I said, you just never know who you are going to impact in your life, whose paths you're going to cross... and I am so happy that all those years ago, a little blond rink rat skated across mine.

~Hayley Wickenheiser

# A Nation
# Held Its Breath

*Hockey captures the essence of Canadian experience in the New World.*
*In a land so inescapably and inhospitably cold, hockey is the chance of life,*
*and an affirmation that despite the deathly chill of winter we are alive.*
*~Stephen Leacock*

I was circulating my classroom, following a geography lesson with my seventh grade class, when Rob's hand shot up. "Mr. Forrest do you think Canada can win?"

A month before, such a question would not have been taken seriously by any Canadian hockey fan. And if answered, the response would have been a confident, if not slightly sarcastic, "Are you kidding me?" But this day I took time to reflect.

It was September 28, 1972. The ideological and cultural "cold war" between East and West was at its peak and the Soviet Union was dominating World and Olympic "amateur" competitions, even in ice hockey.

Hockey was Canada's game, but our best players were professional and not allowed to play for their country. The Soviet's best players were enlisted in the Red Army. They were considered amateurs, even though their sole duty was to train full-time and win World Championship and Olympic medals. But you can't claim to be the best until you beat the best and the stage was set for a hockey supremacy showdown. An eight-game series, four to be played in each country, was to be held in September of 1972. Dubbed "The Summit Series" it would be the first and ultimate competition between full-strength Soviet and Canadian national ice hockey teams.

As a teacher who loved and still played hockey, I knew my students would be fully focused on the games; so I decided to seize the teachable moment and designed a unit of study based on the Summit Series. That month we studied the current culture and the history and geography of the Union of Soviet Socialist Republics and compared and contrasted it with Canada's.

Meanwhile, the Canadian Broadcasting Corporation went all out, preparing to televise all eight games. Legendary broadcaster Foster Hewitt was coaxed from retirement to do the play-by-play. For twenty-seven days in September our country would be hooked on hockey, and the anticipation of victory and vindication was palpable.

My students had been highly motivated in their work and the result was a remarkable learning experience for them and me. To wrap things up I had planned a pizza and soda party. We would mark a successful conclusion to their hard work and laud Canada's hockey supremacy by watching the final game together.

Indeed, all Canadian hockey fans were well primed for success. Finally we would get the chance to show "those Russians" who truly owned the ice. The Soviets were suitably deferential, pleased at being given the chance to improve their game by competing against such great players. But all was not as it seemed and when play started, an unexpected and incredible drama began to unfold.

Just prior to final game time, every student in my class and millions across Canada were wondering: Would the outcome be a triumph or tragedy? Hence my student's unlikely question—"Do you think Canada can win?"

The series opened on September 2, at the historic Montreal Forum. Thirty seconds after face-off, Canada's captain Phil Esposito scored. A few shifts later, unheralded winger Paul Henderson (a replacement for sidelined star Bobby Hull) notched a second goal. As predicted, these Russian pretenders to the hockey throne were no match for Canada's finest. Let the celebration begin. However, the Soviet defense stiffened and their offence went into high gear. Employing incredible speed, pinpoint passing and accurate shooting, the visitors dominated play for the balance of the game. Final score: Soviet Union 7 — Canada 3. Shock and disbelief descended like a wet blanket upon our land.

The next match was in Toronto's Maple Leaf Gardens. Grit, determination and great goalkeeping helped salvage a 4-1 victory and earn Canada a degree of redemption.

Winnipeg hosted Game 3. The very fit and multi-talented Soviet players again dominated play. We now knew their names and were beginning to appreciate their skills. Canada hung on and gained a 4-4 tie, but doubt was setting in and second-guessing was rampant amongst hockey pundits.

Then disaster struck in Vancouver. Soviet Union 5 — Canada 3. Disappointment and dismay reigned. In a now famous postgame television interview, a frustrated captain Esposito expressed the team's disappointment and appealed for support. Down two games to one with one game tied, Team Canada was going on to play in enemy territory. A disheartened group left for Moscow, where they would have to win three of four games to avoid an unthinkable series defeat.

All of the games in Russia were played at the Luzhniki Ice Palace in Moscow. Canadian fans had responded and 3,000 avid supporters were in the stands. In Game 5 Canada started strongly and built a 4-1 lead, but to the delight of the home crowd their team came back to record a 5-4 victory. The Soviets needed only to tie one of the remaining three games to claim victory in the series.

Despair, if not panic, now gripped most fans. But in Game 6, a desperate Canadian team, down by two goals, rallied in the third period. Henderson shot the game-winning goal. Canada 3 — Soviet Union 2. There was hope. Game 7 was even more dramatic. With the score tied and just minutes remaining, Henderson again saved the day with a game winner. Canada 4 — Soviet Union 3. Game 8 loomed and it was a must win.

It was time to answer Rob's question.

"Yes Rob, I believe we can, but it will be a very close game." I pointed to his desktop. "Your map of the Soviet Union looks impressive.

Good work! All right class, let's finish up. The game starts in thirty minutes."

That final match would be the most watched television broadcast of any kind in Canadian history. The country came to a standstill as a nation held its breath.

Two periods of Game 8 had been played. You could literally hear a pin drop in my classroom. The third and final period was about to start. Despite enthusiastic cheering from my students and me, Team Canada was losing 5 to 3. But defeat would not rest lightly on their shoulders. Against all odds Esposito scored early, making it 5-4 and then midway through the period Yvan Cournoyer tied the score at 5.

My kids started chanting "Go Canada Go!" but the Soviets knew even a tie would ensure a series victory for them and went into an almost impenetrable defensive shell. They stymied us again and again. Suddenly, though it was not his regular line, with just thirty-four seconds remaining, Paul Henderson jumped over the boards and joined the rush. And then, in the immortal words of Foster Hewitt: "Here's a shot! Henderson makes a wild stab at it... Here's another shot! Right in front. They score! Henderson has scored for Canada!"

My classroom exploded and a nation exhaled as one with a joyous cheer that would resonate forever in Canada's sporting history.

Canada 6—Soviet Union 5. O Canada.... Hockey is our game!

~John Forrest

# Olympic Spirit

*When I'm in Canada, I feel this is what the world should be like.*
*~Jane Fonda*

Few people have the opportunity to attend Winter Olympic Games. Not only did I have that opportunity in 2010, but I was able to watch the host country Canada play for the gold against its archrival and my home country United States in the most popular sport north of the border.

What struck me on Saturday, the night before the epic gold medal matchup, was the pride Canadians displayed. Not necessarily in playing host to the world or even in their usual kindness, but in their love of hockey. It was never more apparent than that evening, hours before they were to face off against the Americans, as citizens filled the streets—displaying flags, yelling, celebrating, and excited about a rematch against an underdog, less talented USA squad.

Team Canada had been embarrassed on their home ice a few days earlier by the U.S. in a sport that is more important than most everything in that country. It's their expertise. Their pride and joy. It draws absolutely no comparison to anything in the United States. Not baseball. Not football. Nothing. It is their life. And for them, on Canadian soil... er, ice... in the gold medal Olympic game, stacked with talent and expectation, in a rematch against their rival who had already defeated them, there may not have been a bigger game in their history. And the price of the ticket I purchased proved it.

The excitement boiled over to the Canada Hockey Place the next afternoon—the final day of the 2010 Winter Olympics. The crowd was 17,000 strong, packed with red and white, one with a sign declaring: Hockey is Canada's game. Only a few speckles of Americans wearing blue could be seen—maybe 500, surrounded by hockey-crazed, eh-saying Canadians. When the home team jumped to a 2-0 lead midway through the second period, it was obvious they were headed towards a gold.

Then, a little magic started happening. A goal five minutes later brought the Americans within one, but desperation clearly set in as the third period wound down. The Americans pressed. Hard. Knowing the clock was ticking and the chance at a second upset of the Canadians was slipping away. With a little over a minute remaining, the United States pulled their goalie, sending in an extra attacker, and with twenty-five seconds remaining Zach Parise tied the game—sending hope through the American fans, and doubt through those wearing a Maple Leaf.

Canada was devastated while Americans had flashbacks of the 1980 "Miracle on Ice" Olympic gold medal winning team. Their fans were nervous, doubtful, and fearful. That is, until Canadian hero Sidney Crosby scored in overtime—the arena, and subsequently an entire country, erupted in celebration. It spilled into the streets—people honking, parading, and yelling, as if their country had been saved. In a sense, it had.

Canadians didn't expect to lose. There was no choice—gold medal or failure. The U.S. won the silver medal against all odds. They lost the game, but won silver. But had Canada lost, the silver might as well have been filled with chocolate. Their country proved that they are the best in the world at a sport they invented. They were proud of it and didn't hesitate showing that pride. For hours. Never rioting, but celebrating. Never taunting, but cheering. Never tasteless, but happy. On top of the world, literally.

As I was leaving town that night, my not-nearly-as-happy self experienced two timeless memories with Canadians. While walking down the street, a guy drove by beeping his horn and pumping his fist out the window as everyone around returned a yell and a fist of their own. He noticed I wasn't very excited and stopped his car, looked at me, and said, "Hey man" as he pumped his fist. Sporting my USA hat, I looked up solemnly and tired, as if my country had been defeated, not knowing if he realized I was an American, and gave him a thumbs up and a congratulatory wink and nod. He said "Yeeaaah!" as he continued down the road cheering and beeping.

While driving out of town, I drove through an intersection only to be greeted by a swarm of red and white crossing the street. I was stuck, partly in the intersection and partly in the opposite crosswalk. People walked around my car, without a care in the world, cheering. As a couple passed in front of me, the girl stopped and put her hand on my hood while waiting until I made eye contact. I looked up with my USA hat on, her with a questioning smile, looking as if she wondered if I was mad at the crowd in front of me blocking the street. She gave me a questioning thumbs up, waiting for a smile, a cheer, or something. I grinned, and then beeped my horn a few times—the storm of people let out a roar, including her.

I was off, heading south of the border and leaving the 2010 Winter Olympic Games: exhausted, tired, and poor. But when I thought about it, the experience was worth every penny. And I loved the Canadians for their love of hockey.

~Jim Bove

# 110% Viewing

*You've got to love what you're doing. If you love it, you can overcome any*
*handicap or the soreness or all the aches and pains,*
*and continue to play for a long, long time.*
*~Gordie Howe*

I'm sure glad we easily won our preliminary round match-ups. It's not that I wasn't ready for overtime or a shootout. The beer fridge was full and the pizza was pre-ordered. But after those first three games, I definitely needed the break.

When you face the possibility of elimination in any round of Olympic hockey, you better be prepared and you better be in shape. I started my training in the spring of 2006 right after Team Canada tanked in Turin.

I knew that in order to make it past the preliminary round, I had to change my game plan. No longer could I allow myself to be fully emotionally invested in every game. No longer could I flip back and forth between channels watching two games at once. I had to learn to pace myself.

So this year I made some trades. I bought a new TV with a faster remote. And I traded the rec room sofa for a new rocker-recliner with a built-in fridge.

I also developed a new winning attitude. Instead of just jumping into Olympic hockey viewing unprepared, I used the NHL season as my training camp. By watching game after game, I prepared myself for any eventuality.

If I fell asleep or ran out of beer during a game, I didn't panic. I learned to take those setbacks in stride, improve my viewing ability and move on. And almost without exception, I was able to put in a winning performance in the next game.

I have to give a lot of credit to the coaching staff as well. My wife and daughter were nothing but supportive, especially in the weeks leading up to the Olympics. Although I suspect that the acquisition of a second TV had much to do with that support, it was appreciated nonetheless.

Focus is also a key in sports-viewing success. My usual scattered viewing approach had to be jettisoned. No more multi-sports viewing. Winter now meant watching hockey games only.

So, gone were the weekend sports-viewing binges. No more football games. No more basketball doubleheaders. No more golf tournaments. No more overheated remote. An Olympic championship demands laser-like devotion.

Experience is a great asset, too. When you're young and don't need bifocals, you can watch several games at once, stay up past midnight and do it all again the following night. I used to be able to do that, too. But time has taken its toll.

I know I can't do that kind of marathon viewing anymore. But experience has shown me how to pick my spots and concentrate my viewing energy. I may not be able to view as well as I once did but I can view once as well as I ever did.

I think the results speak for themselves. I'm into the medal round and I feel great. As with any playoff run, I've had my ups and downs. I've even had my share of injuries, like the bottle cap abrasion on my right hand during the Switzerland game and the pulled groin from leaning over too far to pick up the remote in the Norway match. But I've learned to tough it out and view through the pain.

Sure, there have been some setbacks. Running out of chips in the quarterfinal match could have been disastrous. Or the failure of the beer fridge in the U.S. game could easily have spelled defeat. In past years, I might have panicked. But my newfound viewing maturity saved the day. Backup supplies of ice and snacks gave me the ability to carry on.

So I'm looking forward to the medal round with a steely confidence and renewed determination. This is just the next step on the road to gold. I'm going to view the Olympics one game at a time. I've come to watch and I intend to give 110%. And if Canada ends up playing for the gold, I know I can take my viewing game to the next level.

~David Martin

*Chicken Soup for the Soul*

# A Dream Come True

*For too long the world has failed to recognise that the Olympic Games
and the Olympic Movement are about fine athletics and fine art.*
~Avery Brundage

I had always loved sports and hockey in particular. As a kid I remember watching with total fascination as all the athletes entered the stadium during the opening ceremonies at an Olympic Games. I even had imagined myself, as kids are prone to do, walking amongst them, though I had no real idea what sport I would be playing. Women's Hockey was not an Olympic sport at that time so hockey wasn't an option, or so I thought.

The moment I put on skates I was hooked. The only issue was that my parents made me wear white skates and the ones I really wanted were black. My first year of skating was as a figure skater, because that was what you were supposed to do if you were a girl at the time. Nothing against figure skating, but it just wasn't for me.... I wanted to play hockey. And as I skated that first year, I always kept one eye on my brother's hockey practices. I was always watching him play. I wanted to play too, but whenever I asked, I always got the same answer – "Girls don't play hockey."

When I was six years old, I started to really watch a girl named Jennifer Minkus who played on my brother's team. I still remember her name because she became the final and winning argument I had for my parents when it came to them allowing me to play. They had no comeback when I simply reminded them that "Jennifer plays!" They respected her and her family so much and she became a role model to me without her even knowing.

The next year I was playing on a boy's team. I was only seven, my hair was cut short and, like the rest of the team, I would arrive already dressed for the game. I never remember hearing anything negative, but my parents heard things from time to time. As a kid, it doesn't even occur to you that people might have an issue. As it turned out the team didn't really understand that I was a girl until the end of the year party... which turned out to be a swimming party!

We had been living in Northern New Jersey and my first team was the Ramapo Saints. I played in the Mites division and continued to play there for two years before we moved back to Canada. It was exciting for me at the time to finally be playing the same sport as my brother. I had always been a tomboy and I idolized my older brother. I had played street hockey with him, even wearing some of his cast-off clothes sometimes. He just seemed to be the coolest person I knew.

After we got back to Canada the opportunities to play women's hockey improved. We moved to Brampton, Ontario, which, at the time, had the world's largest women's hockey association — the Brampton Canadettes. I just loved to play and even though a lot of my friends quit during their teen years, I kept playing. My first major tournament was the Canada Winter Games held in Prince Edward Island in 1991. By 1994 I played in my first women's hockey World Championship, and then in 1998, the Olympics!

Even now, more than thirteen years later, I remember so vividly walking into the stadium in Nagano for the opening ceremonies. It was one of the best experiences of my life. It felt like I was having an out of body experience. There I was walking into the Olympic stadium yet I was also picturing myself watching as a little girl at home. It was a surreal moment. And I was thinking, "Wow, can you believe it?" It was almost as if I was talking to that little girl... to me. It was a truly amazing, unforgettable moment. I could see myself in my old house, glued to the TV, entranced by the opening ceremonies, dreaming of the day… and it all came back to me in an instant. The endless times my parents had driven me to practices and games. All the training and workouts, plus all the people who had helped me along the way, including coaches and friends. There are so many people that are involved in getting a player to the Olympics or to a national team or the NHL for that matter. It was all of those people that I was thinking about when I entered that stadium.

The Canadian women's hockey team was the favorite that year and the feeling that I had come all this way and that I was representing my country and for the first time ever, women's hockey, well it was overpowering. We wanted to bring the gold home that winter, but we lost to the U.S. in the gold medal game. I was crushed. I thought that I had let my team down, especially because there were older players there who would never get another chance to win gold at an Olympics. It wasn't until about six months later that it finally registered as a win. It finally dawned on me: "Hey, we brought home a silver medal in the Olympics!" It was the first Olympic Games to include women's hockey and we got the first silver medal.

Losing that game definitely made me a better player. We learned so much about ourselves from that loss. I intensified my training, and I became a better leader. We all became better players and better people after the challenging time we had in Nagano. Four years later I returned to the Olympics in Salt Lake City, and this time we beat the U.S. team in the final game and brought home the Gold! It was a game we should have never won—the U.S. had their "dream team" and had put so much money into their program. But we managed to play our best when it mattered the most… on gold medal game day!

To this day I believe that if we had not lost in Nagano, we wouldn't have won in Salt Lake City. It was as if we needed that big loss in order to take a serious look at ourselves and become the players and team we did become.

Moving on, I was fortunate to compete in my third Olympics, which I knew was going to be my last prior to going pro. In 2006 in Turin, Italy the Canadian team again brought home the Gold. It was by far the best Team Canada I ever played on as far as talent and depth.

As a young girl, I never knew that I would be able to go to the Olympics as a female ice hockey player, but I had a vision and I was lucky enough to have it come true! From watching the Olympics on TV as a child to playing on the biggest stage in the world! It was truly my dream come true!

~Cassie Campbell-Pascall

# Golden Tickets

*The most important thing in the Olympic Games is not winning but taking part; the essential thing in life is not conquering but fighting well.*
*~Pierre de Coubertin*

When the tickets went on sale for the 2010 Olympics in Vancouver, my husband Rob and I knew we wanted to take our twins. They would be almost the same age I was when the Calgary Olympics were held, and I knew it would be an experience they'd remember forever.

Over a year before the Olympics, Rob and I chose the tickets we'd like and waited as our names were put in a lottery. Months later we found out we had gotten lucky and received our first choice tickets. The kids were thrilled when we told them we'd be travelling to Vancouver to watch snowboarding, the closing ceremonies and the best event of all, Men's Gold Medal Hockey.

Not long before the games started, our seats were randomly selected and our Olympic experience got even better. We had amazing seats to the hockey game. Row 22 in the end zone.

As we loaded up the car to begin the ten-hour drive to Vancouver, the kids were excited and asking questions. "What teams are playing?" "Is Canada going to play?" "Will we win?"

Rob and I exchanged glances. It was still undecided who would be playing in the gold medal round. The game that night between Slovakia and our Canadian boys would determine if we'd be cheering for our home team later that week. After arriving at our friends' home, where we would be staying, we all gathered in the living room and celebrated as Canada secured its spot in the final round against the USA. It was going to be a great game.

The final day of the Olympics arrived, and dressed in our Canadian jerseys, we took the sky train downtown to Canada Hockey Place. Canadian spirit was running rampant, and everywhere we looked people were wearing red, waving flags and cheering. As we walked to the arena, we stopped to watch an impromptu game of pickup between fans and the local police force.

The festive mood continued as we stood in long lines waiting to clear security. Chatting with people, we lost count how many times the kids were told, "You have the coolest parents ever." And asked, "Do you know what your tickets are worth?"

They didn't. We did.

The game was every bit as exciting as the build-up had been. We cheered when Canada scored and rallied when the USA returned fire. By the end of the third period we were up 2-1 with only seconds left. The roar of the crowd threatened to lift the roof of Canada Hockey Place. We were all standing and screaming. And then, with only twenty-four seconds left, the noise stopped.

USA had scored.

In the following moments, confusion reigned as we all looked at each other with bewildered expressions. The kids asked, "What happened? I thought we were going to win."

A few minutes later, in overtime, when Sidney Crosby scored right in front of us, we did win. Up in the stands, we hugged and cried while the boys on the ice did the same.

And to everyone who'd asked the kids if they knew how much their tickets were worth, they finally had an answer — Gold.

~Elena Aitken

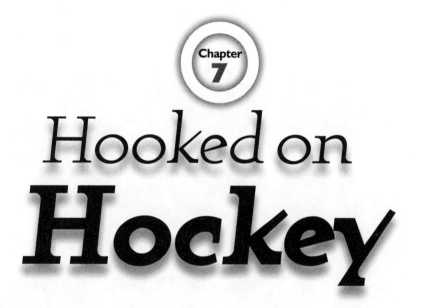

Chapter
**7**

Hooked on
**Hockey**

**Dreams & Inspiration**

# 60

# Eat My Shoes

*A successful person is one who can lay a firm foundation*
*with the bricks that others throw at him or her.*
~David Brinkley

I was eighteen years old in the summer of 1993 when I got an unexpected call that would totally change my life. It was my agent calling, saying that I had just been drafted into the NHL in the third round! How could this be? I was playing for the Czech Junior hockey team at the time, spoke absolutely no English, and had never been outside Czechoslovakia for more than a week or two at a time and certainly not ever to the United States. My sights had been set on playing professional hockey in my home country, like my dad. The NHL wasn't even a dream at that point.

Like many kids in Czechoslovakia, I learned to skate fairly early, at age four, and started playing hockey a year later. The choice for many was either soccer or hockey and I chose hockey because I wanted to be like my dad. I was a pretty good player, better than most, but certainly not the best. Still, within ten years I was playing for my hometown junior team HC Motor České Budějovice, I was the captain of that team, and I was also playing for the junior National team kind of "on the bubble," playing some of the time but not a regular starter.

So there I was, seventeen years old and playing junior hockey. The summer came and I got a job waiting tables, making ten times more than I had playing hockey. It was during that summer that my parents and I talked it over and we decided to take a chance. I would spend the next year concentrating only on hockey. I had saved up a little money and my parents also helped me out.

Then on January 1, 1993 something happened that changed things for me dramatically. Our country peacefully separated into two countries: the Czech Republic and Slovakia. That was good news in so many respects, and it meant that now there were only half as many candidates for the national hockey team as there had been. Basically, it opened a door for me, and I started playing a lot more.

We were playing teams like Russia, Sweden, Germany, and Finland, and because we were playing other countries, there were always scouts in the stands. During that year I had gotten an agent, and through him I got a meeting with the European scout for the Philadelphia Flyers. He must have seen me at those games and I guess he was impressed. One of the factors that maybe made me noticeable was that I was a player who passed the puck a lot. I think maybe I was the kind of player that made the teammates around him better. I knew I wasn't the best player, but I knew I was good.

The summer of 1993 came around and I went back into training, hoping that someday I would be able to play high-level professional hockey for my country. Back then, because we had only just come out of the communist regime, the media coverage was not that great, so honestly, I wasn't even really thinking about the U.S., or the NHL because I didn't hear that much about it. I think I also dreamed of maybe going to Canada to be on one of the junior teams there.

I was therefore incredibly surprised when my agent called me and said that the Philadelphia Flyers had just drafted me! I was in shock. On the one hand I was so excited and happy, but on the other I didn't know if I was ready to leave my parents and my country. Nowadays it is more commonplace for eighteen-, seventeen- and even sixteen-year-olds to leave home and go abroad, but twenty years ago it wasn't so common. I thought that maybe I should stay in the Czech Republic for two or three more years and play professional hockey there and get better, and then maybe go to the NHL.

Anyway, as soon as I got drafted, my team in the Czech Republic, HC Česke Budějovice, signed me for the minimum salary, which I think was about $120 a month. You see there's a kind of agreement with the NHL that they will reimburse a foreign team if it takes one its players. So my team had finally signed me, but just to get the reimbursement from the NHL. My agent went to my team and asked them what their plans were for me, and the general manager at the time said, "Yeah yeah, you can take him. He's no good. If he ever plays one minute in the NHL I'm gonna eat my shoes."

And they let me go. Just like that.

All they gave me was a pair of skates. I don't even remember if they wished me good luck. There's a saying, "The golden train only comes by once. You better get on it and never get off, because you don't know if it ever comes by again." I was not about to miss my chance, my train… so off to America I went.

When I got to Pennsylvania I immediately started in the minors. In the U.S. you have to be twenty years old to play in the minors, but Europeans are kind of exempt from that, so I started playing for the Hershey Bears in the AHL. And it's really tough in the minors. The money is not so good (about 15 percent of a NHL salary), some of the arenas are not great, and the schedule is non-stop. You play game after game with long bus rides in between. You might play a game one night at home and then right after the game hop on the bus for a six-hour ride to Albany, play again the next night, and then back to Hershey for a Saturday night game, play the game and right after hop right back on the bus for a nine-hour ride for a one o'clock game the next day in Hamilton, Ontario.

That's not an easy schedule. And I did this for three and half years. Sometimes I would go through all of that and not even play; I think I once went ten games without suiting up. You miss holidays, you don't have your family, and for me it was really tough because it took me a while to even learn English.

I was really lucky though. When I got to Pennsylvania I was taken in by a wonderful couple—Doug and Marion Pearl. They showed me everything from how to write a check to how to drive a car. I owe so much to them and I am happy that we still keep in touch. So when I had first arrived I had played a few games in the pre-season as a sort of tryout and the Flyers decided to take a chance on me and signed me to a five-year deal! I was so happy. I mean I didn't know any better. So I played the first three and a half years of my professional hockey career in the minors. And after playing three seasons with the Hershey Bears I was moved up to the Philadelphia Phantoms in their first year. Then in the middle of the season I was called up to the Flyers and have never looked back.

The NHL is so completely different than the minors, different from any other hockey league in the world. Nothing compares to it. Everything about it is first-rate—the arenas, the level of play, the accommodations, the travel, everything. Still I know that I am the player I am today because of all the time I spent in the minors.

Hearing the comment about my former GM "eating his shoes" was a strong motivation for me. It gave me my drive. Of course, at first I was a little hurt by his words and by the fact that my own country did not want me, did not believe in me, but I decided I would prove them all wrong, that I would do whatever it took. That was such a strong force inside me. And I realized that what really mattered was that *I* believed in me! That I knew that I could make it, and I never stopped working. My agent, the incomparable Ritch Winter, to whom I owe so much, always says "hard work trumps talent every night that talent doesn't work." I might not be the best or fastest skater, but I know that I am a hard worker, and I am consistent. I am one of a select group of players that have played over 1,000 games in the NHL, an achievement I am very proud of. Sometimes I think kids who go straight into the NHL get there a bit too easy and don't completely appreciate what they have.

I also feel that what goes on outside the rink really makes the player. People don't know how much training and effort and sacrifice one goes through in order to make it as a professional hockey player. My wife says only half-joking that she and my wonderful kids see more of me during the season than during the off-season, when all I seem to do is train.

They are the reason I do what I do. They are my reward. That, and maybe a little bit knowing that back in the Czech Republic, someone had a fine meal of shoe leather... because I proved him wrong. And more than anything, just being able to play this game I dreamed about and love so much.

~Vinny Prospal

61

# The Young and the Old

*In youth the days are short and the years are long.*
*In old age the years are short and the days are long.*
~Pope Paul IV

There was a seventy-five-year age difference between my eighteen-year-old hockey-playing neighbor, Scott Kosmachuk, and my ninety-three-year-old hockey-loving father-in-law, Bob Atkinson, but when they first met at my house on August 15, 2010, they got along like old buddies. Hockey buddies.

Their lives could not have been more different but they had more in common than you might think, and it was a love of sport — particularly hockey — that was the fabric that wove their separate lives together.

Bob was born in Guelph, Ontario on July 29, 1919 "in a little log cabin I built myself" he liked to joke. But his early upbringing was no laughing matter. When his mother died in 1924, his father was unable to care for his two children so Bob and his younger brother, the late Jim Atkinson, were placed in a Guelph orphanage "for much longer than I care to remember" Bob would often say. But like the resilient 6-foot, 2-inch high school athlete he would become, Bob and his brother endured the "children's home" and were eventually taken in by their paternal grandmother. The boys attended school in Guelph and developed a lifelong love of sport. Bob excelled at swimming, tennis and basketball. To his regret, his grandmother would not allow the boys to skate because if they broke an ankle, there was no money for doctor's bills! Sadly, he shelved his dream of playing hockey and starred in basketball for four years in high school. His team won every league game in his final year. Later, he played basketball on a YMCA team and the year he joined—1938—his team advanced to the Ontario semi-finals.

As the decades zipped by, Bob enjoyed a happy and satisfying life. Among his proud achievements was serving overseas for several years in WWII with an anti-tank regiment in the Canadian Army. He married, had four children, and enjoyed a career as an auditor with the federal government. When his wife, Audrey, died in 2001 he lived alone for many years until he was diagnosed with Alzheimer's disease and temporarily moved in with me and my wife, Kris, until we could find a nice retirement home for him nearby.

For all of his young life, Scott Kosmachuk lived two houses away from us on our street in Richmond Hill, Ontario, with his parents, two brothers, a sister, and a couple of dogs. A gifted athlete, Scott's first love was hockey, so it was a joyous day in the Kosmachuk household when he was drafted in 2010 to play for the Guelph Storm hockey team of the Ontario Hockey League (OHL). Two years later, the strapping 5-foot, 11-inch right winger was one of the team's top scorers and had his sights set on becoming one of Guelph Storm's forty-one players to graduate to the NHL, such as Todd Bertuzzi, currently with the Detroit Red Wings.

When Bob heard that our neighbour was not only a star hockey player but a member of the Guelph Storm hockey club, he said to me one evening: "I'd like to meet this young man." The next day, I relayed his request to Scott's mother, Wendy, who said she would bring her son to the house the next time he was home. A short while later, Wendy and Scott arrived at the door. He was wearing his #24 Guelph Storm hockey jersey! When I called Bob, he used his walker to shuffle to our front hallway. Introductions were made. It is a meeting I will never forget!

I took a photo of the two sports fans while Kris, Wendy and I listened as the teenager chatted about his future hockey dreams. Bob reminisced about his basketball-playing days and spoke fondly of Guelph's hockey teams of the past, including the Guelph Royals, an early 1960s junior hockey team in the Ontario Hockey Association. The Royals were affiliated with the New York Rangers and among their graduates were Rod Gilbert and Jean Ratelle, former Rangers now in the NHL Hockey Hall of Fame.

I watched Scott intently as he politely listened to my soft-spoken father-in-law. I have no way of knowing what Scott was thinking, but I thought of the observation by British writer H. H. Munro: "The young have aspirations that never come to pass, the old have reminiscences of what never happened."

It has been over two years since the two men first met, but because of his infirmity and his Alzheimer's, Bob wasn't able to get out to see Scott play hockey. So my wife and I served as Bob's eyes and ears and cheers at Guelph Storm hockey games. On December 17, 2011, we watched Scott score four points in a Storm win over the Sault Ste. Marie Greyhounds at Guelph's Sleeman Centre. On January 1, 2012, in the same hometown arena, we witnessed our neighbor score the team's first goal of the year, and he added an assist before being struck in the mouth by a stick in a goalmouth scramble. He spent a period in the dressing room having a fractured tooth cared for before returning to the ice late in the third period wearing a hastily-fashioned face cage attached to his helmet.

The photo I took of Bob and Scott, with the young hockey player proudly wearing his Guelph Storm hockey jersey, was framed and placed on Bob's bedroom dresser. During the hockey season, I'd update Bob on the win-loss record of the Guelph Storm and bring him up to speed on Scott's individual exploits on ice. And when I did, a glint would appear in Bob's eyes, and as the fog of his disease would momentarily lift, he always said the same thing: "I know that kid!" And my response was always the same: "Yes, and he knows you!"

Bob died suddenly and peacefully on February 21, 2012 in his favourite chair in his retirement home. Four months later, Scott was drafted by the NHL's Winnipeg Jets! While Bob never got out to an arena to see Scott play hockey, he now has the best seat in the house!

~Dennis McCloskey

# 62

# The Dream

*Victory isn't defined by wins or losses. It is defined by effort.*
*If you can truthfully say, "I did the best I could, I gave everything I had,"*
*then you're a winner.*
~Wolfgang Schadler

My aunt Eileen used to play bingo with Foster Hewitt's sister and she was able to get us seats almost in the camera bay for Hockey Night in Canada. To watch Bobby Hull "rag" the puck for 1:45 seconds while killing a penalty was awesome. "Orr flies through the air." "Henderson scores." "Brett Hull *does* have his foot in the crease." "Gretzky does 'high stick' Dougie." "Bobby Baun scores on a broken leg." Mystery, tales and lore abound in hockey. We all wanted that special moment to keep to ourselves. As Steve Shutt once so eloquently put it, "We thought the glass was there to keep everybody else out. It was ours to enjoy."

Having watched, played and coached the "Royal Game" (Lord Frederick Arthur Stanley of Preston was after all the Governor-General of Canada), there are so many things that I find memorable. Watching my son and daughter start out looking like "Bambi on ice" first and later flying across the rink with the greatest of ease ranks right up there with being present at their births. But of all the hockey memories I have, the one I hold dearest and closest to my heart concerns someone else's child… and his moment of absolute hockey heaven.

I was a coach for the Queensway Canadiens Minor Hockey League, which was blessed with having our practices outdoors at the

Prince of Wales Rink. If the wind was right and you didn't dribble, you could spit in Lake Ontario. We were a house league team and a feeder system for the Rep team. One of our players though, named Petey, had no chance of making the NHL or even the Rep team.

Petey was eager though. His parents always dropped him off fully dressed, skates tied up. If attitude were a skill, he would've been an all-star. It was my estimable pleasure, one particular day, to find Petey ready to go, way ahead of the rest of the team. Five-thirty a.m. comes really early when the temperature is minus twenty Celsius and there is a wind chill factor that causes kids to wear a toque under their helmets.

My skates were tied and I didn't feel like hanging around listening to twelve-year-olds have conversations of great import to themselves. I wandered out to see if Jimmy, my next door neighbor's son—the rink attendant—was done. The junior Zamboni had just come off the ice. The sun was rising over the lake and the Toronto skyline was silhouetted, looking east. Mist from Lake Ontario was swirling nicely, just in our periphery. "Away ya go kid," I said, opening the gate for Petey, sending him out onto that clear, clean and unspoiled sheet of ice. He looked back as if to say "now what?" With an inward smile I threw a puck onto the ice, shrugged and closed the gate. Away he went with all of his dreams of future glory coming alive. Striding and gliding, puck on a string, making perfect passes to perfect teammates who didn't notice that his ankles weren't quite aligned. His blades had never quite cut with such a pristine edge before. It lasted for almost four and a half minutes.

"Hey Coach, can we go on?"

"No."

"But we wanna play."

"Wait."

Petey heard the noise intrude into his reverie. The Stanley Cup was just this close, just a whisper away. He looked over in embarrassment. He knew there were others more skilled than himself. But for a moment he knew—he just knew it was as it should be. He was good. It was my pleasure to share that moment looking into a child's eyes and seeing what can be seen when we dream. I opened the gate again and all of the others flooded onto the ice. Petey's moment had come and gone. He did look over at me, briefly. Our eyes met for just a second. I am not Petey but I wish I had had that special moment. He did and I shared the dream.

~Leighton Kemmett

# Sledge Hockey: A Dream Comes True

*If you can dream it, you can do it.*
~Walt Disney

Our son Nicholas is like most boys in almost every way—he loves action, sports, and playing with his peers. The marked difference is that he has cerebral palsy. His form of CP affects his balance and means that he requires a walker for mobility. It also means that everything he does requires a lot more energy and effort than it does for other people.

When he was three to five years old Nic would constantly ask us (and anyone else who was willing to play) to have a mini-stick hockey game with him on our basement floor. We quickly observed his keen hockey instincts and his healthy competitive spirit. But we also recognized that playing on a hockey team would in all likelihood be something that Nic would never be able to experience. His body just wouldn't move the way his brain wanted it to.

As a six- to eight-year-old, Nic was involved on a team in our community soccer program. With incredible determination, he was able to "run" (with his walker) and play on his team. As he grew older though, the differences between his abilities and the abilities of others became more noticeable and he could not keep up.

His words, his attempts at practicing sporting skills in the basement or back yard, and his sadness made it obvious that Nic would love to play on a team. His goal was never to be a token teammate; he wanted to be a full and contributing team member.

By age nine or ten, when we asked if he might want to go to the arena to watch his friends play a hockey game, Nic would say no. Watching adults play hockey was fine, but having his peers play while he sat on the sidelines was, in his words, "Just too painful to watch."

At about this time we became aware of sledge, or sled, hockey being offered by the Society for Manitobans with Disabilities. However, the muscles and tendons in Nic's legs were too tight; he would likely need surgery to make it possible for him to propel himself on a hockey sled. Surgery to loosen the hamstrings of both legs and the tendons of his left heel and tighten his kneecap tendons needed to wait until he was eleven years old. He also knew that the surgery would be followed by many months of rehabilitation, of learning to walk again, and building up his strength to be able to propel himself on the ice. So he waited and hoped—that someday... his dream to play hockey would come true.

When the surgery date arrived, Nic went into the operating room with courage and determination, and a nervous smile on his face. It was the same winning smile he wears most days, even when life is tough. The surgery was successful, and after being in full-length leg casts for six weeks, he continued on the long and grueling road to recovery, spending up to an hour a day on physiotherapy exercises with much determination.

One year later, at the age of twelve, Nic was strapped into a hockey sled for the first time and began to skate. His face beamed as he glided, tipped, got up and glided some more. It was an experimental run to see if Nic had the strength and balance to propel himself on the sled. There was no doubt that Nic would be a sledge hockey player.

A week later he was welcomed onto the team. We're not sure who was prouder, Nic or us, but we witnessed a sense of worth and a joy that we had seldom seen. We also witnessed determination, respect for his teammates (each player had his/her unique challenges) and a drive to score and win.

Nic played for only a few weeks before the season ended in March but he was hooked. In fall he was back on the ice, practicing his skating on our local rink, and driving to Winnipeg (about seventy-five minutes from our home) each Saturday to practice and play on the Sledgehammers hockey team. His skills have increased tremendously and so has his joy and sense of accomplishment. As we write this story we are preparing to go to Nic's first ever hockey tournament weekend.

Recently we also watched with a deep sense of excitement as Nic taught some of his school friends how to skate on a sledge hockey sled. We borrowed an extra sled and brought it to our local arena during a skating evening. One by one, some of Nic's friends tried their hand at skating with him. He showed them how to hold the special sticks with picks to propel themselves, and then to adjust the grip to pass and shoot the puck. The ability to teach them as they struggled to do something Nic had mastered was a significant reversal as we ponder what it means to be differently-abled.

Something we never knew how to imagine became possible via sledge hockey. Nic is #18 on the Sledgehammers hockey team, a slick skater with a keen sense of seeing plays develop, the ability to make great passes, and a level of defensive responsibility that generally takes more time to develop.

But, most all, Nic feels a sense of belonging as a valued member of a hockey team…. and that means everything.

~Sharon and John Klassen

# Scoring in Life

*You can live your dreams if you can embrace change.*
*It's by taking chances that you'll learn how to be brave.*
*~Nikita Koloff*

Our whole family loved hockey. We would all sit in front of the TV and hockey was a sport we would watch together. When my son Derek turned four, he got his first pair of skates and started to play. I became a hockey mom—taking him to games early in the morning, sometimes at 6:00 a.m. Sitting in cold arenas with a hot tea was how I typically spent Saturday mornings. His big sister Maddie and I were his cheering squad. Little did I know that one day I would be on the ice playing with NHL hockey legends.

It all started with a bold request. I was asked to volunteer for a charity hockey game, to help them sell tickets. It was something I would have normally jumped at the chance to do. It was put on by an organization called Help a Child Smile. They had helped my family in the past. When my daughter Maddie was battling cancer, they were the organization that sent her to Disney World in Florida. They put a smile on her face and gave me wonderful memories. Memories I hold dear, because of the limited precious time I was able to spend with her. Sadly, her life was cut short when the cancer returned and she died at the tender age of fifteen.

Full of life and always positive, she requested one thing of me before she died—that I would live my life fully and be happy. It was that promise that led me to play hockey. I had always wanted to play hockey. Searching for that happiness, I was inspired to try something new, to get out of my comfort zone. No more sitting on the sidelines. I was stepping into the action.

The day I was asked to volunteer, I blurted out "I play hockey." With more confidence than I felt, I asked, "Can I play instead of selling tickets? Could I play in the game, in memory of my daughter—to score a goal for her?" I was thinking I could salute her courage by doing something courageous myself.

I wasn't totally lying about playing... I just left out how well I played. I had recently joined a league of women players. It was a Women's Masters League team, for women aged thirty-five and over. To my amazement, a few were over sixty. We played Friday nights and I was having a blast. I had just started to get comfortable skating around with all that gear on, learning to stick handle. I learned that we played differently than what I had watched in the NHL. When we knocked down opposing players, it wasn't on purpose and we always said sorry and helped them back up. Plus, some of the sweat and heat came from hot flashes, not speed.

After I asked to play at the charity event and didn't hear back, I just forgot about it. Then, I got a phone call—"Yes, you can play. Show up at the arena with your gear tomorrow night." I was so excited I could barely sleep. When I arrived at the arena, in Hamilton, Ontario, they handed me an NHL Alumni jersey. "What's this?" I asked. "I thought I was going to be on the other team, the local team." No, I was to play on the same team as all those hockey legends. Oh, what had I gotten myself into?

I had a separate changing room with another female who was playing for the other team. We chatted excitedly as we got dressed. We even talked about putting on a play fight, but never did. No matter what happened, we knew that we were going to have a fantastic game!

The game opened with our national anthem, "O Canada." I felt so proud standing there on the red carpet, honouring our national flag. It gave me goose bumps. I was really going to play hockey. The fans were cheering as the team was introduced, including little old me — "Sharon Babineau."

I decided this was a once-in-a-lifetime opportunity and I should just have fun. It was my mother's birthday. I held up a sign that read "Happy Birthday Mom!" I had no idea where she was so I skated around the whole rink.

I didn't stand a chance on the ice. I followed the play as best I could, skating with all my might, yet I seemed to go nowhere. Everyone else was flying by me. At one point, they held down the goalie, so I could score, but I was still unsuccessful. At one point, I struggled so hard to get the puck in that I wanted to pick it up and throw it, but my pride prevented me from doing so. There were lots of theatrics, and fake fighting with the referee (also a hockey legend), throwing of sticks and a pie, and mock bad behaviour. It was so much fun!

I was exhausted, skating back and forth, barely touching the puck, definitely out of my league. I was amazed at how athletic these players still were... for their age. I can say that since I too was almost fifty years old.

We played two periods. During our break, I sat in the changing room with hockey legends — Bob Probert, Mark Napier, Mike Krushelnyski, Pat Ribble, and Dave Hutchinson to name a few. I was sweaty and exhausted from playing the first period of the charity hockey game. I was grinning ear to ear, sitting there alongside such extraordinary players. They invited me to sign autographs for the fans with them. I wanted to pinch myself because I thought I must have been dreaming. This was the last place I expected to be. I knew I didn't belong there. I certainly wasn't anywhere near the calibre of those amazing hockey players. I could barely stand on my skates, never mind trying to keep up with them. It was sheer luck that I was there. Actually, it was bravery. It was having the courage to take a risk and put myself out there, to try something new. And that is the real lesson I took away.

In the second period I made contact with the puck a few times. Although I didn't score on the ice, I felt I had scored off the ice. I had one of the most unforgettable nights of my life. I was so grateful for the opportunity to play. The kindness I experienced, the encouragement, all of it was absolutely amazing.

Life is full of surprises. Sometimes you just have to ask for what you want. Stop sitting on the sidelines, get in on the action, and score your goal in life.

~Sharon Babineau

# Deep at the Heart

*A brother is a friend God gave you;*
*a friend is a brother your heart chose for you.*
~Proverb

The first time I held a hockey stick in my hand I was nine years old — my expression a study in bafflement.

"You want me to hit that little black thing?" I asked my big brother Craig through the wool fibers of my scarf. "With this big stick?"

"You don't just hit it," he explained, his breath delivering white puffs into the frigid New England air. "You have to keep me from stealing it away from you."

"Oh. Okay." And I thought, how hard can it be?

As I spent the better part of the next hour either chasing after my brother or picking myself up off the ice, the truth of the situation became clear: Hockey requires many skills I failed to possess, such as the ability to spend more time upright on my skates than falling on my behind.

In my defense, up until my seventh year I lived in Tucson, Arizona, and my winter activities included snow and ice only if my family drove to Mt. Lemmon for the day. My exposure to ice sports was limited to sitting in rapt attention in front of our black and white television watching Peggy Fleming perform in the Olympics.

After we moved to Massachusetts, I was thrilled by the opportunity to learn how to skate. And when we moved to a house situated on the Concord River with our own private cove that froze solid in the winter—perfect for ice-skating and hockey—I donned my ice skates at every opportunity. It wasn't in my future to become a figure skater, but I had fun nonetheless.

Over the course of that first winter my brother Craig and I played hockey many times. My technique never improved. Each time we hit the ice I spent more time chasing after him than he ever did chasing after me. But like that old optimist Charlie Brown allowing Lucy to hold the football for him to kick, I persisted in battling for control of the puck with every ounce of effort inside me. All to no avail.

"Oh, c'mon, kid," Craig coaxed whenever I showed signs of giving up. "Let's play just a little longer. I bet you'll win next time."

Five years older than I, my brother possessed more strength, stamina, and better skating skills. I was the baby sister, easy to persuade to participate in a bout of hockey I had no chance of winning. It was like pitting Bobby Orr against Pee-wee Herman.

Craig invited me to play when his friends were unavailable or he was bored. I laced up my skates and gave the game my all because he was my big brother and I idolized him. Even as I exhausted myself chasing after him, I basked in the sheer joy of his invitation to play and spend time with him.

Subsequent winters did not yield more hockey games in the cove. Craig became more interested in girls and less inclined to best his baby sister on the ice. And with five years separating us, it would be some time before we would call ourselves good friends.

But I've thought a lot about that winter and all of those one-sided hockey games. Ostensibly, those hours spent were child's play, worthy of little remembrance. But the truth, deep at the heart, is that each second resounds as a moment to savor.

We spent hours shoveling snow from the uneven ice, perspiring under layers of clothing, and trying to blow "smoke" rings with the condensate our breath created upon exhaling. We sported numb toes, red noses, scrapes, bruises and torn jeans. Our shouts of "En garde!" echoed across the cove when we fenced with hockey sticks transformed into imaginary swords, the puck abandoned on the ice. And many was the time we stood side by side in forlorn solidarity, staring out to the middle of the river after a hard-placed slap of the hockey stick sent the puck flying far beyond the safety of our thick-iced cove and onto the dangerous mid-river ice.

I couldn't know it then, but those hockey games were both learning experiences and building blocks. I learned that it's okay to fall down as long as I get back up and keep trying; that persistence, even when winning isn't likely, offers its own rewards; and that excelling at an activity isn't necessary for its enjoyment.

And how were those hockey games like building blocks? Each moment spent on the ice with my brother—chasing, pushing, arguing; cooperating, laughing, talking—were of themselves part of the architecture from which we built our relationship, first as siblings, now as friends.

We learned about each other in those days, what we were made of and what we hoped to become. We didn't know it then, but the ice on which we wielded our hockey sticks was a metaphor for the relationship we have been so fortunate to share into our adult lives: strong, solid, and deep.

Anyone who says hockey is just a game… has never really played.

~Lisa Ricard Claro

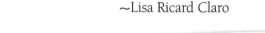

# 66

Chicken Soup for the Soul

# Hockey Mom

*The goal is too small and the goalies are too big.*
~Scotty Bowman

"H e shoots! He scores!" the announcer's voice shouts from the small black and white TV in my childhood living room.

Saturday nights and Hockey Night in Canada were synonymous at our house. Even though my enthusiasm did not match that of my hockey-playing brother, I hoped the Toronto Maple Leafs won the game, the series and eventually the Stanley Cup. I imagined one day I would have children of my own who would love this game and I would become a hockey mom.

The NHL grew in size. I grew up, had children and became a hockey mom when my older daughter began playing the sport. While I outfitted her with all the hockey equipment, her younger brother begged for a hockey stick too. At two and three years old he wielded his red plastic stick, bouncing the matching plastic puck with enough force that I outlawed him from playing hockey in the house. He watched hockey games on TV. He cheered for his favourite, the Edmonton Oilers, and promised he would play hockey like his hero, #99, Wayne Gretzky.

By age five my son's dream of being on a hockey team came true. As I purchased all the hockey equipment, signed up my son and waited for the first practice, he kept reminding me, "Mom I'm going to be like Gretzky. I'll skate. I'll shoot. I'll score lots of goals," while demonstrating his moves at every opportunity.

"Remember," I'd reply, "Gretzky's skated and practiced for years and years. You'll have to learn first and then work hard on all the skills. Don't be disappointed if you can't skate like the hockey players on TV, at least not right away."

Jeremy would smile and assure me he would skate like his hero and score plenty of goals.

Hockey season finally arrived. My daughter chose to change her sport to ringette along with her sister. Three children in three different age groups meant lots of rink time for our family that winter.

I helped my son dress in all his hockey equipment for the first practice session and handed him a real hockey stick. Before stepping onto the ice he turned, smiled and said, "Just watch me, Mom! I'll skate and score lots of goals."

He placed one foot on the ice, followed by the second. He stood for a moment and then let go of the supporting boards, fully prepared to make good on his promise to immediately skate like a pro. He wobbled. His feet flew out from under him, landing him on his backside. I tried not to laugh at the expression of horror and disbelief that crossed his face. But he did not give up. The coach helped him to his feet, steadied him and handed him a chair to push around the rink as he learned the art of staying upright while balancing on the thin blades of this new footwear.

He hated pushing the chair, so he quickly learned to skate. Shortly after he mastered the skill of skating and stick handling his team began to play short games. In one of the first games he slid hard into the boards. The coach took him out of the game when he complained of a sore arm. An X-ray revealed a freak break just above the elbow. Six weeks of healing meant no hockey, no sports or playing rough. Yet an arm in a cast did not slow him down or stop him from loving the game of hockey.

By the end of the first season he gave up his dream of scoring goals like Gretzky and focused on his newfound love of stopping other players from scoring them! All summer he played ball hockey in the driveway with his friends. Most days he chose to play goal. As I watched I realized he possessed amazing reflexes and a lack of fear, key skills for a goaltender.

A new adventure happened in his second hockey season. The coach arranged a road trip to play a small town team. The opportunity to play a real game on a full-size rink filled the entire team with excitement. Jeremy's excitement about wearing full goalie gear for the first time knew no bounds. We drove to the game, where I learned the new skill of strapping the huge goalie pads on to my son. He pulled on the big gloves and practiced handling the goalie stick. The game would consist of two periods with a break between them. At the break Jeremy and another aspiring goalie would change places.

My son, the goalie, led his team onto the ice as I headed toward the stands. I stared at the opposing team. They were huge. I wondered if the coach had made some kind of mistake. How could our little boys play these big guys? The opposing team players were at the upper end of the age group while our boys were all only six years old.

I almost panicked as the first shot on our goalie drove hard and fast toward the net. I almost screamed as he reached to stop it. Shot after shot flew at him or slid along the ice toward our goal. My son stopped many of them. My heart sank with every shot that made it past our goalie and cheered each one he stopped until my voice became hoarse. At the end of the first period, with the score favouring the other team, I headed to the dressing room to help him get out of the goalie gear.

"I'm not going to play goal. Those big guys scare me. Let Jeremy be goalie again. He stopped lots," my son's replacement said.

I stopped undoing the goal pads while the coach asked every player on the team to take a turn in goal. Fear kept everyone but my son from accepting the position for the second period of play. I retightened all the straps, and then Jeremy willingly led his team back onto the ice, his huge grin hidden behind his mask. He seemed to have no fear of pucks flying towards him. He thrived on the task of stopping as many as possible.

My life as hockey mom took on a whole new dimension that

day—the first of the majority of games my son played, almost all of them in goal. It never got easier to watch pucks shot at him or hear the frustration of other parents when he let goals into the net. But I cheered with each blocked shot. My chest puffed out with pride when I overheard comments from friends and strangers about his amazing reflexes and fantastic saves.

"He shoots! He scores!" Those were no longer the words I wanted to hear, but rather, "Look at that save! What a goalie!" After all, some hockey moms have to be the mom of the goalie.

~Carol Elaine Harrison

# 67

# The Great Transformer

*Teamplayer:*
*One who unites others toward a shared destiny*
*through sharing information and ideas,*
*empowering others and developing trust.*
*~Dennis Kinlaw*

My stomach was churning and I could tell my fourteen-year-old son felt the same way. It was his first day as a high school freshman and we had moved to a new school district after I remarried that summer.

Jimmy was a small boy with a large personality who was well liked in the school and neighborhood where he had spent his first fourteen years. All of his friends were going to the high school in our old neighborhood.

When I returned home from work, Jimmy was in his bedroom with the door closed and music blaring. I took a deep breath and knocked on his door.

"Hi honey," I said as he cracked his door open a few inches. "So, how did everything go today?"

"Okay," he said as he began to close the door. "I have lots of homework to do."

"Well, I hope you're hungry," I said, eagerly trying to coax a smile out of my son. "I have beef and onions cooking."

"Okay," he said, and firmly closed his door.

The first week of school was a short one and Friday came quickly. Jimmy couldn't wait to stay with his dad in the old neighborhood and spend time with his old friends. As soon as I got home from work, he was anxiously waiting by the door with his duffle bag packed, ready to go. He hadn't been this excited for a long time.

As the weeks went by, Jimmy began to settle in at the new high school and make some friends. However, on the weekends, he still spent all of his time at his dad's house in our old neighborhood. Sunday evenings were difficult as he faced another week with us and his new school.

During dinner one night at the beginning of the second term, Jimmy said that he wanted to play deck hockey again. He had loved playing the year before, and it was a perfect game for him... fast moving, not much contact, and not too expensive. I knew it wasn't possible for us to make the drive over to the old neighborhood for the afternoon practices and games. However, to my surprise and delight, Jimmy told me that he and his friends at school were trying to get a team together to play at a new facility just minutes from our home. There were lots of discussions around the lunch table at school and over the phone after school. The teammates needed to choose a name, pick out shirts, figure out positions, and get their schedules coordinated. They were on a mission. They were a team!

That season was great fun. As I sat on the hard bleachers with the wind blowing through my hair I watched my son, the new kid in the neighborhood, become part of the team. But he wasn't the only one making new friends. The other mothers and I shared our opinions of the teachers at the high school, the high cost of the boys' tennis shoes, and what we could make for dinner that could be ready thirty minutes after we got home from the games. I looked forward to the games as much as Jimmy did.

In his sophomore year Jimmy and some of his teammates decided they wanted to move on and play ice hockey. I was concerned about the risk of injury but his mind was made up and he tried out for, and made, the junior varsity team.

Now, we moms sat on hard benches in a freezing indoor rink, with our hooded jackets zipped up and gloved hands in our pockets. When we talked we could see our breath in the air. At the first practice, I realized that Jimmy skated fairly well, but could only stop by skating into the boards. He wasn't the only one, and the slamming sound of bodies against the boards punctuated the frigid air. Slowly, but surely, Jimmy improved. He had a natural ability to move his small frame with speed and agility. He skated around, between, and underneath other players. He was a tenacious player who found a way to score.

In his junior year, Jimmy moved up to the varsity team and his teammates picked him to be the assistant captain. He was no longer the new kid in school. He was an integral part of the team, a generous player happy to score himself or assist other players in scoring goals for the team. When he wasn't practicing or playing, he worked on plays and strategies. He grew both physically and emotionally. He still visited his dad on the weekends, but now he had friends in both neighborhoods.

Assistant captain once again in his senior year, Jimmy continued to encourage his teammates to play hard and believe in themselves. He rallied the players when they fell behind. He became a true leader. He did as well in school as he did on the ice and was accepted to the college of his choice. His senior year whirled by in a blur and soon his high school hockey days were over.

Poignancy mixed with excitement filled the air at the end of the year hockey banquet. The seniors were moving on. The players received their varsity letters and smiled broadly for the clicking cameras. Then the coach stepped forward to announce the winner of the Unsung Hero Award. Explaining that it would be given to the player who had made a great, yet unrecognized contribution to the team, he announced Jimmy's name as the winner! A rush of emotions filled my body. I looked at Jimmy and he looked at me. My eyes filled with tears but my smile stretched from ear to ear.

Sometimes in life, we find a wonderful surprise waiting for us. The rough and hard-hitting game of hockey transforming my son from an uncertain boy to a focused leader was certainly one of mine. Hockey... the great transformer!

~Audrey McLaughlin

# 68

# Love at First Lace

*An athlete is a normal person*
*with the gift of an undying passion*
*to be the best and achieve greatness.*
~Amanda Ring

Hockey has taken me to many unforgettable places... from winning gold in the National Championships with Team Ontario in Chicoutimi, Quebec, to travelling overseas to Europe for tournaments, to co-starring in a television commercial for Tim Hortons with Sydney Crosby.

Hockey has also allowed me to be scouted and accepted into a prestigious private school, The Bishop Strachan School, in downtown Toronto. This is where my fondest memories have been made as a student, resident and athlete. As I browsed through baby photos to choose for my yearbook graduation photo, I came across a very special hockey card: myself at age four, outfitted in my brother's hand-me-down equipment. It is my hometown hockey "Rookie Card." I reminisced about how a year before the photo was taken I had a traumatic figure skating experience, by a four-year-old's standards at least, that changed my life.

I was dressed as Peter Pan for the end-of-year figure skating extravaganza. My fellow skater, Tinker Bell, made fun of my "boy's skates" because they were so different from her white dainty figure skates. She told me that my skates didn't belong and I ran to my parents in tears. I told them I was done with figure skating, and I wanted to play hockey like my older brother Jordan. And so, wearing a Peter Pan outfit complete with black Bauer skates and green laces, four-year-old me ultimately made a decision that would change my life forever.

As I look back on that moment, I remember being so easily offended by the insult about my skates, but I am thankful that I chose the sport for which they were made. My life changed then. I'm different than the majority of girls who attend this private school, which is located in a very privileged area called Forest Hill. To be honest, I didn't believe that I would fit in when I was first scouted and invited to tour the school. First of all, I knew that I preferred the cold crisp air of a rink at 6:00 a.m. to the hot sunshine on a secluded beach in the tropics. I preferred concession stand hot chocolate to an expensive latte. I believed that bus trips, not spring break in Punta Cana, would make for the best memories with friends. I felt more comfortable balancing on thin steel blades than in expensive Christian Louboutins, and preferred wearing a jersey pulled over bulky shoulder pads to a slinky silk dress. My signature hairstyle was a messy bun, and the uniform skirt only highlighted my far-from-perfect legs, which were full of bruises and scars.

Most of my spare time was spent on a cold sheet of ice or in a gym lifting weights, instead of in malls, coffee shops, or movie theaters. I didn't wear make-up; I wore "war paint." I wrestled with insecurity about my butt being too big and muscular—it couldn't fit in jeans as nicely as I wished and yet it powered me on the ice. Yet, despite these differences, it took me only minutes to make friends who accepted me even if I smelled like a rink rat and not Chanel No. 5. These friends may seem much different than me at first glance, but deep down we have made relationships that will last a lifetime. They accept me no matter what my crazy hockey schedule might be, and they don't take it personally when I am unable to attend their lunches and parties. They even take time out of their lives on occasion to venture into the unfamiliar cold rinks and support me… and my dream.

As I write this I look around the walls of my residence room and see some of my favorite things: a poster of the Toronto Maple Leafs, a Canadian flag, homemade signs friends have created to cheer me on at games, trophies, and sports photos. No shirtless celebrities can be found on my walls. I hold my rookie hockey card in my hands and laugh as I read that, "body building" was apparently one of my hobbies… as a *four*-year-old! As I read that my future ambition was to "play for the Canadian National Team," my mind jumps back to this past summer. I was chosen to attend the Team Canada Strength and Conditioning Camp earlier in the year. I spent the entire summer training for the final camp. Daily, I woke up bright and early and drove an hour to York University, where I trained with teammates and a strength coach. I gave up parties, vacationing, junk food and a social life to dedicate my time to chasing my dream. I was invited to the final selection camp at the end of the summer but was not selected for the final team.

When I returned home from the airport my parents had left this same rookie card sitting on my dresser. Although the feeling of defeat was strong, I knew I had come so close to reaching the goal that four-year-old Peter Pan had made at a figure skating show. I spent the rest of the day with a tub of ice cream, but I could still see that little girl smiling in the back of my mind. I knew that if I continued to perse-vere and dedicate myself to my hockey dream that someday in my future I would make that little girl inside of me proud, and achieve my goal at last.

As I hold my card in my hands I decide to use it for my grad picture. Not only because I am such an adorable little darling with my huge smile and oversized hand-me-down equipment, but also because it will serve as a message to myself in the future. When I look back at this yearbook, years down the road, hopefully I will see this picture and feel that sense of achievement that I have been working so hard for.

I think back to my younger years, growing up in a small town on the shore of Lake Simcoe. It was the small town hockey player dream: pond hockey in the winter, early morning hockey at the local rink, and Tim Hortons stops along the way. I had grown up being the only girl playing on the boys' teams. As if I didn't stand out enough already with my long brown ponytail, I always insisted on wearing bright green laces on my skates. I was not sure at the time why I chose this color, but now I seem to have come full circle. Through my hockey I again have the incredible opportunity to attend another prestigious school, this time for university. Dartmouth College, the Ivy League institution down in New Hampshire has recruited me and I have committed to playing hockey there for my university career. I will be proudly wearing the Big Green jersey for my future team. Sometimes I think that the little four-year-old version of me really knew what she was doing when she loved those green hockey laces... and I owe everything to her.

~Ailish Forfar

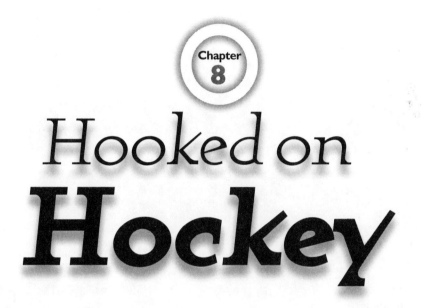

Chapter
8

# Hooked on Hockey

## Life Lessons

# Use Your Courage

*Success is not final, failure is not fatal.*
*It's the courage to continue that counts.*
~Winston Churchill

**D**uring the late 1970s I was blessed to be drafted second overall into the National Hockey League, where I continued to play professional hockey for fifteen seasons. In my rookie season it felt like our Washington Capitals played the Philadelphia Flyers ten times. When I checked, it turned out to actually be only four! Those four games swelled to ten in my memory bank because the Flyers were known as the "Broad Street Bullies" in those days, and for good reason.

Many of our games against the Flyers spiraled out of control into bench-clearing brawls. Before each of these games, every player on our team struggled with the fear of which injuries he might incur during the upcoming sixty minutes of play. I can recall as if it was yesterday how the bus ride from the hotel to the Spectrum was always stone cold quiet. All of our players were deep in thought, pondering what might be about to happen. Fear often grows out of our perception, before any harm has actually taken place.

I learned a very important lesson during my early NHL days: "Courage is not the absence of fear." Courage is choosing to be my best, independent of the fear I am feeling.

A second lesson I learned was the importance of taking action. Some games the only way I could overcome my fear was to take action. After a while the feeling of courage seemed to follow. How we feel affects what we do; what we do affects how we feel.

These are not easy times. My wife Jenn and I have observed many families around us going through hard stuff. But just like those difficult games against the Flyers, this is not the time to shrink from the challenge; this is the time to grow and develop our personal courage.

I explore the connection between the inner game (including our courage) and the actions that we take (our performance) in my latest book, *Hungry!* Again, inner feelings and belief are always the drivers of our outer performance, and the inner quality of courage not only drives our personal performance, but inspires it in the people around us.

My wife Jennifer and I are both passionate about adding value to people's lives and developing leaders worldwide. We accomplish this through speaking at leadership conferences or delivering long-term interactive leadership development sessions. During these sessions I have been challenging leaders across North America with this simple thought: The only thing that I can guarantee leaders in today's economy is… problems! If this is true (and I believe that it is) then developing the courage to tackle these problems head-on becomes essential.

As you and I battle through the fear generated by our own "Philadelphia Flyer" situation, let's remember these simple but powerful concepts:

1. "Courage is not the absence of fear."
2. How we feel affects what we do; what we do affects how we feel.
3. Courage and integrity form the foundation of character.
4. Personal courage inspires team performance.
5. When tough times hit, be mindful of Churchill's "It's the courage to continue that counts!"… and Christopher Robin's timeless instruction to Winnie the Pooh: "Promise me you'll

always remember: You're braver than you believe, and stronger than you seem, and smarter than you think." A.A. Milne

~Ryan Walter

# My Dad the Coach

*Leadership is practiced not so much in words as in attitude and in actions.*
*~Harold S. Geneen*

Growing up in the family of a famous professional hockey player and coach was just about as exciting as life can get. There were always new challenges, new opportunities and something unexpected almost every day.

My dad, Billy Reay, played for the Montreal Canadiens for eight years. He was an assistant captain of the team from 1948-1952 and played with Maurice "The Rocket" Richard, Elmer Lach, Butch Bouchard, Jacques Plante, Bernie "Boom Boom" Geoffrion and many other great players. Two of those years he helped them win the Stanley Cup. Talk about exciting!

A coaching career began immediately after his playing days, but coaching was not a new venture to him. He had coached the Sydney Millionaires in the Cape Breton Senior League and the Quebec Aces in the Quebec Senior Hockey League during the 1940s. Through an unusual set of circumstances he became the coach of the Toronto Maple Leafs in 1957 and assembled a team that included Johnny Bower, Bobby Baun, Frank Mahovlich, Bert Olmstead, George Armstrong and many more Maple Leafs greats. Coaching the Leafs ended abruptly at Christmas two years later when the Leafs decided to replace him as coach. The core group of players on that team went on to win several Stanley Cups.

After a year out of hockey and a time of renewal and soul

searching, Dad reinvented himself and re-launched into the coaching world. That's when I began to draw closer to him, to go to the rink with him on a regular basis and to really understand his psyche. For me, going to the rink and on road trips was no different than any kid going to work with his father, other than the fact that, during the hockey season, our name would be on the front page of the sports section just about every day… the good, the bad and the ugly!

The first stop along the route to becoming the coach of the Chicago Blackhawks was a two-year assignment with the Sault Sainte Marie Thunderbirds, an Eastern Provincial Hockey League team. The Thunderbird organization was unique. Their mode of transportation for the team was unconventional; instead of a bus or train they used two stretch limousines. Dad was the driver of one and he duly appointed the other based on that night's performance/heat allocation… I'll explain. On those cold northern Ontario nights not much heat got back to rear seats of the limo, but the guys up front got pretty toasty. Each player's nightly game performance determined his seat selection. The players made a joke out of it.

There were a lot of young men of character on those Sault teams. Guys like Denis DeJordy, Matt Ravlich, Doug Robinson, Pat Stapleton and Norm Guimond. Some would follow Dad to his next coaching assignment in Buffalo. A few, such as Stapleton and Ravlich later followed him to the Chicago Blackhawks. My favorite guy on the Sault team was a sniper named Freddy Hilts. He would let me sit in the back of the limo with him while his teeth were chattering from the cold and I would ask him questions. I liked Freddy… I remember he was always chewing on a toothpick.

The Sault team was very successful and after the second season Dad was promoted to the American League to coach the Buffalo Bisons. It was a step up — the Bisons traveled by bus.

Coaching is an art. It's more than just X's and O's and strategy. For those gifted at coaching, it's about getting the absolute best out of each player in game situations. Dad's request of each player was that "he give everything he's got every game, no more no less." He knew that a 100 percent effort resulted in good results over the long haul regardless of what team you were playing.

A subtle part of coaching that many individuals overlook is that hockey players are "whole" people. They have wives, children, health problems, financial concerns, responsibilities with parents and a whole host of other things going on, just like everyone. Dad understood these things firsthand. As a young man he had worked to support his family financially, and he also had a handicapped sister, who he was very close to, who needed a great deal of help. Later in life while he was playing for the Canadiens, my mother required special attention and care from complications of a grave illness secondary to childbirth. Dad knew intimately that all these things have an impact on a player. He and my mother did everything they could to assist players and their families during stormy times, knowing that it was impossible to "give all you have" when your life is in turmoil.

There were hundreds, even thousands of acts of kindness during his coaching years, and more time working behind the scenes to help players and families than anyone will ever know. One of the many, many examples I remember vividly is how he once went out of his way to route the limos past a penitentiary in northern Ontario whenever he could so one of his players would be able to have a short visit with his incarcerated father. On one trip I asked Dad what the heck we were doing and he simply replied, "Taking care of business," with little explanation. Do you think any of the players on that team ever forgot those moments?

Buffalo was another great experience. The Bisons were a class act and the envy of many organizations. I got to sit up front in the bus when they traveled! A handful of the guys off the Sault team joined the Bisons and in Dad's second year they finished in first place and won the Calder Cup! And then, Dad was off to the Chicago Blackhawks.

What an adventure! Chicago Stadium, Michigan Avenue, O'Hare Airport and incredible fan support on top of joining a team that included future Hockey Hall of Fame players Bobby Hull, Stan Mikita, Pierre Pilote and Glenn Hall, made Chicago a fantastic stop in the big show. More importantly, the team ownership was first rate and Dad was able to be consistent with his compassionate, caring approach of taking care of the needs of the players and their families, and asking for "everything they've got on game night" in return.

Dad said that coaching hockey was like having twenty-five sons. For me, it was sharing my dad with twenty-five brothers and their families. Our conversations around the dinner table at home frequently focused on how we could help certain players' situations. My mother was a very wise person and she was Dad's quiet, behind-the-scenes confidante. Mom also had a special way of interacting with the players' wives, making sure their needs were met and their families were cared for. Those intimate conversations at the dinner table were cloaked in a very strict rule; what was talked about in our house did not leave our house. Period, no exceptions. Ever. While he was a kind and caring man, he was tough when he needed to be.

Much can be written about the Chicago coaching experience. A fourteen-year run is almost unheard of in professional sports. Tremendous teams with great character and a lot of success, but also with times of uncertainty and chaos. During that period Bobby Hull made a decision to move to the World Hockey Association. It was a financial decision for Bobby that might have been averted had cooler heads prevailed during discussions. There was also a trade that took place while our family was on vacation in Manitoba one July. Dad was not aware of the trade. I was learning to drive that year and we were in the car headed to our daily golf game at Sandy Hook Golf Club, on the shores of Lake Winnipeg, when we heard the news on the radio. I was immediately instructed to change my route to the nearest pay phone. I stayed in the car but I could hear his voice from inside the pay phone from thirty feet away. Not a good day. Unexpectedly, the Blackhawks also traded some of his "sons" to Boston: Ken Hodge, Fred Stanfield and Phil Esposito. Being upset on these occasions doesn't describe his demeanor adequately. He was rip-roaring mad! Those players went on to fortify the Bruins roster and ultimately win several Stanley Cups.

Christmas was a special time of the year for Dad. I'm not sure if it was because he grew up in a family of six children—or whether his spiritual side took hold—but early on in his tenure he convinced the Blackhawks ownership to have a Christmas party for the players and their families. Santa would come, everyone would receive a gift and it would be a day to gather together as a family. The owners embraced the idea and went the extra mile. Not only would there be gifts for all the kids, the players would receive a special "significant" gift, such as a watch or color TV, as a remembrance for that year. Keep in mind this was the 60s and 70s—players were not making the kind of money they are today. It was a really a nice gesture to reward the players for filling Chicago Stadium every game.

The Christmas party became a tradition, something that everyone looked forward to and was the envy of the league. For the young players, the rookies, Dad did something very special on his own. He gave them new skates for Christmas as a surprise. When Dad was young he never had a pair of skates of his own. He shared skates with his siblings until he got his first job, carrying papers for a Winnipeg newspaper and playing on the company-sponsored team.

So what does all this have to do with being a hockey coach?

Dad operated with five guiding principles, as a coach and as a father and husband:

1. Be a good example. It's not what you say; it's what you do!
2. Take full responsibility for yourself.
3. Never ask another person to do something you are not willing to do yourself.
4. Be fair, firm, and consistent.
5. Praise in public, criticize in private… the rest will take care of itself.

You see, there's more to coaching than changing the lines!

~Bill Reay,
son of Billy Reay, former Montreal Canadiens player;
Toronto Maple Leafs; and Chicago Blackhawks coach

# There's No "I" in Team

*I am a member of a team, and I rely on the team,*
*I defer to it and sacrifice for it, because the team, not the individual,*
*is the ultimate champion.*
~Mia Hamm

I love hockey. I mean I r-e-a-l-l-y love hockey. I love hockey more than snow days, summer, or even Halloween candy! I love hockey so much that I wanted to play after my brother's funeral because I knew it would make me feel happy. I wanted to score a goal for him. I ended up scoring four.

I play center forward and I love the feeling when I get a break-away skating in and out of players and trying to "top shelf" the puck. I love taking the risk to skate and score even if I miss.

At the end of the year we had a banquet where the coaches handed out awards. I was pretty sure I was going to get one because I was one of the lead scorers on our team. They handed out five awards and when the last one was announced, and it was not for me, I was devastated. It took everything within me not to cry. I bit my cheek and tried really hard to smile and be happy for my teammates who did get one. When we got into the parking lot I was choking back the tears. I couldn't wait to get into the car and really let it all out. When we got home I had a long talk with my mom and told her how I felt before bed. I fell asleep with a crying headache.

When I woke up in the morning there was a card waiting for me on the kitchen table.

*Dearest Aedyn:*

*I just wanted to write you a note of encouragement because I know you felt disappointed about not getting an award tonight. Do you remember how I told you that everything happens for a reason? And, how most of the time, when we are in the moment of what we might think is unfair, we don't have the full picture? We only have the small square of the GPS screen like in Dad's car, not the whole "life map." In the end, it is best to say "It is what it is" and choose joy and happiness anyway. No one can ever take away your choice to choose to be happy regardless of what's going on around you.*

*Dad and I were talking tonight—exchanging stories about how beautiful you are, how smart you are, how athletic, kind, and funny you are. And I was crying so much because you are just the whole package—"it"—everything! And what I realized and we hope you do too, is that you don't need an award to tell you how great you are. You are strong enough and smart enough to just know it and feel it in your soul.*

*Close your eyes. Put your hand on your heart. Breathe deeply until you feel your beautiful spirit floating up. When you do, love that moment. You only need to know in your heart. We know it.*

*Love you so, so, so, much.*

*Mom and Dad*

*P.S. I hope you love this card. We bought it in Ireland. If you read the back you'll learn about dreaming. Don't ever stop dreaming or believing that dreams come true, because they do! Just not always with the timing we think they should!*

*Love you more than words can say.*

This year at our tournament when I was coming out of the change room, my coach grabbed my arm and told me that he doesn't measure our games by the goals that are scored. He told me that he appreciated that I could play defensively and set up plays and that's what hockey is all about.

When I thought about what he said later on, I realized that he was right. I realized last year I was focused on scoring and keeping the puck to myself, but that this year I had given a lot of effort to passing and working as a team player.

In that moment, I knew why I hadn't earned a trophy, but more than that, I realized that there is no "I" in team.

I'm so grateful that I learned that life lesson.

~Aedyn MacKenzie, age 14

# Hockey's Lessons on Life

*It's too easy when you're not winning to look for excuses and point at others for reasons. You can say "Oh well, it's this guy's fault or they don't do this well" or you can say "I've got to play better and contribute more." You've got to find another gear and come up with big games.*
~Sean Burke

G rowing up in Canada, hockey was more than a part of life. Hockey was winter's routine. Hockey was our television viewing. Hockey was fun.

School was what happened between hockey games—we'd come to school early for a game in the schoolyard, get in a few minutes during recess, eat quickly and rush to continue the game during lunch. For me, the most memorable image of elementary school was all of us grabbing our sticks and heading to the playground. Hats, gloves and coats were an afterthought. We were superstars, we were legends, and we were our own heroes. To this day, thirty-eight years since grade school, I can still remember all the boys in my class and their particular talents—the good players, the mediocre, and the poor players. If I was forced to choose my hockey team from my old eighth grade class, I still know who I would choose.

From hockey, I learned many of life's most important lessons. First of all was to give your all… never quit. Play all-out. Don't quit. When I think back, I learned that from my dad. I remember a hockey game where my team was losing badly — 8-0. I saw an open puck and rushed up the side to score. It was no great achievement, the other team had totally dominated us and they had put in their 2nd or 3rd string goalie. No matter what, I scored. I was thrilled.

When I left the game, my dad, who had been watching, said, "You scored."

"Yeah, but they creamed us," I replied.

"You didn't quit, and that's what matters. It's okay to be bested, but never walk away beaten."

Wow. That was a powerful lesson.

Another thing I learned was that you are part of a team. If my teammate went into a corner, into a scrum with the other team, I would be right there behind him. When I was in a scrum, I knew my teammates were right behind me. Hockey is the greatest of all trust exercises.

Among my hockey heroes, I more recently had the opportunity to witness one in real life, doing something that was above and beyond the feats achieved on ice. In the 1990s we would frequent a sports-themed restaurant called Don Cherry's — owned by Canada's most famous (and sometimes controversial) broadcaster, Don Cherry. He had won the Stanley Cup twice as a coach. I met him a couple of times in passing. His Saturday night routine involved delivering his broadcast between the first and second periods of Canada's National Hockey Broadcast — Hockey Night in Canada. Following his weekly broadcast, he would drive home from the hockey arena or TV studio in Toronto and stop in at his restaurant.

Don Cherry's restaurant, on a Saturday night, was filled with kids in hockey sweaters, accompanied by their parents and coaches. It was a big event for these kids to go to Don Cherry's, eat and watch hockey on the multiple screens, play the various hockey games in the lobby and be surrounded by an amazing collection of memorabilia. Something akin to a believer walking into a shrine... it was wonderful to watch these kids immersed in the legends and heroes.

Faithfully, Don Cherry would enter the restaurant on Saturday night, acknowledge the regular patrons and staff, and make his way around from table to table. Enjoying banter with the kids, signing autographs, answering questions and interacting with the kids and adults who were there. He was so gracious and giving of his time. I later learned that during one particular period, Don Cherry's beloved wife was dying and he faced other challenges. Yet on Saturday nights, he would seldom fail to visit with the guests in his restaurant. He was saying thank you to those kids, parents and coaches who made the trip to celebrate at Don Cherry's. The kids were usually wide-eyed at seeing him in person.

Don Cherry was often controversial, but on those Saturday nights he embodied all that is great about Hockey. He remembered that, for those kids, life was hockey. Other stuff happened, like school and family and chores. It happened between hockey games.

If all hockey taught me is don't quit, play hard, support your teammates and give it your all, then I can take those lessons anywhere and score.

Thanks hockey.

~Peter J. Green

# The Hockey Coach

*Courage is fire, and bullying is smoke.*
~Benjamin Disraeli

My second son, Derek, was in the first grade and was having difficulties in school. His teacher was hard on him because he was the funny one; he always had to be telling a joke and his humour tended to be on the physical side. He would jump up on chairs or try to do back flips in class in order to get attention. And he did get attention, just not the kind that he was hoping for. He was being bullied.

Each day he would come home upset. He was afraid to go to school; he would refuse to get up in the morning, his eating patterns changed and he became very thin and pale. His smile faded as the weeks of bullying turned into months. The school did everything they could to help us but the bullying continued.

It was late February when things changed for Derek. He was walking home from school and it was dreadfully cold. His hat had been stolen and his snow pants were soaking wet after he had been shoved into a puddle. Our neighbour Cody, who had only recently finished high school, spotted Derek walking home from the bus and noticed how cold he was. He ran out of his house straight away and wrapped Derek up in a warm, wool blanket. Cody walked the rest of the way up the street and knocked on the door to speak to me. I saw how sad Derek was and I fell to my knees to hug him and help warm him up.

I wasn't sure if he was bored, or he was just simply an amazing kid, but Cody offered to spend some time with Derek every day after school. Cody waited at the bus stop for Derek to get home from school and he took him out on excursions. At first I didn't know where they went, but Cody had him home promptly at six. Initially there was no change in Derek, but after three days he came to me and asked me if I would buy him a pair of hockey skates. I looked at him; his little six-year old expression was serious as he waited for my reply. I smiled and said, "Alright." For the first time in as long as I could remember, his face lit up with the biggest smile. My heart melted and I knew that something great was happening for my son.

After I bought those skates for Derek, he spent every day with Cody learning to skate and learning to manoeuvre a hockey stick across the ice. A few times Cody allowed me to come to the arena in order to witness the skill Derek had acquired in only a few short weeks. I could hear Derek's laugh as he joked with Cody on the ice. It was music to my ears.

At the end of March, Cody asked if Derek could play in a hockey game. Cody was an assistant coach for the house-league hockey association in town, and he had special permission to allow Derek to play in one of the final games of the season. We were hesitant because we knew that Derek had only just learned to skate, and we were afraid of him getting hurt. But Cody assured us that he would be right there the whole time.

The day of the game we were so nervous for our little boy. But Derek had gotten up early that day, had eaten his breakfast in front of the fireplace and was half dressed by the time we got up that morning. As a family we all piled into the van and drove to the arena. Anxiously we waited for the game to begin. Cody took care of everything. He had a hockey sweater waiting for Derek and all of the equipment he would need. All suited up and ready to go, Derek joined the rest of Cody's team in their box.

Derek sat on the bench for the entire first period. We weren't sure why and we could see Derek's smile fade slowly as the game wore on. My eldest son whispered in my husband's ear during the second period and afterward got up and walked around to the other side of the ice in order to speak to Cody. By this point Derek was nearly in tears as Cody urged him to go onto the ice.

Derek was timid as he skated around during that second period. When he was on the ice he stayed far away from all of the other players, and steered clear of the puck. By this point I wasn't sure I even understood why Cody had wanted him to play in the first place. My "mom" instincts were kicking in and I wanted to get my son off that ice.

The third period looked like it would be much of the same. Despite my yelling and encouragement from the stands, Derek remained far away from the action. Slowly two players from the other team had made their way over to where Derek was skating, and they tripped Derek, causing him to fall on the ice. As his head hit the ice, his mouth guard fell out and he bit his lip. Blood was flowing from his bottom lip and dripping down the front of him. The events unfolded in slow motion and I stood up screaming like a mad woman.

My eldest son pulled on my sleeve and tried to get my attention, but I was more concerned about what was happening with Derek. The referee placed the two players in the penalty box and then directed Derek to the opposing team's net. The referee dropped the puck in front of him and pointed toward the net. I glanced quickly at the scoreboard and realized that there was very little time left in the last period and the game was tied. (Scores didn't really make much difference in this age category, but it was our movie-magic moment so I mention it for that reason). I was still on my feet as I watched my son positioned directly in front of the net, and slowly my son took aim, lifted his stick in order to shoot that puck into the net. I had never seen Derek use that much concentration. The puck flew effortlessly past the goalie and right into the net, and the goal was awarded to Derek's team. After a few more minutes of play, the period was over and Derek had scored the winning goal. The sound of the cheers and applause from the stands made Derek smile and laugh as he skated off the ice.

After the game my eldest son finally got my attention, and it was then that he told me that the two boys who had tripped Derek were the two bullies who had been tormenting him all year in school. They were brothers who rode on the same bus as Derek. As I stood outside the change room waiting for Derek to come out, their father approached me in order to apologize for his sons' behaviour. We told him what had been happening all year and he promised that he would make it right.

Derek was not bullied again after that day. We witnessed our son's smile and sense of humour return, and we look back and realize that if it had not been for the selfless efforts of a young teenage boy and the game of hockey, our son might never have found his humour again. Cody continued to coach Derek long after that hockey game, and when Cody left for college that fall he left behind a young boy who could stick handle with the best of them, a boy with confidence and a killer punch line!

~Jennifer Litke

# The Sound of Opportunity

*A lifetime of training for just ten seconds.*
*~Jesse Owens*

The summer before I started college at St. Olaf, I was terrified. But not for the usual reasons. I was okay with moving 600 miles away from Grand Rapids, Michigan to Northfield, Minnesota, a place where I knew few people.

What worried me was the hockey team that I was joining; I was one of six freshmen on the women's varsity squad. Until I arrived at school in the fall, I had only skated with one of my future teammates, another girl from Michigan. I was terrified that I wouldn't be good enough; that I would spend the whole season on the bench; that I would be the worst player on the ice. That summer I had countless nightmares of stepping on the ice for the first time with my college team and making a fool of myself. I was scared of the unknown.

I was simultaneously excited and afraid of the opportunity to play for the Oles. When we met with Coach Buzz in September for pre-season team meetings, I was jittery and filled with mixed emotions. During one of these meetings, Buzz told us a story about the renowned UCLA basketball coach John Wooden, whom he highly revered. This story involved a few players from the 1964 and 1965 UCLA champion basketball teams. One player sat on the bench for most of the 1964 season. Five minutes into the championship game against Duke, this player relieved a teammate and got his chance to play. He played extremely well and stayed in the whole game. The next season this same player returned to the court instead of the bench. During the 1965 championship game against Michigan, this player was relieved by another teammate who usually rode the bench—a similar but reciprocal situation to the year before.

Buzz finished the story by emphasizing the importance of preparation and readiness. You never know when your opportunity will present itself and you do not want to miss the opportunity because it might be your only one. Buzz always says, "When opportunity comes knocking, don't complain about the noise."

I never forgot that story. It lingered in the back of my mind throughout the dreaded two-a-days, the rigorous practices, the tiring dry land training, and most of all throughout the day of October 29th, 2010: our first game of the season; the first game of my collegiate career. That was also the first time in my eight years of competitive hockey that I ever got nervous for a game. I remember my arms shaking as I pulled the St. Olaf jersey over my head. I sat in the locker room tapping my fingers on the bench on either side of me. My feet twitched incessantly in my skates, the tips of my blades nervously dancing about in the air.

With an abundant roster, not everyone dressed for the game. One or two girls had to sit in the stands, so I was honored to just wear the jersey and occupy the players' bench. Although I was in the lineup that night, I was the fourth forward on the fourth line. I hoped I would eventually rotate in and take a shift at wing at some point during the game. Seven shifts passed as I waited anxiously on the bench. Between my shouts of encouragement to my teammates I kept reminding myself of the story Buzz told us during the pre-season meeting. I did not have time to feel sorry for myself. I knew I had to be ready because I never knew when my opportunity to play might arise.

"Maybe," I thought, "in the last game of the season... maybe in tomorrow night's game... maybe in the second period of this game... maybe..."

"Right now, Tara. You are up next. Get ready," Buzz called from the other end of the bench.

What? Right now? My heart began to beat fast and my shoulders shook with agitation. What if I wasn't ready? No. I had to erase that doubt. I had to be ready. No question.

With adrenaline pumping through my body I could hear the pounding of my heart. That was all I could hear. The noise of my heartbeat drowned out all other sound. I was ready. I had been preparing for this moment ever since that meeting in September, ever since I heard coach's story — the story that inspired me to be ready for my opportunity, no matter when it came.

This is how I remember the moment of opportunity knocking: My skates hit the ice and I zealously propelled my body forward. I raced into the offensive zone just as my teammate sniped the puck at the opposing goalie's pad. It bounced right out to me in the slot. My arms quivered with anxiety and nerves but still I pulled the puck back on my stick and launched it at the net.

Time slowed down. The world stopped. All sounds ceased. All sound except for the thumping of my heart. Ba-boom. Ba-boom. Ba-boom.

The puck seemed to saunter through the air, leisurely floating toward the net. My impatience built up in my tensed muscles as I watched the puck sail in slow motion.

The instant the red lamp lit up, the world burst back into life. The first thing I registered was the noise. The exclamation from the horn. The shouts from my teammates. The roar from the crowd. I stood in disbelief despite the reassuring cheers.

After exploding into sound, the world exploded into motion. The referee's arm vigorously pointed at the net, skates scurried in my direction, fists and sticks pumped into the air. One moment I was alone in the slot, the next I had four teammates rushing at me, flashes of white and gold blurring my vision. Just then, reality hit me. I had just scored my first goal during my first shift of my first collegiate hockey game.

I love recalling that remarkable moment: being surrounded by my teammates in front of the opponent's net. That shift was my opportunity knocking. That goal was my response to the noise. I did not know when my opportunity would present itself. I had to be ready. Turns out I was.

Even though the noise immediately following the goal was loud, chaotic, and thundering, it was also exhilarating. The cacophony of the buzzer, the fans, and my teammates was beautiful harmony in my ears. After scoring that goal I continued to play well and received a lot of playing time throughout my freshman and into my sophomore year. I will never complain about the noise—the sweet noise of opportunity knocking.

~Tara Reyelts

# Game Scents

*... to be a child, to be a child! To have the roads and the days all stretching out forward and upward and away.*

~Gary Jennings

When you play hockey as a child, the love of the game really never leaves you. As an excited young mother, I signed up my five-year-old son Sean to play Mite hockey in the local league. I'd played organized hockey in high school and had often wished I'd started when I was younger. I couldn't wait to see my son in action. He already knew how to skate and the basics of the game. And he'd learned the rules while watching our favorite NHL team play on television.

"He's a natural," I told everyone. "He's really got talent. I think he will definitely make the Travelling Team."

Sean's eyes shone every time I praised him.

Although we visited a local store that sold used sports equipment to pick up most of what he needed, we shopped at a sporting goods store for his skates. You simply couldn't skimp on skates. The right pair could make all the difference. So I closed my eyes and handed over my credit card to pay for the latest version of the best youth skates on the market.

Sean hugged the box to his chest. "Thanks, Mommy!"

On the morning of placement evaluations we got up early to dress. Sean's thin little-boy body looked so adorable and funny bulked up in all his pads. I asked him about nineteen times if he had to use the bathroom, remembering how I'd more than once had to get completely undressed because I'd forgotten to go.

"I'm fine, Mommy," he said. He sat down at the kitchen table to eat his cereal, swinging his feet back and forth, not touching the floor.

"Should be fun today," I said. "Are you excited?"

"Yep," he said, munching.

"I'm sure you'll be great. Just remember what I told you about keeping you head up and what Papa said about holding your stick."

"I'll remember, Mommy, don't worry. I'm going to be really great!"

At the ice arena, we made our way through the crowd of parents and players. Everyone from the Mite program would be evaluated and placed on a team based on their performance today. I said goodbye to Sean at the door of the locker room. The coaches and assistants were helping the players with their skates and helmets this morning.

As I walked through the double doors into the chill air of the arena, I felt dry, cold air crackle inside my nose and noticed a faint scent of... something. Does ice have a smell? No, it can't. Maybe it's the Zamboni?

And that's when it started....

It was like someone turned up the volume on all my senses. My heart raced. I could hear the skate blades cutting the ice and sticks slapping against the puck and voices calling out. Bodies slammed into the boards and elbows thudded into other players. I was fourteen years old and I heard my coach's voice, "Skate! Get open! Get in front of the net!"

And then—just as suddenly—it was over and my mind returned to the present. I walked up the metal steps of the bleachers and took a seat directly at center ice in order to get the best view.

My friend, another hockey mom, came through the doors and saw me sitting alone. She waved hello and then disappeared for a few minutes. When she returned she held an insulated cup in each hand. Quickly climbing the steps, she sat down next to me and handed me a cup.

"Thanks," I said. "Is Jacob ready?"

"Yes, barely. I had to drag him out of bed," she said. "Do you know when we get the results from the evaluations?"

"Not for a few days," I answered.

Then I sipped my hot chocolate.

And it happened again....

The smell took me back to a long-ago Saturday afternoon. Sweat-dampened, helmet-flattened hair lay plastered against my flushed face and my fingers and toes were numb with cold. The sweet and sumptuous scent of hot chocolate filled the kitchen as we laughed and told stories of our exploits in the game: the long pass, the breakaway, the double deke, and the short-handed goal.

"There he is!" My friend pointed toward the mass of players on the ice. There were at least thirty five-year-olds out there and I couldn't pick out her son. But I saw my own. He was wearing my old high school socks—green with white stripes.

He seemed so very small. And it was obvious he wasn't the fastest skater.

He's still young compared to some of the others, I told myself, clutching my mittened hands together.

For two long hours I sat with my friend in the cluster of other parents as all of our kids went through the basic skills testing. I felt tense with apprehension each time it was Sean's turn to perform. He wasn't the biggest or fastest, but he wasn't the smallest or the slowest, either. I thought he did very well for his size—in fact some of the other parents were impressed at his stick handling. But I soon began to feel like I'd set him up for disappointment. I'd told him he was going to be great. I'd told him he was going to make the Travelling Team! Would he be crushed when he didn't? Would he be devastated when he realized that there were quite a few kids who were better players than he was?

At the end of the evaluations, I met him in the locker room. All the parents and coaches and kids were crowded together. Loud excited voices echoed between the cement walls. We found a spot near the door on the end of a bench. I quickly helped Sean take off his skates and put on his shoes so we could get out of there. I hustled him to the car. We buckled ourselves in and started for home.

As the tang of his sweaty equipment filled up the close quarters inside the car, another memory washed over me.

I was riding home in a mostly empty school bus with the other ten members of my girls' hockey team. We'd spent all day at a tournament far from home. After squeaking out wins in our first two games, we'd been slaughtered by an older, bigger, more skillful team. Our spirits were about as low as three hockey games in a day and a final nine-to-nothing loss could make you.

"You girls should be proud of everything you did today," our coach said. "You played with heart. That's all that matters and I'll never ask for anything more."

My eyes teared at the memory. I knew just what to say to Sean to make him feel better. Glancing in the rearview mirror, I saw him looking at me. He smiled sleepily.

"That was the most fun I've ever had, Mommy," he said. "I can't wait to play in a real game."

I smiled right back at him. "How about I make some hot chocolate when we get home?"

~Leanne Fanning Pankuch

# What's the Big Deal Anyway?

*To play the game is good, to win is better, but to love the game is best of all.*

*~Author Unknown*

As a small town Canadian girl (with three older brothers), it seemed only natural that I should learn how to skate. However, as a child, each time I grew an inch taller the tendons in my feet did not. They merely stretched. Every growth spurt I went through meant days of agony, and skating was hardly on the radar at a time when I could barely walk. Therefore, like many childish things, I left it behind.

That is until, as an adult, some wonderful coworkers encouraged me to come out and join them at their weekly pickup game.

Against my better judgment, I scrambled up some gear, bought some old used hockey skates (as this was surely only going to be a one-time deal) and found myself alone in a change room. Well, technically, it was the puny figure skating office. As the only girl, it beat the alternative.

Now, imagine yourself alone in a room with a bag full of equipment and no clue what to do with it. I came out with shin pads and hockey pants over my jeans. Damned if I could figure out that garter getup.

I wobbled down the long rubber path until I found the entrance to the ice surface. Then I nearly threw up. What the hell was I doing?

I had no right to be there, I couldn't even skate! It was going to be the biggest embarrassment of my life.

One by one, my coworkers skated onto the ice, clapping me on the back as they went, teasing, laughing, encouraging. Naturally, I thought they were nuts.

Once they'd all hit the ice and were busy skating around, I ventured out with a death grip on the boards. Stick, what stick? It was rendered useless because then I'd have to let go of the boards.

Gradually though, I relaxed. I let go. I held my stick. I even began to skate. Then, as I was making my plodding way up and down the boards, lo and behold a puck landed on my stick. And THAT is when it bit me. The hockey bug I'd heard people talk of. That puck was MINE, dammit!

Over the next couple of years, I took skating lessons, went to hockey school, and of course, kept showing up for the weekly pickup games. Hell, I even played net on occasion.

I adored hockey. But why? Was it the fact that they didn't care how stupid I looked, how many times I fell, or how grossly un-cool I might have appeared? Or maybe because I learned that I didn't care about those things? Or perhaps it was the sheer adrenaline rush of getting a puck on your stick, making a pass, taking a shot, scoring the ever-elusive goal and then imagining a crowd going wild.

Now, nearly nine years later, I still play pickup with many of those same people each week. I still hear that imaginary crowd every time I score a goal, and I'm still as bitten with the sport as I ever was.

Hockey has a lot to teach a person, no matter what age or ability. If you already play, then you already know. If you haven't played, then there are no words to explain it. All I can tell you is to grab a pair of skates, borrow a stick, meet some friends, hit the ice, and then write your own story.

~Tammy E.A. Crosby

# What Hockey Taught Us

*Every accomplishment starts with the decision to try.*
~Author Unknown

Every head in the locker room turned as my seven-year-old daughter pushed open the door and strolled into the room filled with seven- and eight-year-old boys and their parents. The boys shot surreptitious looks our way, as if looking to see if that really was a girl on their locker room bench. It was our first introduction to the world of youth hockey.

When I was seven years old, one of my friends played on the boys' hockey team. She had to get a court order in order to play. Thankfully, the acceptance of girls in hockey has grown and there are even girls' hockey leagues. Just not in Kansas. Truthfully, there's not much hockey in Kansas at all. Playing hockey is definitely an anomaly for any kid in this part of the world, and even more so if you're a girl.

How my daughter decided at the age of six that she wanted to play hockey, I'll never know. I'm not even sure she had ever seen an entire game when she announced one spring morning that she wanted to play hockey. We patted her on the head and told her that was nice, thinking she'd forget about it. Two months later, she asked me again when I was going to sign her up for hockey.

After diligently checking into hockey programs in the area, I discovered the only hockey programs were mainly made up of boys, with just a few girls in each program. With trepidation and visions of frozen pieces of rubber flying at my daughter's pretty face, I signed my daughter up for learn-to-play-hockey classes.

My daughter is about as far from your vision of a hockey player as you can get. She's the smallest kid in her class. She's got a mop of blond, curly hair that is the envy of anyone who has ever wanted curly hair. She's Shirley Temple with a hockey stick.

We really figured hockey would be a passing fancy. She would get out on the ice, realize it was hard to skate and cold and decide she wanted to do something more traditional. We should have known better. This child has been anything but traditional her whole life. After sixteen weeks of learn-to-play-hockey classes, eight stitches in her chin from falling on the ice without her chin guard and countless tears over not being able to perfect the hockey stop, we showed up to turn heads in the locker room for our first night of youth hockey.

I think my daughter thought she was going to step on the ice and be the next Wayne Gretzky. She never thought it would be hard to learn to play. She never thought she would be the worst player on her team. Most of the boys she was playing with had been on skates almost since they could walk. She had a lot of catching up to do and little help from a mom who can barely stand up and skate in a circle and a father who has never been on skates.

But she had what a lot of kids don't have at age seven—determination. She wanted to play hockey more than anything else—and she wanted to be good. We went to every clinic, took private lessons and wore out our welcome at free skate. We even built a homemade ice rink in the back yard during the winter. When she scored her first goal, it was cause for huge celebration.

That first hockey year wasn't easy. It's never easy to learn something new. It's even tougher when you're the only one like you doing it. She was the only girl on the team. While most of the boys were nice and encouraging, it was still tough to be the one that always stood out.

Her coaches were great. They told her how much they loved her polka-dot stick and her pink skate laces, yet treated her like a hockey player on the ice. The parents loved her. They rooted for her to get better all year. When she scored her first goal, every parent was in line to congratulate her.

More than a year later, we still can't keep her off the ice. She has her eye on the travel team next season. Instead of hearing "Who's the girl?" from the other teams' parents, we hear "Who's #8? She's really good." Heads have stopped turning when she walks into the locker room, and now there's another girl on the team.

But that first year of hockey was life changing for my daughter. She learned more from hockey than she did in her entire second-grade year at school. She learned the value of determination. She discovered that following your dreams may require hard work and even some blood, but it's worth it in the end. She became a champion of the underdog and began to stand up for kids who were being picked on at school because she knew what it was like to be different. And she gained confidence that she could be exactly who God made her to be, even when it flies in the face of society's conventions.

And her parents? Well, we learned that you can't keep your kids from their passions, even when you see the road ahead will be bumpy. We learned stitches aren't the end of the world. We learned that when your child doesn't fit society's mold, it's okay to make a new one.

And we have hockey to thank for all of that.

~Lori Fairchild

# 78

# My Hockey Scar

*Some people skate to the puck. I skate to where the puck is going to be.*
*~Wayne Gretzky*

By the time I was fourteen years old, I was still struggling with some of the finer points of dealing with and showing sensitivity towards other people. I wasn't a bad kid, but like many young people, my worldview was egocentric. Meaning that my expectations were such that I was horribly shocked when things didn't go entirely my way.

I had the good fortune of being friends with Billy, a classic spoiled rich kid. Billy was a bit on the wild side and was not exactly a scholar, having been left back in school two different times—the result being that he was a sixteen-year-old with a driver's license in grade nine. His father had given him a new silver Trans Am for his sixteenth birthday and predictably, Billy trashed it within about six months. But before he did, young Billy enjoyed a brief period of enormous popularity.

So, I was rather excited when Billy called me up one day in April to say that his dad had given him a pair of hockey tickets to the Avco Cup finals, where the Edmonton Oilers were hosting the Winnipeg Jets. The Oilers had made it easily to the finals that year on the back of the seventeen-year-old rookie phenomenon, Wayne Gretzky, but Winnipeg also had a very good team and a win that night would clinch them the Avco Cup.

Billy picked me up in his Trans Am and after an alarmingly quick ride to the Edmonton Coliseum, we arrived just in time for the game.

Of course, Billy's parents had gold seats, located in about row twelve and lined up just inside one of the blue lines. We grabbed some food (Billy's treat!) and took our seats, feeling pretty good about ourselves.

Just as the opening face-off was to begin, a very portly gentleman started to push his way into our row with a series of "excuse me's." This person was surely 300 pounds, and had great difficulty maneuvering within the tight spaces of the packed stands. After much grunting and groaning, the man wedged his considerable girth into the seat directly to my right.

Perfect! Now I was completely unable to see the play at the far end of the ice on account of his protruding stomach. And being the nice boy that I was, did I suffer in silence? No, I most certainly did not. I spent the remainder of the first period and more than half of the second complaining bitterly to my friend. In fact, we probably spent more time making barely-whispered fat jokes than we spent watching the game. I'm sure the poor man heard many of these exchanges as I noticed that his complexion grew increasingly redder as the game went on.

Did we stop? No. But what happened next helped me learn a bit about the concept of karma.

Winnipeg was making a rush down the ice and their star player Terry Ruskowski wound up and unleashed a wicked slap shot. Just as he shot, Wayne Gretzky of the Oilers stuck out his stick blade and deflected the puck out of play. Out of play and into the crowd, where it struck a young teenage boy right in the face, shattering his glasses and knocking him out cold.

I never saw it coming. Instead of watching the game, I had turned away and was whispering yet another fat joke into Billy's ear.

I regained full consciousness as I was being carried up the stairs by two St. John Ambulance attendants, and I remember hearing Billy say that he had picked up what was left of my glasses. He handed them to an attendant and went back to watch the game. As an adult, this complete lack of attentiveness seems insulting, but really, what else was a sixteen-year-old going to do?

Anyway, they took me to a medical room deep within the recesses of the stadium and a doctor examined me. He determined that there was still some glass in my eye, so an ambulance was called. As I was being loaded into the ambulance to be taken to a hospital, somebody handed me the puck. Needless to say, I missed the rest of the game, which the Winnipeg Jets won. The last WHA game ever played in our city.

Some minor surgery was required to remove the remaining glass, and for the next two weeks I was required to wear a patch over the eye, a testament to my youthful stupidity… but a great lesson.

While I did lose the puck playing street hockey not long after that, I still have the scar just above my eye, courtesy of Mr. Wayne Gretzky, and the good story that goes along with it!

~Jeffrey Scott Hamilton

79

# The Life Lessons of Hockey

*Children have to be educated, but they have also to be left to educate themselves.*

*~Ernest Dimnet*

There are so many things to love about hockey—the speed of the game, the thrills of wild goals, the tenacity of the players. But what I treasure most are the life lessons it teaches my son. These are ideas that cannot be learned in books.

Lesson One—Do it yourself.

At age three, we slapped skates and a bicycle helmet on my son and enrolled him in the local Mice on Ice class. I remember holding my breath as he began to skate, wobbling with a PVC duct-taped walker to steady himself. I followed him onto the ice, only to be quickly shooed away by the instructor. She glared at me and barked "No parents!" This would be the beginning of many parent oustings. I learned that many life lessons would not be taught by me.

Lesson Two—Work hard.

Somewhere in the second or third year, my son realized hockey is hard. It means enduring pain, getting knocked down, finding a way to keep going, doing it again. Hockey became the reference point for fractions, long division, volunteer projects, writing research papers and difficult relationships. When my son would begin to complain about how challenging something was, it became "just like hockey."

Lesson Three—Be wild sometimes.

I love hockey's ability to unleash "the cowboy gene." Nowhere else in life do kids have the permission to run free, scrap it out and even get a little crazy. In school, church, restaurants, and at home, kids are forever being "shushed" and told to settle down. I love that my son gets to take a healthy risk with the wildness of hockey. My theory is that by engaging his cowboy side, it will eliminate the desire for unhealthy risks like drugs, alcohol and fast cars.

Lesson Four—The team is everything.

There is something magical about watching a team come together. My heart swells every time I witness kids heading over to encourage a goalie with a stick tap after he just let in a goal. It is a beautiful thing to overhear positive words from teammates, coaches and other parents. It is so easy to be critical, but using words to build each other up is an amazing experience.

Lesson Five—Celebrate everything.

Even with an epic loss in hockey, there is always something to celebrate, whether it is a single amazing pass or a funny, fluky goal. Noticing the bright spots, however small, is a hidden message for always finding the good in life. For my son, it was the losing seasons and the missed goals that were the things that taught him the most about true character. Going for almost three years without ever scoring a goal, my son faced a huge self-esteem battle. We tried everything to encourage him from practicing in the garage to special lessons and camps. Nothing worked because he didn't believe it was possible.

I'll never forget the day he finally scored that goal. You would have thought he had gone to the moon and back. We had a special dinner; we played loud celebration music on the way home. He was king of his world. I was so proud of him, but not for scoring the goal.

I was proud that he didn't quit—he kept going and grinding it out until that miraculous goal came. He learned how to find it in himself to keep trying, to go for it anyway. For that, I am grateful to the great game of hockey. It showed my son that anything is possible. As they always say in hockey, "Good things happen when you put it on the net." And when you don't too.

~Cara McLauchlan

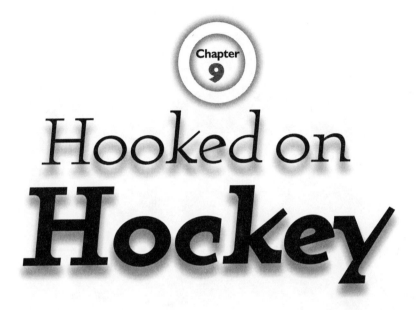

# Hooked on Hockey

## Spectacular Spectators

# 80

# More than a Game

*At the end of the day, a loving family*
*should find everything forgivable.*
*~Mark V. Olsen and Will Sheffer*

My grandson Travis was three years old when his mother bought him a video of *The Mighty Ducks* movie. "Best purchase ever," she said. "He watches it for hours."

Little did she know the importance that video would have on their lives. When Christmas came that year, I was told if I wanted to escalate my grandmother status a notch, I should purchase Travis a hockey stick. His eyes shone when he saw it, and all the other gifts lay dormant while he played and played with the stick. My basement became a hockey rink that year, and I felt like I'd given him the moon.

"It's just a phase," I told my daughter. "Baseball is just around the corner." It wasn't hockey I objected to, but the fact there were no programs within miles of their farm. Where would he play? And I lived even farther away. How could I attend all the games?

By the time he started school, the hockey phase was still with us. No matter how many basketball or baseball programs Travis participated in to please his parents, he'd always rush home to play pretend hockey.

There were more hockey gifts—NHL table hockey, NHL action

figures, jerseys, and all kinds of hockey sticks. He was obsessed and begged to play on a team.

Travis was in the second grade when it all changed, and I got the call. "Mom, on the way to school today Travis was quiet—too quiet. I asked him if he had a problem, and he said, 'I want to play hockey.' Mom, he had tears in his eyes. Well, I crumbled and told him we'd find a way."

I was worried, but his parents, Carey and Bob, worked it out. They purchased hockey gear and signed him up for a team fifty miles away in Kansas City.

I waited by the phone anxiously to hear how the first practice went. Travis didn't know how to skate very well, and the physical aspect of hockey could be defeating. Carey finally called. "Mom, he fell and fell, but wasn't the least bit discouraged. Know what he told me? He said, 'Mom, this was the greatest day of my life.'"

For the next year, they drove 100 miles roundtrip to Kansas City twice a week so Travis could get hockey out of his system. But the year stretched into the next year and the next. I was amazed at the dedication of his parents. The cost was tremendous. Gasoline was soaring and the equipment costs were off the charts. They scrimped and plunged ahead. Bob cleaned out the extra barn and the two spent hours playing rollerblade hockey on cement. Travis worked on speed, stick handling and shot release each evening. It became a ritual. Homework, hockey in the barn, then dinner. I just shook my head and attended as many games as possible, and each time I made the trip, I was rewarded by the fun and excitement hockey provided.

Five years later Travis was still committed. So were the parents even though they were no longer together. The divorce was hard for all of us. I loved both Bob and Carey and tried to remain neutral. I was an outsider hoping tension would ease for Travis's sake, but raw feelings, tears, and anger continued.

Even though Travis was upset, he channeled his emotions into hockey. "It was a bad day when they told me they were separating,"

Travis said. "I love them both, but I knew I couldn't do anything about it, so I focused on my hockey game."

The first season after the divorce, I didn't know what to expect. Both parents wanted to watch their son, so this family would be thrown together weekly by hockey games.

I wrestled with how to act. If I was congenial toward Bob my daughter might consider me a traitor, and if I ignored him... well, that wasn't my style. I walked into the Line Creek Ice Arena and my eyes met Bob's. I couldn't resist and hugged him like old times. My daughter was late, and by the time she arrived, Bob and I were sitting in the bleachers side by side. Carey sat on my other side. The game started. A few minutes into the competition found Bob and Carey talking across me giving each other commentary on the unfolding game in front. No one would ever have suspected they were emotional enemies.

Travis skimmed the ice at breakneck speed. I watched, heart swelling, breath held and eyes focused on #96. Defense from the opposing team did nothing to restrict my grandson from fighting his way toward the goal. One second short, the goalie was unable to block the shot and Travis raised his stick in triumph. His skill was undeniable but more important was the developing comradeship between my daughter and her ex-husband. They gave each other a high-five and clapped in sheer admiration.

Outside the rink, emotions healed at a rapid pace as they called back and forth to see who would be taking Travis this week or the next to practice. They talked about hockey, how Travis was doing in school, and how each of them was doing. Oh, there were tense times, but there is little doubt hockey played a huge part in bringing compassion and civility back into Bob and Carey's life. Travis is now fifteen and playing high school hockey. Carey has a new person in her life, and Bob is making a new life for himself—and they are friends once again. And I have a trophy puck on my desk inscribed, Travis Treanor Six Goals in One Game—5-11-11.

I give a lot credit to Bob and Carey and the people they truly are, but also know that aside from their son, they still had a common thread. Had it not been for hockey, and the fact this family had to see each other on a weekly basis, all that anger and ill will might have festered for years.

~Arlene Rains Graber

# An Audience of One

*My father gave me the greatest gift anyone could give another person, he believed in me.*

*~Jim Valvano*

When I was young, I loved to play hockey. The memories that I have of the game are wonderful, but one memory stands out above them all. It wasn't a specific game, or winning the league trophy, or being named the most valuable player. It was something more tangible, something more lasting, and something that has encouraged me and stayed with me throughout my entire life.

My father showed up at every game to cheer me on, and his smile is what I remember most. It didn't matter to him who was winning, or how well I was playing. What deeply mattered to him was that I was his son, and that he was proud of me no matter what the score was. He taught me that success wasn't always based on winning, but rather on having the courage to compete and the confidence to try your very best no matter what the outcome.

The most memorable moment for me was when we made it into the playoffs, and we had to play in our opponent's hometown. The size of the other team and the unfriendly crowd made it all so intimidating. My father could see in my eyes that I was losing my courage even before the game had started. He quietly took me aside and told me, "Play for an audience of one." He went on to say, "Don't focus on the unfriendly crowds, or the size of the other team; simply focus on the game and whenever you get discouraged, look for me, for I will be cheering for you." So, when my heart grew faint, my eyes searched for him and saw him with a big smile and an encouraging look. I saw him cheering me on in spite of the odds, or the score, or the crowd, and this gave me the strength and the courage to do my best. Every game after that I would look for him in the crowd, and he would hold up one finger reminding me of his words: "Don't worry about the crowd, just play for an audience of one."

A few years back my dad passed away, but this important lesson has carried me through many difficult times. We all go through seasons in our lives when we feel like we are playing in a large hostile arena, listening to those voices that tell us, "you will never make it," or "you're not good enough… so why try, just give up."

Through those challenging times, what has kept me in the game of life is this lesson I learned when I was young. Only this time it wasn't my dad I looked for, it was God. I would picture God looking down on me smiling from ear to ear, cheering for me at the top of His lungs and drowning out all those negative voices. I would see Him standing to His feet and clapping His hands with joy, not necessarily because I was actually winning or making all the right plays but simply because I was trying to do the very best I could.

Did I mention that after every game my dad would give me a big hug and tell me how proud he was of me? Well, I imagine that when this game of life is over, and we meet our heavenly Father, He will be grinning from ear to ear. I suspect that you will be greeted with the biggest hug you could ever imagine and He, like my dad, will tell you how proud He is of you. So remember to stay in the game and don't listen to the crowd, simply play for an audience of one.

~Ken Freebairn

# Poetic Justice

*Hot coffee and cold winter mornings are two of the best soul mates who ever did find each other.*
*~Terri Guillemets*

Hot chocolate fails to reach cold toes
Sweetened by frosted air
Heaters overhead, rectangular suns
Blaze color not heat.

So we stamp
We cheer
We yell
We put chilled fingers to blue-tinged lips,
Cloudy whistles of derision for the ref's call
And we slap each other on the back—"Great game!"
And leave the flotsam of our celebration to be swept away
　　while the Zamboni circles.

~Valerie Coulman

# A Night at the Arena

*The glory of sport is born at the moment when the game*
*and the person become one, when all the complexity of one's life*
*finds a moment to emerge in the game.*
*~Timothy Shriver, Ph.D.*

We live in an area that has a long history of ice hockey. Games have been regularly played in Hershey, Pennsylvania every year since 1931. We have a host of college, high school and junior teams here but we are best known as the home of the AHL Hershey Bears hockey team.

My favorite memories of seeing the Hershey Bears play come from the years when they were still playing in the 7,200-seat Hersheypark Arena. Now they play in the modern, 10,500-seat Giant Center just a few hundred yards away. I'm not knocking the new venue, as it is an amazing place, but the old Arena has a charm and a history that will never be replaced.

I didn't have much knowledge of hockey when I attended my first few games, but that didn't matter much. As soon as I walked through the Arena doors, I could hear the hum of the crowd waiting for the game to begin. The excitement was contagious even though I knew nothing of the game itself.

I remember looking up at our seats near the top of the Arena. It felt like it took forever to get there, but really it was only about ten minutes. The stairs were very narrow and short so you had to be careful when going up and down since it was easy to trip. Once we got to our curved wooden seats, they were narrow too. I guess people were thinner back in 1936 when the Arena was built.

Finally settled, I got my first view of the crowd and the ice. Though it seemed like we were far up, I still had a great view of the ice. The motor of the Zamboni could be heard even in the highest seats and I marveled at how the driver knew just where to turn the corner. The announcer told us about sponsors, pointed out pages of the program and urged us to buy tickets for the raffles to support the junior hockey team.

It was hard not to succumb to the call of the vendors who carried every snack you could imagine up and down those narrow stairs. A flash of my hand and a loud "over here" was all it took to get cotton candy, popcorn and a drink heading my way. I loved the way food and money moved in the stands from person to person, very slowly. You don't see cooperation like that too much any more these days and it struck me as such an old-fashioned idea, but a great one.

I was savoring those first crunchy kernels of salty popcorn while watching the Zamboni exit the ice. And then in a huge rush of energy, there they were, the Hershey Bears! Skating like madmen over the ice, but moving gracefully, which was amazing considering they were the size of grizzly bears in their "Hershey chocolate" brown and white uniforms.

Noise filled the air as folks whistled, shouted and applauded their welcome to the Bears. Some members of the team raised a glove in greeting, others showed off their strength by slamming the pucks against the boards. Eventually the opposing team took the ice as well and received a positive, though not nearly as loud, welcome from the crowd.

Next the announcer asked us to stand, which was pretty hard to do in a small seat with an armful of snacks, but I managed. I remember I was surprised to hear both the American and the Canadian national anthems play over the sound system. It gave me a warm feeling of pride that all the players and fans paid their respects to both countries.

After that folks settled back in their seats as a powerful feeling of expectation filled the Arena. The game was about to begin as both teams stood motionless, sweat already dripping onto the ice. It was quiet as everyone waited for the puck to drop. As soon as it did the fans went crazy and things never got quiet again.

From the moment the puck first hit the ice to the final buzzer, I sat breathless on the edge of that narrow seat waiting to see what would happen next. It didn't matter that I didn't know the game was divided into periods, or that a biscuit was a puck, or even what a hat trick was.

What mattered was that I was a part of the living, breathing sport called hockey. In no other sport will you find such passion and energy brought to life before you. From the players on the ice to the fans in the stands, everyone has a piece of this game and loves it. Including me.

~Shawn Marie Mann

# 84

# Hockey Grandparents

*Grandchildren are the dots that connect the lines
from generation to generation.*
~Lois Wyse

he local arena was coming to life. The clanking of pipes echoed the sounds of pucks hitting the boards as slumber-wrinkled baby-faced boys and girls shuffled towards smelly dressing rooms. I stood back admiring the parade, watching my husband carry a hockey bag bigger than our grandson.

Reflecting on my four brothers' hockey days, I thought of how the boys made their own way to the rink with a hodgepodge of hockey shirts, hand-me-down skates, and taped-together equipment in old army surplus kit bags. There were few parents at the rink in those days. And no grandparents that I remember. Parents sent children out to play—with one rule: "Be home by supper."

"Different world back then," my husband said. "Can't compare."

But being the worrier in the family, I pressed on. "Playing the game of hockey is expensive," I said. "And super-organized. Doesn't all that seriousness take some of the fun out of just being a kid?" He gave me his just-enjoy-the-game-look, but he was right. As I watched the kids, my concerns dissipated.

I had to admit that the passion for hockey was indeed alive. Probably still thriving in every one of Canada's small-town rinks.

Rinks where a cup of hot chocolate is an absolute necessity to warm aging bones. Where overdressed children in sweaty socks and knee-pads play their personal best.

Through my window of protective glass, I watched our team listen attentively to the coach's instructions for the big game—against the best in the league. Pucks flew over the boards and players hit the ice for drills. Like a ballet on ice, they moved as one, performing push-ups, squats and stretches. I looked at my grandson, Mitch, and in my mind's eye saw him as a toddler in our back yard, clutching a sawed-off hockey stick, falling down, getting up and falling down again.

"Come on, c'mon, let's get this game going," yelled an impatient fan. A hush fell over the crowd. They were remembering the previous Saturday's game when a young referee politely asked a woman to watch her language. When she refused, he blew his whistle, stopped the game, and pointed to the door.

Tagging along with both of our grandsons—the Baker boys—we've been in almost every frigid rink of our corner of Nova Scotia. And yes, every time my feet felt like sticks of steel, I sent vibes of envy to snowbird friends down south. But how could an equatorial breeze compare to the rush of frosty air on a minus twenty degrees Celsius Saturday morning?

Hockey to grandparents, however, means more than withstanding winter's weather. It's the suspense we experience as we search the ice for our grandchild's number. It's the pride we feel as we watch him looking through the maze of a mask, trying to find us in the stands. And when he weaves and bobs, then passes the puck, it's that momentary wave of warmth that brings us back, game after game. When it's over, it's the love that overwhelms us when he says, "Good game today Nanny and Poppy. We almost won."

The boys and girls—on both of our grandsons' hockey teams—have blossomed over the years. When they were five years old, in their Timbit hockey jerseys, my husband and I would take newspapers along to games. Markets rose and fell as wobbly legs skated from one end of the rink to the other. Today they skate faster and shoot harder. Taller and wiser, they're coordinated, focused—and able to play well. They practice shinny hockey in driveways, on frozen ponds, and on quiet streets.

Part of the joy of childhood is a sense of play. But in the game of life there are rules to follow. It's important for children to take responsibility for their actions. The young hockey players we watch all get pats on the head when they come off the ice. They also get to share in the agony of defeat as well as the joy of victory.

Behind the goalie window we waited with other bleary-eyed older folks for the game to start. Bundled up against the cold—in Frenchy's faux furs and fuzzy scarves—we cradled fleecy blankets and insulated cushions to keep our backsides off cold bleachers. The whistle blew and we headed for the stands. The puck dropped. The game began.

Our grandson, who usually played left wing, was playing centre. Crouched over, he was focused and ready for the face-off. As the game progressed, the opponents skated around our players like the *Cirque du Soleil*—executing the art of puck control. It was evident our team was having problems but they stick-handled and skated their hearts out. "Way to go," shouted the crowd.

"I think they're tired," said my husband. "Stay with it, you can do it," he cheered. Before we knew it, the score was tied. Overtime loomed. With seconds to go, Mitch came up on a breakaway, deked an opponent and passed the puck to a teammate who quickly took a wrist-shot to the top corner of the opposing net. The puck dropped right on the goal line. Everyone was holding their breath. There was a scramble in front of the net and when another player got his stick on the puck the noise was shattering. He scored! Players piled on top of the boys as if they'd won the Stanley Cup. Spectators screamed their support and in his excitement, the coach hollered, "I'm taking everyone out for pizza." Shouts of children bounced off the walls. We were all laughing—enjoying a game where everyone would go home a winner. A game filled with fun and laughter. Lots of laughter.

~Phyllis Jardine

# 85

# That Constant Face

*When all is said and done,*
*it's not the shots that won the championship that you remember,*
*but the friendships you made along the way.*
*~Author Unknown*

I t seemed as though every winter of my childhood was spent inside a bitterly cold ice hockey rink, toting around signs in support of my brother's team and erupting in cheers when they scored. Brian and I were born a year apart, and although I didn't play hockey until my teens, I learned every facet of the game and experienced the triumphs and defeats with him.

Year after year, beginning when I was eight years old, I stood on the frozen metal bleachers watching as he and his team moved the puck masterfully down the ice and bombarded the opposing goalie with shot after shot. I often stood in awe, admiring the way these young boys were able to gel so well, seemingly reading each other's minds as they made cross-ice passes from blue line to blue line.

As each season drew to a close, the players, parents and siblings would become one big family in a giant igloo, and it was always tough when the team lost a season-ending playoff game, but we knew there would always be next year.

Before I knew it, the "boys in blue" were suited up for the high school's team, the Buccaneers, playing in the most elite division in the state. Game after game, I stood in the stands, one of the few hundred students who comprised the "Pirate's Cove" cheering section. The

Cove wasn't just at home games. Having been a co-pilot during many trips to opponents' rinks, I often led a carpool of students to away games. There may have been more bodies than seats in the van from time to time, but we loved our team and did everything to be a part of the rowdiest cheering section in high school sports. I would often look in the rearview mirror and smile at the blue-and-white painted faces geared up for that evening's game.

When it came time for the state quarterfinal game, the Cove was ready. A week earlier, we watched our boys destroy their rivals in the final round of sectional playoffs, and after a two-hour trip to the arena, we were raring to go. A sharp blast from the blue line put our boys up 1-0, sending the fans into a frenzy. Looking up at the clock, I knew that both teams had an aggressive offensive attack, and that a one-goal lead certainly would not be enough. Two unanswered goals by the opponent ended the season for our team. It was almost too much to bear.

As I watched the boys slumped over the bench and sobbing, I realized that hockey was much more than a game. It had become a way of life, and for the families who had been together for the past decade this was the end of an era. This time, there wouldn't be a next year. The boys I had watched grow up and leave it all on the ice in that final game would be graduating in the spring. I felt empty inside, and I feared the next winter would be as cold and empty as the barren, snow-covered trees outside the rink.

A week after that final game, I got a text message from one of the boys on the team, thanking me for always being that constant face in the crowd. With that simple thank you, I knew that although winter would never be the same, I was truly blessed to have spent the past twelve years with such a wonderful hockey family. What a rewarding experience it was to watch some of my favorite players mature from the "boys in blue" into truly exceptional young men.

~Sarah McCrobie

# The Anti-Fan

*We can't all be heroes,*
*because somebody has to sit on the curb and applaud when they go by.*
*~Will Rogers*

"Stuff a sock down your kid's throat!" That was the cry I heard one night directed at my father as I once again stood in the cold Clarkson College hockey arena and cheered for the other team.

Clarkson College, now Clarkson University, is a small post-secondary institution in Potsdam, New York. Known for its engineering school, Clarkson is even better known for its hockey team.

For over sixty years, the Golden Knights have been a perennial top-ranked hockey power. As a Division I NCAA team, Clarkson often contends for top collegiate honors.

I grew up in Potsdam in the 1950s and 60s watching the Clarkson hockey team. My dad taught at the university and every year he would buy a pair of season tickets, which he shared with my brother and me.

When you grow up in a small town, hockey night at the local college is a big deal. Walker Arena barely had room for 2,000 people so it was packed to the rafters for every game.

The building was full of Clarkson students, residents from the town, and faculty members and their families. And everyone was cheering wildly for their local heroes. Everyone, that is, except me. I was cheering for the other team.

I'm not sure what started me on my quest for infamy. After all, what did I possibly have to gain by being the only person in Potsdam cheering against the hometown college team?

I think it started out as an assertion of my Canadian identity. We had moved to Potsdam from Canada in 1957 when I was seven years old and, as long as I lived there, I still considered myself Canadian.

So when teams from Canadian universities like McGill, Queen's and the University of Toronto came to play Clarkson, I felt that it was my duty to support the Canadian team. Never mind that back then ninety percent of the Clarkson players were Canadian; in my mind they were the American team and I was therefore duty-bound to cheer against them.

But that initial inspiration soon gave way to a different motivation. For a kid, it just became fun to be different, to be the crazy kid who stood and cheered when the other team scored and everyone else fell silent. So I started supporting all the visiting teams, even the other American ones.

I liked taking on the role of the outcast, the miscreant, the anti-fan. It granted me a unique status, albeit one with certain risks.

"There's Martin's kid again," one adult fan might say. "Too bad he can't get him to shut up."

But my dad never intervened. He may have been slightly embarrassed by his son's antics. But he never told me to stop and sometimes I'm sure I saw a smile cross his lips when I jumped out of my seat cheering a team like Princeton or Boston College or Michigan when they scored.

But this wasn't just an impish gesture on my part. I think it also appealed to my juvenile sense of fairness. It just didn't seem right that the visiting team would be drowned in cheers and noise when scored upon, but be greeted with nothing but silence when they managed to score one themselves.

So I did my best to be a one-kid cheering section for the other team to let them know that they had fans, or at least one fan, too. I celebrated their victories and I suffered their losses as if they were my own.

As I grew into my teenage years, I gave up my role as the visiting team's cheerleader. After all, the last thing a teenager wants is to be singled out. So although I still secretly pulled for the other team, I kept those feelings to myself.

It's been forty years since I've been to a Clarkson game. I understand that they now have a big modern arena that seats twice as many fans. I'd love to see them play in their new home. But even today I can't guarantee that I'd be cheering for them.

~David Martin

# 87

# Skate-Walker

*It may be that all games are silly.*
*But then, so are humans.*
*~Robert Lynd*

**M**y coworker and I, both make-up artists, stood at the Lancôme cosmetic counter cleaning our make-up brushes. We worked at the Dillard's store in Brandon, Florida. I pointed the end of my powder brush toward a group of people walking by wearing Tampa Bay Lightning jerseys.

"Is there a hockey game tonight?" I asked.

"No," she said. "But there's a promotion in the men's department, and one of the Lightning players is making a special appearance."

"Oh." I scooped up my clean brushes and placed them in a glass cup. Special appearance? I shrugged. I didn't read *People* magazine and I wasn't a celebrity worshipper. Although I respected many professional athletes, the people I found most interesting, famous or not, were driven, lived passionately, and had that extra something special.

A cute guy about thirty walked by our counter. Wow, I thought. Great posture. Actually, he didn't walk. He glided. A former dance teacher, I notice the way people carry themselves, and this guy moved like no one I'd ever seen. He had dark hair and wore a fitted, navy pullover tucked into khaki pants. I watched him "skate" down the cosmetic department's tile floor.

Of course! I thought, proud of my detective skills. He's a hockey fan who plays hockey. The guy, Skate-Walker, appeared driven, passionate, and definitely had that something special.

I turned to the other artist. "Be right back."

Clusters of jersey-clad folks assembled between men's sweaters, suits, and stacks of denim. I scanned the crowd of about fifty for Skate-Walker. Thank God I was having a good hair day and wore a skirt and boots instead of a pair of baggy trousers or my Mr. Rogers'-like cardigan. Where are you Skate-Walker?

The hockey fans looked to the area about ten feet to my right. I glanced over. What? Skate-Walker? The cute guy with great posture stood on a small, three-foot high wooden platform signing hockey sticks.

He caught me staring.

"Hi," I said.

"Hi," he said, Sharpie in one hand, hockey stick in the other.

Words I couldn't stop blurted out of my mouth. "Don't worry," I said. "If you fall off the platform, I'll catch you."

Catch you? No, you did not say that, Cynthia! Dork.

Skate-Walker glanced down at the floor, back at me, and smiled, nodding. "Thanks. Good to know."

The store manager standing on the other side of the platform handed him another hockey stick, and I went back to my counter.

The next day I begged the men's manager for one of the two remaining sticks. Score! I sat it upright on the passenger seat of my car as I drove home that day. I treasured my singular piece of sport equipment, not because it was autographed by a pro-hockey player, but because the man who signed it moved like no one I'd ever seen.

The Tampa Bay Lightning won the Stanley Cup the following year, 2004, and I gave my hockey stick to a friend diagnosed with cancer. Skate-Walker had brightened my day the year before, and now he lifted the spirit of my friend.

I wasn't born into a family who went to ball games, wore team jerseys, or drank out of mugs stamped with sports insignia. My mother's background was classical music, musical theatre and dance. My father encouraged me and my brothers to appreciate the jazz music of

Miles Davis and Thelonious Monk. But meeting Skate-Walker stimulated desire for new venues of entertainment.

I became a hockey fan. Although I didn't like wearing hockey jerseys, I bought season tickets and a Swarovski crystal lightning bolt necklace.

Maybe the Tampa Bay Lightning players weren't ballet dancers, but with their sticks as their partners, they glided with stealth and seamless flow. Seating in the stadium wasn't as comfortable as the red cushioned seats at the symphony, but I found the skates slicing the ice, the sticks smacking the puck, and the occasional bullhorn both symphonic and exhilarating.

If I needed to cough during a performance of The Florida Orchestra, I'd bury my face into a balled-up sweater. But at a hockey game, I could cough my head off and no one would scowl. I'd never shout, "Great job, van Gogh!" in an art museum. But I've yelled, "Go Lightning!" at the top of my lungs more times than I can count. I'd be kicked out of the public library if I laughed, talked too loudly, or ate nachos. But at The St. Petersburg Times Forum, primal behavior flourished. The pace, fury, and fun of hockey games complemented my artistic side perfectly.

My love affair with hockey began in 2003, but I remember the day the guy with great posture skated by my cosmetic counter, the smile he shot me when I said I'd catch him, and the look on my friend's face when I gave him the autographed hockey stick. I do a great imitation of Skate-Walker gliding across the floor. But there's only one Martin St. Louis. And he moves like no one I've ever seen.

~Cynthia Mallick

# 88

# Priceless Hockey Heirlooms

*If becoming a grandmother was only a matter of choice,*
*I should advise every one of you straight away to become one.*
*There is no fun for old people like it!*
*~Hannah Whithall Smith*

**M**y little grandson was only three years old when he decided he wanted to play hockey. So he began taking skating lessons, desperately struggling to find balance on his tiny skates. But after two years, the hopelessness of learning how to skate was getting the better of him and he became terribly discouraged. "Grammy, I want to play hockey. I don't want to learn how to skate," he told me on more than one occasion. "I'm always falling down and it hurts." Truthfully, after all the lessons, by the end of the second year the poor little fellow could still barely skate.

His parents repeatedly tried to explain he needed to be able to skate in order to play hockey, but little Max insisted he could play the game even if he couldn't skate. So when he turned five, the registration age for hockey, his parents signed him up anyway. Max eagerly anticipated getting on the ice in full gear with his very own hockey stick.

I think Grampy and I were even more excited than he was. We'd been there for every single skating lesson, and were determined not to miss a hockey practice or a game. We only hoped he wouldn't be discouraged when he got on the ice.

At the very first hockey practice, much to our astonishment and Max's complete surprise, the moment he set foot on the ice he skated quite a distance before falling. Watching from the stands, our hearts were in our throats until we saw the beautiful smile that lit up his rosy cheeks when he got right up and tried again! And he never looked back! The hockey gear and padding had taken the "ouch" out of falling on the unforgiving ice and he was no longer afraid of hurting himself. Additionally, he instantly caught on to using his hockey stick for balance and it worked like a charm. That hockey gear had given him the confidence he needed to believe he could do it.

The initiation year (age five to six), as hockey families are well aware, means the earliest possible ice times. This makes perfect sense to me now, since small children tend to rise earlier than adolescents. But whoever makes up the schedules for ice times certainly doesn't consider grandparents when they do. It seems they have absolutely no idea how difficult it is to get old bones moving at the crack of dawn in the freezing cold.

Nevertheless, brutally early Saturday and Sunday mornings, hot coffee in hand, cushions for the icy cold spectator benches and a warm fleece blanket to throw over our knees, we were determined to be there every step of the way through our little grandson's hockey adventure. No ferociously frigid temperatures, bitterly cold arctic blasts, or blinding snow and ice storms were going to keep us away.

And Max always looked for us in the bleachers—a proud wave from his tiny, thickly padded gloved hand when he spotted us right there next to Mommy. His quick smile assured us he appreciated having his fans there. He also knew beyond a shadow of a doubt he was our favourite hockey player!

Max's first hockey team was called The Pirates. With a fierce name like that, one would envision an unruly cluster of miniature hockey players in knee-length jerseys creating havoc on the ice. But in reality, these girls and boys were learning how to have fun with a sport that's been around for more than a century. They were learning the "real" game without the brutality and utterly senseless skirmishing that quite often happens in the national league. They were also gaining self-confidence while learning the concept of being team players, respecting each other, accepting discipline, and understanding that in life there are rules to be followed and consequences for crossing lines.

Our son, Max's father, did coaches' training so he could be right there on the ice with his little boy. And he positively glowed as he watched his son's rapid progress. Over the course of that first year, little Max blossomed into a confident little man and a great skater, whose love for the game of hockey turned into a passion.

My grandson's initiation into hockey was a déjà vu for me, because it seemed like only yesterday I was at the arena watching my son learn how to play the game. Although as I recall, in my youth the bone-chilling cold didn't seem to bother me. But I will endure whatever it takes without one complaint for as long as this journey continues. And whether or not my little Max ever becomes one of the greats, to me he's already the greatest hockey player there ever was!

This worthwhile expedition into freezing cold arenas at the crack of dawn has generated the warmest family memories this hockey grandmother has ever known! And my cache of priceless hockey heirlooms continues to grow.

Who knows, I may be watching the next Gretzky. In any case, I'm privy to a front row seat, free of charge, to some of the best hockey there is. It's good clean hockey played with lots of heart, an abundance of determination, and oodles of fun.

~Annabel Sheila

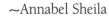

# 89

# Numbers Game

*While we try to teach our children all about life,*
*our children teach us what life is all about.*
*~Angela Schwindt*

When I was two months into my pregnancy, the very first thing I bought for the baby was a little Pittsburgh Penguins outfit. I presented it to my husband as one of his birthday gifts, and he was so happy he could have burst. Jason loved hockey. He was devoted to his Penguins. He played roller and ice hockey. It was safe to say that regardless of our future child's gender, the child was going to be raised knowing about pucks, sticks, and Mario Lemieux.

Our baby, Nicholas, wore that Pittsburgh Penguins outfit and lots of other hockey-themed attire as he grew older. His eyes were bright and took in everything, but he was slow to walk, slow to speak words. At age two, he couldn't even form sentences or interact with other children. Then the diagnosis came: autism.

To say this was devastating would be an understatement. But Nicholas was still the same boy to us, a very happy-go-lucky kid most of the time. We simply had to learn how to connect with him—and how to connect him with an outside world that could be so overwhelming.

A change in jobs brought us across the country to Phoenix, Arizona. Jason's new work schedule freed up his evenings to watch hockey on television at home. Nicholas began to watch too. He didn't seem to follow the actual game play, but there were several other things he did love. Nicholas enjoyed game shows like *The Price Is Right*, full of exuberant people and bright lights. The crowds during hockey exuded that same enthusiasm, and he would cheer and dance until sweat soaked his hair.

Then there were the numbers.

Nicholas adored counting and math. During his game shows, he was more excited about the price of a car than the car as a prize. When a goal was scored in a hockey game on TV, it was clear he didn't understand what that meant to the team. But it did mean an increase in numbers, and that was a miraculous thing. He would squeal and dance with joy regardless which team scored—much to his dad's chagrin.

All of this pleased Jason, but he still had one big wish to fulfill: for us to attend a National Hockey League game together as a family.

The Phoenix Coyotes played just thirty minutes from our house, and we supported the hometown team (unless they were against the Penguins, of course). There were a lot of big "ifs" involved with taking Nicholas to a game. First of all, a crowd like that is a challenge to any child, not just one with autism. Then there was the noise. Nicholas was hypersensitive to sound and often covered his ears in public. Loud noises made him cry and scream. He loved flashiness and excitement on television, but reality was something else entirely. What if he had a total meltdown? I worried that we were going to spend a lot of money on tickets and then leave early, mortified by our son's misunderstood behavior.

There was only one way to know—we had to give it a try.

Nicholas was three years old and starting to speak in sentences. I kept telling him about the game and what to expect. "There will be lots of noise. You can wear your hood to cover your ears. It's going to be a real live hockey game and lots of fun."

"Lots of fun," he echoed.

As we stood in line to enter the arena, Nicholas was wide-eyed as he looked around. So far, so good. We went inside. Nicholas gasped. "Stairs!" he said.

These weren't just stairs—they were escalators, one of his favorite things in the whole world. He squealed with joy as we went up to the next level.

The crowds were thick on the 200 level. I was getting more anxious, wondering when my child would explode in a tantrum.

Jason pointed to the right. "Our seats are this way." He walked forward.

"No!" Nicholas yelled, anchoring himself against a pole.

I looked at Jason. Oh, no. The tantrum was starting.

"Numbers go up!" Nicholas said, pointing the other way.

That was it. We were going backward in the numbers, not forward. Jason nodded and smiled. "We can walk around the long way."

Nicholas chanted all of the seating area numbers as we passed. He gasped in awe when they started over at 200 and had no problem counting up to our seating section. We went down the stairs and found our seats.

The game was about to start. I tugged Nicholas's hood up. He already sat with his hands over his ears, but his expression was of curiosity, not alarm. How would he handle it when the game started, with all the horns blaring and people chanting? The lights dimmed and the announcer began to speak.

I watched Nicholas more than the ice. He stared slack-jawed at the light effects and then focused on the Jumbotron. "Zero, zero, S-O-G zero, two, zero, zero, zero," he said.

"That's right," I said. "The first period is twenty minutes and no one has scored a goal yet." I coaxed him to stand for "The Star-Spangled Banner" when it played. "There are fifty stars on our flag," I whispered.

"Fifty," he whispered back, bouncing in place.

We sat again after the anthem. The game started. Nicholas continued to watch the Jumbotron, breathily counting down the seconds on the clock. I looked across Nicholas to Jason. My husband was intent on the game, leaning forward against his knees.

"See, little guy? The Coyotes have the puck," Jason said. "Number 19 is their captain, Shane Doan."

"Nineteen! Doan!" Nicholas squealed. He almost bounced out of his seat.

Music began, echoing through our seats. "Let's go Cah-yotes! Boom, boom, boom-boom-boom. Let's go Cah-yotes!" Everyone around us began to cheer. I joined in and looked at Nicholas. His eyes searched mine and I recognized a flare of understanding.

"Let's go Cah-yotes!" he yelled, waving his little fists in the air.

This was like the game shows and hockey games he watched at home. He got it. Nicholas didn't need to grasp the mechanics of hockey to have a good time. It was about fun, pure and simple, and he soaked in the crowd's energy like a sponge.

"Go, Doan!" yelled someone behind us.

Nicholas half-turned, then looked back to the ice. His little eyebrows drew together in concentration. "Go, 19!" he yelled. His voice was so small against the crowd, but Jason and I heard him loud and clear.

~Beth Cato

# The Look

*Sometimes I fall asleep at night with my clothes on.*
*I'm going to have all my clothes made out of blankets.*
~Mitch Hedberg

My husband is giving me "the look" again. It's a look I completely understand. It's a look that says, "Remember the Rangers game?"

It was 1994 and I had taken a full-time job in Manhattan at a private investment firm. My job was to do the "clearing." Doing the clearing is what Wall Street refers to as reviewing every trade that has settled from the previous day and making sure it settles with an accurate commission, price, and the precise number of shares. In other words, it's like balancing a very big, fat checkbook.

It was not the kind of work that made me happy. I'm an artistic person. I like writing songs, playing music, reading poetry. Numbers are just not my thing. But I landed the job and as they say, "a job is a job," and my husband and I had just moved into our first new home. A home with a mortgage that needed to be paid!

So, I was thankful for the job. But the hours for this position were very long and on top of that, I had a long commute. I started work at 7:30 a.m., as the stock market opens at 9:00, and all portfolio managers (like my boss) need to know their stock positions in order to begin their day of trading.

On this particular day, while drinking my third cup of coffee, the trader asked if I'd like to go to the Rangers game that night. It was

Game 7 of the Conference Finals at Madison Square Garden between the New Jersey Devils and the New York Rangers.

In my caffeine-induced state, I said yes, knowing my husband is a big Rangers fan and that we had no plans for the evening. I am not a Rangers fan, nor a hockey fan. I like my New York Mets baseball but other than that I have no real interest in sports.

My husband, on the other hand, was thrilled to be going. The tickets were not only free, but the seats were right up front. The extra bonus was that since we'd be out late, my boss had provided us with his car service home.

It was an exhilarating night. The crowd was electric with loud jeers of "1940" filling the arena. "That's the last time the Rangers won the Stanley Cup," my husband explained through the noise. The New Jersey fans were taunting the Rangers fans with that fact.

The clock was ticking and the place was alive, but I was fading. And I mean fading fast. My caffeine high had hit an all-time low and I had a wave of exhaustion like I'd never known before.

"Mark," I said to my husband. "I'm so tired all of a sudden."

"Okay," he replied, as he watched the action on the ice.

"These hours are killing me. I need to go home now."

He stared at me and asked if I were kidding. With tears in my eyes, I said, "No. I need to go to sleep. Please let's go."

Suddenly, the people were shouting for joy and jumping out of their seats. The game had been sent into overtime by New Jersey, with only seconds left on the clock.

"Can't you last just a little longer?" My husband begged. But, I couldn't. I had been suffering with sleep deprivation from the new job and I could barely keep my head up.

With the thrill of elation in the air, we called the car service, which conveniently met us outside and began our trip home. I rested my head on the backseat while the driver turned up the radio for my husband, who leaned forward on the edge of his seat to listen to the game.

It was the moment of truth. The final goal was about to be made.

Unfortunately, at that exact moment, we entered the Midtown Tunnel and lost all radio reception.

Shell-shocked, my husband sat back as I slipped in and out of consciousness. As we exited the Midtown Tunnel and the radio reception was restored, we listened motionless as the sportscaster announced that the Rangers had won the big game. The Rangers, my husband's favorite team, would be going to the Stanley Cup Finals!

I fell asleep as he sat silently.

Now years later, at a party, I am reminded of that night as one of our friends is talking about hockey and asks my husband innocently, "Do you remember that game in 1994 when the Rangers made it to the Stanley Cup Finals?"

That's when I get "the look."

~Mary C. M. Phillips

# Hooked on
# Hockey

## Slice of Ice

# 91

# The Ritual

*It's not necessarily the amount of time you spend*
*at practice that counts;*
*it's what you put into the practice.*
*~Eric Lindros*

I t was 4:30 on a frosty January morning. The crisp snow crunched under my boots as I walked down the middle of Lakeshore Road. A police car pulled up beside me, rolling down the window.

"Walking down the middle again, eh John?"

"Well, Officer Munroe, the sidewalks aren't plowed yet and the road is."

He smiled. "Can't afford to let one of our best defensemen get run over. What's the coach going to work on this morning?"

"Penalty killing I think. We play Streetsville tomorrow night and it will be a rough one. First place is at stake. You coming?"

I was on my way to hockey practice. At age fourteen, few teens would relish rising at 4:00 a.m. on Saturday and walking three miles to attend a 5:30 a.m. two-hour long workout; but I did. The year before I had earned a spot on a real hockey team. We had uniforms and coaches, played scheduled games and had organized practices. Whether a game or practice, I was always eager to get on the ice. And this walk was part of my practice ritual.

"Wouldn't miss it! Want a ride the rest of the way?"

"No, can't change my routine now. But thanks anyway."

He gave me a flash of his bar lights as he drove off.

Pat the rink rat was opening the main doors as I arrived.

"Right on time," was his greeting.

"You too," I replied and headed downstairs.

Dressing room number one — always. Black rubber matting covered the floor. Swabbed after the previous night's games, the odour of disinfectant hung heavy in the air. Skate-scarred wooden benches lined the green cinderblock walls. No lockers, just rows of hooks above and a single shower stall, dripping.

I hung my gear and began to dress. Always left side first, a superstitious part of my ritual. Long johns, sweat socks, cup and garter belt, then pants, shin pads, game socks and skates. Shoulder pads followed by elbow pads and finally my blue practice jersey. Good to go. Pause to reflect. Teammates beginning to arrive.

"Hey Ken, hi Bud."

"Always first, eh John?"

"Always. See you out there."

I pulled on my gloves, palms still stiff with dried sweat. They would soon soften. Stick in hand, I clomped my way up the ramp to the rink.

The freshly flooded ice surface gleamed, reflecting the powerful game lights above, accenting the brilliant red and blue lines that governed play. The goal nets were set in place, defined by their crimson posts, challenging me to roof one.

I dropped my helmet on the bench and stepped from the gate. A few tentative strokes to test my edges and shake down my gear, followed by longer strides to loosen; then as I circled the net I turned it on and let it go. Head down, seeking top speed, my blades sliced the frozen surface, legs driving, frigid air pouring deep into my chest as I powered into the turns. One lap, now two, pushing for more speed; lungs and legs burning; enough! I coasted, bent at the waist, stick across my knees, sucking wind, sweat breaking out. I was ready.

Others trickled onto the rink to join me and begin their warm-up routines. The goaltenders arrived, followed by Coach Danby and his assistants.

"John get your helmet on," yelled one of them. I responded with a wave of my stick and complied. My father was one of those coaches. He had driven to the rink. He wasn't part of my ritual... yet.

The sharp blast of a whistle split the air and practice began in earnest.

Skating drills first. Full circuits at speed, stops and starts, line to line, skate the circles clockwise, counterclockwise and backwards. At last, pucks on the ice and shooting drills began—forehand, backhand, from the point. Pick the corners, or at least hit the goalie.

Time-out for instruction. Review the power play and explain the new penalty kill and then practice it at speed. Five on four, five on three, then two on ones. Time flew, but we all watched the clock hoping—and with just fifteen minutes left Coach Danby called for a scrimmage—our reward for a tight practice.

Game on as the red sweaters battled the blues for bragging rights. Body checking was forbidden but tough play was permitted, and we competed as hard against our teammates as we would against tomorrow's opponent. We scored! They scored. We scored again! Time ran out and we won the honour of skating the last circuit, while they retreated to the dressing room.

I was always last off the ice. Helmet in hand, a vapourous cloud rising from my head, I stood slip slipping my skates, surveying the now scarred and snow-covered ice, visualizing it cleaned and ready for tomorrow's game with Streetsville. I was ready for them.

Back in the dressing room, skates off, numb toes tingling as feeling returned, I sat, still fully dressed, enjoying the delicious ennui of exhaustion. I had left it all on the ice, but my ritual was not yet complete. My father appeared in the dressing room doorway.

"Riding with me? Mum will have breakfast waiting."

"You bet!"

"Then hurry up!"

Our car was warm and waiting. I stowed my gear in the trunk and sank into the shotgun seat.

Dad reached across and tousled my still damp hair.

"Good practice son!"

"Aren't they all?" I replied.

~John Forrest

# 92

# You're Gonna Love This Game

*Every time a puck gets past me and I look back into the net, I say,*
*"uh-oh."*
~Bernie Parent

It began as a bewildering, tersely worded text message: "In a jam—wanna play net tonight?" I stared at the message for several minutes, contemplating an appropriate response. A decade earlier, I had lived for hockey, playing goalie in several leagues. Didn't matter if it was roller or ice—any surface, any game, anywhere—I would never turn down a chance to play.

As it's been for generations, my love for hockey was passed down from my dad. At a young age, I remember the first time I asked to stay up late and watch a game on TV with him. His face was a mixture of surprise and joy. He looked at me and simply said, "Sure Son, you're gonna love this game."

Over the years, I eventually learned to play the game. It's funny thinking back to those days. I was pretty good, and unfortunately, I knew it. There was a cockiness that I can't help but laugh about now. No matter how the game unfolded, or how good or bad my form, there was an unwavering confidence within me that the next puck would be stopped. Sometimes I wonder where that youthful, unabashed, reckless self-assurance crawled off to die. Delusional or not, some days it would be nice to have that total unjustified confidence now that I am an adult.

No catastrophic injury or event ended my hockey days; rather, it was a series of life changers that slowly whittled it away. Marriage, career, house, children. Life evolved, and I found a peace and happiness that I never anticipated. Some days I would visualize a return to the sport that had given me so much joy, but those moments became fewer and farther between. And for nearly nine years, the hockey gear lay in a garage cabinet, gathering dust.

I continued to stare at the text message, pondering my options. I briefly wondered how far down the depth chart they had gone before asking a goalie who hadn't laced up his skates in nearly a decade. As I stared at the screen, another text arrived, then another. Despite the butterflies already churning in my gut, and the fingers that trembled as I typed the message, I managed an impassive reply: "Sure. Sounds fun."

Time crawled for the rest of the afternoon. I finished my day's work and returned home to gather my gear and head to the rink. I arrived long before the start of the game, and picked a remote corner of the locker room to don my gear. Despite the years, there was a comforting familiarity as I laced up the skates and slid on the pads. Confidence began to creep into my psyche. After all these years, what if I played really well? What if I managed a shutout?

Nice dream, but there would be no shutout that night. Fact is, goals were flying in left and right. Sure, there was some legitimate talent out there, including a few players who had played at the collegiate or semi-pro level, but they weren't the only ones scoring. The accountants, teachers, and male nurses were finding the net too. A seven-year-old who was watching his daddy turn me into Swiss cheese asked during an intermission, "How come they are scoring so many goals on you?" I didn't know how to respond, so I sprayed him with my water bottle.

It was probably my worst-ever performance in goal, but a peculiar thing happened—I had the time of my life. I hadn't laughed so much in years. Many of the players were the same group I grew up playing against in my younger days. They were all a decade older and a decade balder, but it was still "the guys." There was the same locker room trash talk as ten years ago, like a never-ending tale that keeps getting told week by week, piece by piece. (How could they possibly remember my mother's name after all these years?)

The experience was strange, but awesome—like reuniting with a sweaty and slightly dysfunctional family again. The perils of expectations were evident—several of the stars from ten years ago were unemployed, or worse, uninspired. The screw-up who we thought wouldn't amount to anything obtained a master's degree and now works with at-risk children. A night of lessons—some painful, most humbling, all necessary.

The next morning, I woke up physically a mess. Pulled hamstrings, swollen knees, aching back, and for some reason my right arm couldn't be lifted above my shoulder. But there was also a goofy smile that I couldn't seem to get off my face.

As I sat down to breakfast with my family, the sound of an incoming text message interrupted the morning chatter. "Nice job last night. Want me to put you on a team for next season?" This time, there were no butterflies and no conflicts. I immediately typed a simple, one-word reply: "Absolutely." I smiled and sat in silence for a few moments.

The silence was broken by my six-year-old son. "Dad, how was hockey last night?" he asked. I replied, "It was fun, and looks like I'll be playing a lot more." He thought for a moment, and then timidly asked, "Do you think I could come out and watch you play sometime?"

My face was a mixture of surprise and joy. I looked at him and simply said, "Sure Son, you're gonna love this game."

~Rob L. Berry

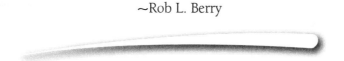

# 93

# The People
# You Meet

*I like to follow my favorite team and talk sports with my band or fans.*
*You won't believe how many musicians are sports fans.*
*We have so much time on tour that we need these outlets for relaxation.*
*~Garth Brooks*

I thought it was a pretty simple question, "What brings you to Los Angeles?" Yet the man beside me at the bar, in the faded blue Michigan T-shirt looked at me as if he were meeting an alien. Normally that might bother me, but tonight I had more important things on my mind. I was watching my beloved Los Angeles Kings—and we were losing. Badly.

My eyes refocused on the television screen above the bar; play had just resumed.

I was in love with hockey. Nothing, not even professional beach volleyball, could compare to the thrill of watching grown men skate around a rink. I was absolutely hooked from my first game and could never get enough of it. Thank goodness Los Angeles had a professional team. Even if they rarely won, it provided me the chance to watch my favorite sport.

Bam! The guy smashed into the boards and I flinched. I wanted to get back to my seat to be closer to the action. Watching hockey on a TV was just not as thrilling as seeing it live. I made a mental note to thank my friend Felice again for getting us free tickets. A model and actress, she was a wonderful friend who had moved from New York to pursue a film career. Dating the current goalie meant that our seats were close to the ice, in the "wives and girlfriends" section.

After the first period was over, we had entered the VIP lounge of what was then fondly called the Fabulous Forum (a few years later, as corporate sponsorships took hold, it would sport the name Great Western Forum). In fact, this was the 1980s, now nicknamed "PG" hockey. No, not the movie rating. Pre-Gretzky.

"Will that be all?" The efficient bartender handed me my drinks and was looking for payment.

"Drat!" I muttered. Not at the price, but because we just lost the puck. I had the sinking feeling that this season might not improve.

I caught the man next to me smiling in recognition. Earlier, he had explained that he was from the Midwest. We joked that in this town of transplants, many seeking fame and fortune, only people originally from cold climates truly appreciated this great sport. I had mentioned that I would not be surprised if most of my friends thought the Kings were the latest reggae band, but my pals would find that equally funny because I don't know anything about music. He looked amused. The conversation quickly turned to include recent player trades, how certain lines were ineffective, and strategies we'd use to turn the club into a winning franchise, if we were in charge.

How wonderful it had been to talk to someone in this city who knew his hockey and shared my passion.

Play stopped and he answered my question, "What brings you to Los Angeles?"

"My work," he replied.

"Aren't we both lucky that we have jobs that allow us to live in this incredible city? I love it—the beach, the sun, the people. How could anyone not relish living here? And we get to watch hockey to boot? Truly amazing. Enjoy the game. I hope we turn it around."

He smiled at my bubbly enthusiasm, nodded his agreement and I hurried back to the table where Felice was waiting for me.

As we left the VIP bar, she asked, "So what did Glenn have to say?"

"We just chatted about the Kings. He really knows his hockey, but he told me he's from the Midwest, so that makes sense. He's bummed about this losing season, too and..." I stopped short.

"How did you know his name?" I asked my friend.

Felice looked at me in disbelief. Her often-photographed hair flying in all directions, she started shaking with laughter.

"Jennifer, that is classic. You were talking to Glenn Frey."

"Who's that?"

"Used to be with the Eagles—you know, 'Hotel California.' He sings 'The Heat Is On' and 'You Belong to the City.' Perhaps you've heard of him?" she asked incredulously.

Oh, that Glenn Frey! No wonder she knew his name. No wonder he was highly surprised when I asked him what brought him to Los Angeles.

"Well, he sure knows his hockey."

~JC Sullivan

**94**

# I Married a Zamboni

*There are three things in life that people like to stare at:*
*a flowing stream, a crackling fire and a Zamboni clearing the ice.*
~Charlie Brown, Peanuts

I was thirty-seven in 2009 when I got married. By that time I had an established career as a lawyer with the U.S. Government. Before my wedding, a number of people asked me if I planned to change my last name—something that has gone out of vogue for some women in established careers. My standard response was: "Wouldn't you?"

If you are a hockey fan, as I am, the answer is undoubtedly "You bet!" Who, in their right mind, would give up the opportunity to take the coolest last name ever—Zamboni? Not me. As a kid, I can remember eagerly anticipating the time between periods when that magnificent machine would come out and do what nothing else in the world can do... clean the ice methodically and perfectly. I remember my mom telling me the name of the machine was a Zamboni. Of course at the time I thought that was what the machine was named. I hadn't realized that Zamboni was a name brand, like Xerox or Kleenex. I thought it was the perfect name for the perfect machine. I love everything about the Zamboni machine: its boxy shape; the pattern it creates when cleaning the ice; and the beautiful shiny ice that it leaves in its path.

Imagine my delight when years later I met this wonderful guy named Zamboni. I loved the last name so much that I didn't use his first name at all. I just called him Zamboni. It was only after our relationship got more serious that I made an effort to use his first name, because I thought my family would think it weird to call my boyfriend by his last name. But that wasn't the case at all. When I first introduced him to my mother, she said: "So you are the Iceman." They hit it off immediately.

After changing my name to Zamboni, I couldn't wait for people's reaction when I introduced myself. "Did she really say her name was Zamboni?" But the reactions have not all been what I expected. Sure, if I'm in a hockey town like Pittsburgh or Boston there are signs of recognition. The most commonly asked question I get is: "Are you related to the family that invented the Zamboni?" My answer is "Yes." I have no idea if we are or not, but who am I hurting by claiming some relation to the inventor, Frank J. Zamboni? And, in a weird coincidence, my dad's first name is Frank and his middle initial is J.

I am incredibly disappointed when someone asks, "How do you spell that?" WHAT?? Who does not know how to spell Zamboni? Obviously not a hockey fan, I imagine. My husband had warned me that it happens more often than you would think. Something about the name starting with the letter "Z" throws people for a loop.

The second most commonly asked question I get is whether I have driven a Zamboni. My answer to this question depends on the audience, because there are two truthful answers: no and yes. No, I have never driven an actual Zamboni machine. But yes, whenever I am in the driver's seat with my husband as a passenger, I am indeed driving a Zamboni. One of these days I will submit a résumé to be a Zamboni driver and hope to at least get an interview for the job.

~Kate Zamboni

95

# The Frozen Tundra of South Carolina

*Coming together is a beginning. Keeping together is progress.*
*Working together is success.*
*~Henry Ford*

A decade or so before the term "epic fail" became part of the American popular vernacular, people living in and around Florence, South Carolina were using some variation of the phrase in response to the announcement that a minor league hockey team—to be called the Pee Dee Pride—was coming to town.

While Florence isn't technically located in the Deep South, it is close enough. Just to put things into perspective, I'm a native of North Carolina, which most Americans would consider a Southern state, but around here they consider me a Yankee.

This is an area devoted to fishing and farming, barbecue and Bud Light and banana pudding. It is home to a couple of small liberal arts colleges and two regional medical centers. Neighboring Darlington County is literally the birthplace of NASCAR racing, and the entire Pee Dee—so called due to its proximity to a river of the same name—is a place where Southeastern Conference (SEC) football will forever reign supreme.

Even in January, seventy-five-degree days are not a bit out of the ordinary, and many folks take pride in wearing shorts year-round. Skiing is done on water, and skating is done on hardwood. The use of ice is essential for boat coolers and glasses of sweet tea, but for sporting events, not so much.

Florence is many things, but it could never be described as a hockey town. So while the addition of the Pee Dee Pride's hockey games to the Florence Civic Center's schedule of events may have generated mild curiosity in some quarters, mostly it was met with a kind of bemused disinterest.

I couldn't believe it. I had moved to Florence from Chicago only a couple of years earlier, and while the Windy City might be considered a viable hockey market by virtue of the fact that it has an actual NHL team, the Blackhawks weren't exactly packing their big-city arena. How could we hope to do any better? The Civic Center, after all, was a venue about which I had often remarked that if Abraham Lincoln rose from the dead and embarked on a motivational speaking tour, it wouldn't sell out in Florence. I was only half joking.

At first, it seemed my naysaying was right on target; the early going was rough. The Pride, from the head coach down to the administrative team, truly had their work cut out for them in Florence. They not only had to educate the locals about the game, but they had to give us some reason to care about it.

I attended one of the first exhibition games, just to scope things out. In social settings, I had pretended to care about the Blackhawks during my time in Chicago, but never having watched hockey as a kid, I felt no real connection with the game.

I considered hockey too fast and difficult to follow, and kind of barbaric, as occasionally a couple of players would drop their sticks, rip off their gloves, and go about the business of trying to beat one another to death for no apparent reason. At least half the crowd thought a Zamboni was some kind of fancy Italian pastry. Plus, it was cold in there. Not good for shorts.

The curiosity factor won out, however, and on opening night I loaded up the kids and a couple of complaining friends and headed out to watch the game. To my complete surprise, the Civic Center was nearly full. The crowd was welcomed, the players were introduced, the puck was dropped, and I started checking my watch.

Then, the strangest thing happened. In one of those serendipitous moments when the unlikeliest of unions occur, the people of the Pee Dee and their Pride proved to be a case of love at first sight. The place was rocking.

Perhaps it was the sheer proximity of thousands of people coming together in the same place at the same time, with no real idea of what they were going to see. Perhaps it was that anticipatory concert-hall feel of being in an enclosed space, waiting for something momentous to happen. Maybe the University of South Carolina Gamecocks had no home game that weekend and people had nothing else to do. I guess I'll never really know.

But I do know this; it worked, and it was spectacular. The field of competition was frozen solid and the boundaries were clearly delineated, but demographic, racial and socio-economic lines simply melted away.

I looked over to see my ten-year-old dancing hand in hand with an older lady whose other hand was clutching a cane. Both of them were bellowing out shaky but enthusiastic harmony to Queen's "We Will Rock You." CEOs of mega-dollar corporations were high-fiving members of their custodial staff. Parents and their teenagers were actually hugging one another in public, and didn't even seem embarrassed by it.

None of us really knew what we were cheering or booing for, but it didn't matter, because we were doing it together.

The Pride became the hottest ticket in town. The arena was always full. Head coach Jack Capuano, who went on to become head coach for the NHL's New York Islanders, could have run for mayor and been elected in a landslide. The players achieved rock star status, given standing ovations in restaurants simply for coming in and ordering a burger.

Pride jerseys were the number one most requested gift from Santa for two or three Christmases in a row. In a scene reminiscent of the Great Cabbage Patch Wars of the 1980s, I got lucky and snagged one for my son. The Civic Center opened its ice to the public, and youth hockey leagues were organized. Some of those young players, who otherwise would never have picked up a puck, went on to earn athletic scholarships, and hockey paid for their education. The entire area got an economic boost as new businesses opened around town, selling foreign objects like pucks, blades and the kinds of facemasks Southerners had theretofore only seen in horror movies.

It was a mutual love affair, between a small town that was experiencing something big, and athletes hanging onto the bottom rung of their sport's ladder who were experiencing the adulation normally reserved for the likes of the New York Yankees coming home with a World Series trophy.

Eventually, the novelty wore off, and the honeymoon ended. Attendance declined, and after eight years in Florence the team announced that it was moving on. But to this day the sight of someone on the street sporting a ragged Pee Dee Pride T-shirt or faded ball cap unfailingly provides me a nostalgic smile and a brief moment of camaraderie.

The poet Adrienne Rich once said, "A year, ten years from now, I'll remember this; not why, only that we were here like this, together."

But the people of Florence will remember why, and so will I. We will remember something that, for a brief period of time, brought us together, made us happy, provided us a reason to spend more time with our family and our friends, gave us something new, and made us care about it.

We will remember hockey.

~Cathy Elliott

# 96

# Texting on Ice

*Being a sports fan is a complex matter, in part irrational but not unworthy,*
*a relief from the seriousness of the real world,*
*with its unending pressures and often grave obligations.*
*~Richard Gilman*

Nonviolence, that's my credo. Well, okay, I'll admit to stomping on a bug or two, but as for fistfights that draw blood... I'd rather not indulge. All of which makes my friends wonder why I love hockey.

It's the action, the adventure, the "shusssshing" sound of skates on ice, the clap that sounds like lightning as the players hit the boards. Turn on a national football game and I can't keep track of the pigskin, but switch to a hockey game and I have no trouble following the puck. It hasn't been scientifically proven, but I'm thinking the Great Goalie in the Sky hardwired my brain for following that little black dot.

What makes it even more amazing is my inability to remember what the hockey terms mean. As the announcers spew forth excitement and terms by the dozens, I smile and nod as if I know them all, while mentally applying my own definitions.

Icing: What I spread on a cake.
Hat trick: Pulling on a knit cap without mussing my hair.
Checking: What the grocery store girl does with my groceries.
Backcheck: What the girl does when she misses something.
Lie: What I do about my age.

Blind pass: Going around another car on the freeway while putting on eye make-up.

Butt-ending: The location where rappers wear the waistband of their pants.

Face-off: Removing all my make-up, or in other words, taking my face off.

Forecheck: The fourth check in the checkbook.

Neutral zone: Somewhere between the Federation and Romulan territory.

Double minor: Twins under the age of eighteen.

Power play: The DVD machine in fast-forward.

Offside pass: Driving around another car on the right side.

Zamboni: A brand of fruit-flavored ice cream.

However, as my hubby will attest, lack of knowledge for the technical aspects has never hampered my love of the game.

During the 2011 Stanley Cup Finals, my husband had flown to visit his mother and I looked forward to watching the games uninterrupted on TV. I'd told him the dates and times, but felt certain he would never watch since he enjoys football over hockey. Just as the action started and the Boston Bruins scored a quick goal, my phone chimed, telling me of a text message. Groaning, I picked it up and read the note from him. "Wow, did you see that goal?"

Being a novice at texting, I looked down at the phone and laboriously typed, "Yes. I saw. But I am tring to wacth the game so don't keepsending me…"

Chime! Another text from him. "Wow, a second goal. Fantastic!" I looked up to see the Bruins' players slapping each other's backs. I gritted my teeth in frustration at missing such unparalleled action and tried to text back without looking at the phone's itty-bitty screen—while still watching the game. My thumbs flew faster than a greased puck on thick ice and I looked down just before hitting the send button.

"Thdkc dkeoc tlelkstk ,ldj djocijm?"

I stared at the phone, trying to figure out what I'd meant and as I did, it chimed a text again. "A third goal! The Bruins are hot tonight! What a game!"

Back to the present. Let us consider the term "spearing." A move in which a player illegally jabs, or attempts to jab, the point of his stick blade into another's body. I wonder how many years I'd get in prison for trying it on my husband during this year's Stanley Cup Playoffs... if he texts me during the games.

Probably not too many, right? After all, nonviolence is my credo, and there are no rules against spearing with a phone.

~Cindy Beck

# The Ride
# of Her Life

*Cherish your visions and your dreams as they are the children of your soul,*
*the blueprints of your ultimate achievements.*
*~Napoleon Hill*

G rowing up in the South, where it rarely snows and where
ponds almost never freeze over, I didn't know a thing
about hockey. Which wasn't a problem until my daughter
became engaged to a man who was into the sport big time.

"Help!" I begged my friend Jeanette, who had grown up in Detroit
as a rabid Red Wings fan. "Teach me everything you know about
hockey."

"Relax," she said. "Hockey's not hard to understand. I can teach
you about rules and stats and famous players and a lot of other stuff if
you want. Or I can tell you what I love most about the game."

"Let's start there. What do you love most?"

"Zambonis."

I suppose she could tell by the look in my eyes that I didn't have
a clue what she was talking about.

"You know, the giant machines that resurface the ice. Ever since
I was a little kid and saw my first hockey game, I've wanted to ride a
Zamboni. Who knew I'd be more than sixty years old before I got the
chance?"

Jeanette and her husband Steve traded Detroit for middle

Tennessee in the 1970s and supported the minor league hockey teams that came and went in a state not overly enthusiastic about the sport. When Nashville snagged the Predators in 1998, the couple was thrilled and quickly became ardent fans. "I still have the commemorative puck I got when we went to the opening game," Jeanette proudly told me.

And though she loves the action and excitement of the game itself, her favorite part of any hockey outing is what goes on between periods. That's when the Zambonis appear and begin to work their magic, making the chopped-up ice smooth and perfect again.

Jeanette and Steve's son, Tim, is also a huge hockey fan, though lifelong chronic health problems have kept him from being able to play the sport. When he was just thirty-two years old, Tim suffered a stroke. "It was a tough time for the whole family," Jeanette said. "As Tim's primary caregiver, there were many days when I wondered how I was going to dig out of the deep emotional hole I found myself in."

Steve came up with an idea he was pretty sure would help.

"He called a friend whose business was a major Predators sponsor," Jeannette told me. "The next thing I knew, I'd been granted permission to ride a Zamboni."

"You're kidding."

"Nope. All I had to do was show up at the arena—wearing one of Tim's Predators T-shirts, of course—and sign some papers. About halfway into the first period, I was escorted to the bottom of the building where the Zambonis are parked."

"So you just hopped aboard?"

"Not exactly. I'd recently had knee replacement surgery, which of course I purposely didn't mention, so the driver had to help me find the toe holds and climb into the passenger seat. I had no idea how huge those machines are until I sat on top of one."

"But you didn't chicken out?" I asked.

"No way. I buckled my seatbelt and off we went. And for as long as I live, I'll never forget how it felt when we burst out of the dark tunnel behind the goal and into the arena. Everything was so big and bright and noisy. I felt like a rock star and the Queen of England all at the same time. As we went round and round in smaller and smaller circles, I waved to the crowd the whole time."

"What happened when you were done?"

"Well… nobody asked for my autograph. But I did get to watch the Zamboni guys empty more than a ton of shaved ice into waste bin before I went back to my seat. Pretty cool. And I still haven't told you the best part. You'll never guess who the Predators were playing that night."

"Don't tell me…."

"Yep. The Detroit Red Wings. What more could a true-blue hockey fan ask than that?"

~Jennie Ivey

# 98

# Holy Moly, What a Goalie!

*How would you like a job where, every time you make a mistake,*
*a big red light goes on and 18,000 people boo?*
*~Jacques Plante*

As the great Canadian goaltender Eddie Belfour once said, "One minute you're a slug, and the next minute you're a hero...." Truer words have never been spoken, both about the game of hockey in general, and about being a goalie

Hockey is a fast game. In a matter of one second the entire game can change, and the radical shift in momentum can be felt both in the hearts of the hockey players and the fans observing the spectacle. When that one-second game changer happens as a result of a faulty goalie play or a wrong movement, which it often does, the goalie is left in a situation no one wants to be in. Of course, the opposite side of that undesirable situation is the goalie making the save that literally saves the game for their team. Clearly, being a goaltender is no easy task, and it certainly is a position full of a roller coaster ride of emotions, passion and competition.

I started playing goaltender at the young age of seven. Along with loving the transformer-esque aspect of the equipment, I idolized NHL greats like Eddie Belfour, Martin Brodeur, Curtis Joseph, and my ultimate favorite, Patrick Roy. Their memorabilia lined my walls, and stood proudly beside my house league hockey trophies. The decision to become a goaltender reflected these two traits surely, but what I didn't realize at that age was the immense impact this choice would have on my life.

Playing rep hockey from the age of eleven until eighteen definitely taught me some valuable lessons. Mental and physical strength were necessary attributes for every aspect of the game. Solely in terms of the mass amount of preparation, goaltending is not a simple physical game. From lugging around that heavy equipment in the dead of winter to the lasting sting of repetitive wall sits, being a goalie often results in sore muscles and tired bodies before even stepping out onto the ice.

Mental preparation before games, especially important games, would leave me with a combination of nervous and excited butterflies floating around in my stomach all day long. It was a feeling that thrilled me. And as my math teacher discussed the lesson for the day, my head was in a far away place, playing out particular saves in my mind.

When I was on the ice, the butterflies wouldn't leave until I had made the first save of the game and felt the adrenaline rushing through my bloodstream. And once that first wave of adrenaline hit, the rest of the game was played with such intensity that the only thing crossing my mind for the next hour was the small black disc zooming around the ice.

Of course, being a goalie can be less than glamorous. Sometimes I'd end up dotted with purple bruises the next day because my chest pad had shifted up and the inside of my arm was exposed or a piece of equipment failed to its job. Often getting hit that hard left me puck shy for the rest of the practice, as I was unwilling to turn my body into a human target board, to the annoyance of my coach, teammates, and mostly myself. I've been sat on, stepped on with skates, and hit so hard in the mask that I saw cartoonlike bird figures fluttering in front of me. Yet, come game time, I would do anything to put myself in front of the puck and make the save. To hear my dad in the stands chanting "Holy moly what a goalie!" Or my excited mom screaming my name, or even the team cheering for me was the only reward that I ever wanted.

The thing is, when I tell people I have played goaltender since I was seven years old, I get one of three responses: 1) The "Well, you know what they say about goalies, being crazy and all." (I guess there's quite a bit of truth to that statement — who in their right mind would willingly stand in front of a hard rubber disk being shot at them?) 2) The stunned, open-mouthed response. (Maybe it's because I seem normal, contradictory to the all goaltenders are crazy theory?) Or 3) My personal favorite: "That's the most expensive position, your parents must have been so upset the day you came to that conclusion." (Very true, goalie gear racks up a pretty penny.)

But none of these responses can adequately capture the reality of being a goaltender, on any level. The responsibility, the mental toughness, the physical agility and strength combine to create a position so thoroughly difficult, yet so rewarding. Being a goaltender instilled an incredible level of confidence in me, especially as a child. Of course, I still feel a pang of guilt and embarrassment if I watch any goalie, from any team, get scored on too much — mostly because I've been in that position before.

One thing is for sure; I wouldn't take back the tears, the bruises, and the mental and physical exertion for anything. From seven-year-old me admiring the position because of NHL greats and having my parents help me put on the league's broken-down equipment to seventeen-year-old me making my final save of my rep hockey career with girls I'd played with for years, I treasure every second and opportunity of my time playing goal.

"Holy moly what a goalie!"

~Daniella Porano

# 99

# The Geri-hatricks

*It's not the men in my life that count—it's the life in my men.*
~Mae West

After forty years of marriage, my husband and I have shared many fun adventures together, such as living on a houseboat when we were first married, rafting down the Colorado River at the bottom of the Grand Canyon, buying and moving a huge barn to our property so we could reassemble it and renovate it ourselves... you get the picture. Oh—and because we couldn't afford to have our home built for us, my husband surprised me by enrolling me in a plumbing, wiring and carpentry class when I was pregnant with our second of three children so I could be a certified helper. We obviously don't fit into any box that's remotely considered "normal."

And so it is that my husband, who just turned seventy-five, still has a passion for ice hockey. Not watching it... playing it! Throughout our marriage, he has belonged to many different hockey leagues and played in a variety of pickup games; largely dependent on what age group he was in. Now that he is a senior-senior, he still plays twice a week. My favorite team of all the ones he has played on is his current over-seventy group: the Geri-hatricks. Is that a genius name or what? The men who play with him come from all walks of life, from one who is a mortician to others who are journalists or doctors. In fact, the mortician suffered a mild heart attack one night during a practice, and it was largely thanks to a doctor on his team that this man is still alive and skating.

The men who share ice time with my husband come from the Washington, D.C. metropolitan area, which includes parts of Maryland and northern Virginia, where we live. That is why two years ago the Geri-hatricks were invited by the Washington Capitals professional hockey team to skate during one of their intermissions on a game night. The "boys" were all thrilled.

I nominated myself to be the head cheerleader, as I'm admittedly loud and enthusiastic. I had a great time gathering items for our large fan section, since the logo for the Geri-hatricks is a set of false teeth, biting down on a hockey stick. I found in a catalog some of those long-handled grabbers, with the top of them being plastic false teeth! You squeezed the handle and the teeth at the top of the pole opened and closed! They were hysterical! I also bought colorful pom-poms for us to shake, as well as inexpensive medals we could place around our husbands' necks after they had skated, changed, and returned to their seats.

One of our married daughters happened to be in town and joined our cheering section. Right before the Geri-hatricks took to the ice, my daughter saw her father and the other men all lined up in their uniforms and she said to me, "Now I think I know what you and Dad felt like whenever you came to watch any of us in our activities. I'm a nervous wreck!"

The crowd went wild when the Geri-hatriks were introduced and began warming up for their brief exhibition. The announcer seemed as excited doing the play-by-play for their mini-game as he was when the Capitals were playing! There was a little concern at one point when an eighty-two-year-old player fell and didn't get right up. Others noticed and helped him get vertical again. He wasn't injured, fortunately.

Through the years, I've heard wonderfully funny stories from my husband about his fellow hockey players. My favorite was about a goalie with tri-focals who wasn't able to see the puck very well as it quickly passed through the different lenses of his glasses. Many of the players have had various parts of their bodies replaced or repaired. My husband is going to have knee replacement surgery this spring. He's put it off for several years, because he's concerned it might end his hockey career. But several other Geri-hatricks who have already had this surgery have assured him he will only play better afterwards.

On a hook in my husband's office hang several medals he's won with his teammates in the Senior Men's Olympics. One of them is even a gold medal! On his wall are photos of the different teams he's played on in these national competitions. I smile whenever I pass them.

So here's to the Geri-hatricks who enjoy fun, fellowship and falling down together as they show younger hockey players just how enduring this sport can be.

~Bobbie Wilkinson

# 100

# Girl in Goal

*There is no position in sport as noble as goaltending.*
~Vladislav Tretiak

It's November 15, 2006, and I am mid-season of my first year of all-girls hockey. Because of my grade level and ignoring my late birthday, I was the youngest player on my team by at least three years. I arrived at the rink expecting to do the same thing I had been doing for the past two months, which was to play my shift and come off as quickly as was permitted. But when I walked into my dressing room I noticed a significant absence as I went to take my regular seat along the far wall of the change room. Our goalie was missing. Akiko, they told me, was too sick to come to hockey that morning. The rest of my team knew as well as I did that we would be playing against a girl named Jasmine who had the hardest shot in our league, which essentially guaranteed that no sane person would be volunteering to take to the pipes that day. The only person who had no idea of the perils that lay across the red line was my mother. "Em, why don't you play goal?" I felt my stomach sink and my spirit lift all at the same time. Without knowing that I actually had a choice in the matter, I gave my quiet consent. I was about to play goal.

I followed the rink manager to the storage room, where he picked out a pair of ancient goalie pads, a glove, a blocker, and a stick well past its due date for a tape job. With the help of my team captain Lesley, her father, and my coach Sandy, I wrangled with the rudimentary gear I had. I managed to strap the wrong pad onto the wrong leg at some point, but it wound up working itself out. I took to the ice, and I staggered awkwardly towards the crease. I took a couple of practice shots during warm up so I could find my footing, but well before I was ready, the game began. The first few minutes went rather well—I stopped my first shot, and managed not to fall down. But once their slap shot player took to the ice the trouble started. I remember looking up to the point and seeing Jasmine with her stick held high. I remember watching the blade carve through the air as it made its way to the puck it was aiming for. I remember watching the puck sail towards me in slow motion; though I knew that it was the fastest shot I'd ever seen. I remember how it felt when the puck missed my padding and landed on my upper leg with a force I'd never before felt, and I remember falling to the ice with tears in my eyes, and the puck beneath my knees. Play stopped, and I could feel my tears pooling from the pain caused by the tiny piece of vulcanized rubber that had just been shot at me by the scariest person I'd ever seen. My coach and captain came over to me worriedly, and I remember my coach asking me, "Em, are you okay kiddo? Do you want to come off?" to which I replied, "No, I'll stay on," I somehow heard myself saying. I finished the game, which wound up being our first win of the season, and from that day on I became my team's back-up goaltender. Had I decided to come off the ice, I probably never would have tried goaltending again.

At the conclusion of that house league season, I realized that I loved goaltending more than anything I'd ever done. I remember turning to my mom on my way back from an optional 8 a.m. practice and asking, "Mom, have you ever had a passion? Because this is mine," concluding my phrase with all the certainty a twelve-year-old could have mustered. After taking that half year to learn as much as I could, I tried out for a Bantam BB team and made it, and wound up playing AA by my second year of Bantam and competing against goalies who had been playing the position for the better part of their lives. I now have many tournament championships, provincial and regional awards, shutouts, and other hockey awards to my name that I've earned at the AA level, which is the highest level of non-provincial women's hockey available in Ontario. This year I am the starting varsity goaltender for the Bishop Strachan School Bobcats, and I'm preparing myself for what will be the final stretch of my high school hockey career.

It's said that Canadian babies are born with skates on, and I'm inclined to agree. Cumulatively I have been playing hockey for twelve of my seventeen years of life, I have been playing goal for five. I quite honestly cannot imagine my life without it. The girls I've met, the saves I've made, the (very few) goals I've scored, and the magnificent game I've played are no longer just something I did to fill up my spare time. Hockey is my life now. It is so entwined with our Canadian identity that we can no longer extricate ourselves from it. The beautiful thing about our game is that we find ourselves unified over something as simple as a black chunk of rubber, the cold of our northern climate, and a warm spot in all of our hearts left by the years of tradition we see carried on by our sons and daughters as they take to the ice in our place.

~Emily Papsin

# The Gentle Tough Guy

*I went to a fight the other night and a hockey game broke out.*
*~Rodney Dangerfield*

I dreamed my whole life of making it in the NHL—a dream I know I shared with a million other kids. I grew up in Montreal, and to say my home was an extremely strict household is a supreme understatement. My father is from Haiti and he firmly believed that children had to be controlled with his belt. My mother tried to temper his behavior but she was not able to make much of a difference, which led to a divorce during my youth. It was a tough childhood, but I have to say, my dad's domination and pressure did prepare me for my life. I learned how to work hard, and be prepared for my school and sports and ultimately, my career. Sports were vitally important to us and he pushed my brother and sister and me all incredibly hard.

I struggled as a young black athlete in a predominately white sport. When I was twelve the racism got so bad my dad pulled me out of hockey for a year. I loved hockey and decided to play again despite the fact that I was treated so badly by my opponents, their parents and even my own teammates who sometimes shouted racial slurs at me. I acted as if it were no big deal because there were way too many people to fight back. It deeply affected me but I never wanted to show people that I was hurt. Racist remarks were aplenty on the ice and off, and I had my heart broken many times when I would be the best player/top scorer in a hockey camp to make a rep team, yet when the final teams or the inner-city rosters were posted my name would not be on the list, for "some" reason. My parents wished that I would let hockey go and find another sport, but my dream wouldn't die.

I told them that if I quit, it would only prove that those ignorant people were right. I had to persevere, to achieve my dream. I swore that I would prove all the people who verbally and otherwise abused me wrong when I made it in the NHL. My dad didn't support me... even he didn't believe that I could actually make it. But that just fired me up even more, and I excelled at hockey. Soon people could not ignore me anymore. I started making the school teams. Scouts from the Quebec Major Junior Hockey League started watching me. On May 30, 1992, I was sitting in Maurice Richard Arena in Montreal waiting for the draft notices. And when the St. Jean Lynx team called my name, it was the most beautiful day of my life till then. I played Junior for two years and somewhere along the way I realized that as good as I was, in every level I moved up there were amazing players that were better than me; better skaters, better shooters, just better. I knew I was a great player, but also knew that I had limits.

Around that time a mentor of mine took me aside and told me that one of the things that I had going for me that set me apart from the crowd was my size, my muscle density, my balance and my ability to hit. It takes a very good player to make a good hit. It takes great coordination and balance and most of all timing. Of course, like any player, I loved scoring goals, but I recognized his advice as the truth. If I wanted to make it in the NHL, I would have to be a fighter, a tough guy, and an enforcer. When I accepted and decided to put all of my focus on that, things really happened quickly.

In July 1995 I was drafted in the second round to the Edmonton Oilers. I spent one more year in junior and then two more years in the American Hockey League, in the Oilers farm team, called the Hamilton Bulldogs. Then got "called up" to the big league and became the Oiler's tough guy. It was such an amazing accomplishment; I had made it to the NHL! Tough guys are so important to hockey. They play a very important role and what a lot of people do not realize is that they serve to actually keep hockey safer. They protect the "skills players" on their teams—the Gretzkys and Messiers of the sport and they enforce the rules, so opponents do not take advantage and deliberately injure one of these star players and take them out of the game.

I became one of the most feared enforcers of the game of hockey, and pretty much the entire time, I was scared. I mean, really scared. On game days, most players take an afternoon nap, to conserve and build energy. In all the years I played hockey, I had a hard time sleeping—I was always filled with anxiety about the games and fights to come. It is a very stressful position to play, and I had to fight some of the toughest guys in the world. And I was at the top of the heap. I was unanimously awarded the "Best Fighter" award from *The Hockey News* in 2003 and five years later, I was still named the number one enforcer by *Sports Illustrated*. And I did all this on my terms; I never bad-mouthed or trash-talked any of my opponents. I would always invite them to have a fight. Believe it or not, that is how it goes—one player extends the invitation, and if the opponent does not want to fight, they can turn down the offer. For instance, they might say, I just want to play my game tonight, and that is that. Pretty civilized, huh? Well, not when the fighting starts. I won most of my contests. I think out of around 100 fights in my career I only lost about five or six... but I never would say anything bad about the other player after the fact. When speaking to a reporter or the press, I would only say, "It went very well for me." I respected those other players so much, and I knew the courage it took to do the job they did. I never wanted to make them feel worse than they already did. I didn't even really want to fight, but it was my job.

And over the years I did my job for the Edmonton Oilers, the Phoenix Coyotes, The Pittsburgh Penguins and the Montreal Canadiens. I had a great career, but it had to come to an end. In August 2010 I retired and I guess you could say I went from tough guy to pacifist. Firstly, I was blessed to become a father to beautiful twins—a boy and girl, the loves of my life. The desire to take care of and provide a healthy world for them led me to my other passions.

In 2009, I had actually become a vegan after watching a documentary called *Earthlings*, all about the mistreatment of animals. Within ten minutes of watching that film, I was sobbing like a baby, and being the extremist that I am, in that moment I totally changed who I was and have never ingested another piece of meat or animal product. I took it even further and got rid of all the leather in my home, as well as becoming a part owner in two raw vegan restaurants in Montreal called Crudessence.

Veganism is a philosophy and a way of life for me and for my family and I am a very vocal and active advocate for the movement. I am a spokesperson for World Vision whom I am working with in association with the National Hockey League Players Association (NHLPA) to rebuild the Grace Children's Hospital in Port-au-Prince, Haiti, which was destroyed by the devastating earthquake in January, 2010. And I also became a member of the Green Party, recently being named to their Deputy Leader position. My children and my charity work are my passions. Our world is in crisis—climate change and so many other environmental issues are a real threat and we all have to wake up and do something.

When I became a father, it was the happiest day of my life. I promised to protect my son and daughter and that means trying to do the best I can for the world so we have a thriving planet to leave to my children, to all the children. Even though I was an enforcer in the NHL for fifteen years, I am committed to living my life with compassion and consciousness and I am honored to be known as the "gentle tough guy."

~Georges Laraque

# Meet Our Contributors

**Elena Aitken** lives in Okotoks, Alberta, where she spends her time hanging out with her busy twins, training for various athletic events and writing romance and women's fiction. She's published four novels and is hard at work on the latest release. Learn more at www.elenaaitken.com.

**Sharon Babineau** is a mother, decorated military soldier, hockey player, volunteer, keynote speaker, and founder of her daughter's charity Maddie's Everlasting Wish foundation. www.maddieswishproject.com. Sharon has learned the spirit cannot be broken; she shares that wisdom and insight with her audiences. E-mail her at Sharon@mindbreak.ca or visit www.mindbreak.ca.

**Cindy Beck**, humor blogger and co-author of *Mormon Mishaps and Mischief* (MormonMishaps.com), majored in insects and graduated sum kinda buggy from the University of Wyoming. She seldom shares that, however, because then people ask her to crawl under their houses to check for termites. Visit Cindy at bythebecks.com or bythebecks.blogspot.com.

**Rob L. Berry** received his Bachelor of Arts degree from California State University, Bakersfield and continues to reside in Bakersfield with his wife and two sons. Rob is a member of Writers of Kern and has previously appeared in *Chicken Soup for the Soul: Count Your Blessings*. E-mail him at robberry74@gmail.com.

**Jim Bove** received his bachelor's degree from Radford University (VA) and his master's degree from Michigan State University. He is the Community Outreach Facilitator for the Redmond Police Department in Redmond, WA and is a lifelong Washington Capitals fan. E-mail him at bovejame@hotmail.com.

**Michael Brennan** has played pickup hockey all his life and still manages to keep up with twenty- and thirty-year-olds. Best skating anywhere? The five-mile long canal in Ottawa where one slap shot means the puck goes for miles!

**Georgia Bruton** lives in Longwood, FL with her husband Steve. She loves to write and is the author of *Escape*, a young adult novel, as well as other writings. She is also the grandmother of three: Rachael, Gabriel, and Liam.

**Cassie Campbell-Pascall** was the first woman to do colour commentating on Hockey Night in Canada, the only person male or female to captain two Olympic Gold Medal Canadian hockey teams, a three-time Olympian in ice hockey, the recipient of Queen's Diamond Jubilee, and the first female hockey player in Canada's sports Hall of Fame. Learn more at www.cassie77.com.

**Beth Cato** is an active member of the Science Fiction and Fantasy Writers of America, and a frequent contributor to *Chicken Soup for the Soul* books. She's originally from Hanford, CA but now resides in Buckeye, AZ with her husband and son. Information regarding current projects can always be found at www.bethcato.com.

**Matt Chandler** is a newspaper editor and children's book author from Buffalo, NY. When he isn't writing, he can usually be found playing golf or hanging out with his wife Amber and his children Zoey and Oliver. E-mail Matt through his website, www.mattchandler.net.

**Lisa Ricard Claro** is a freelance writer whose work has been published in magazines such as *Writers' Journal* and various other media including newspapers, online, and multiple anthologies. For more of Lisa's writing, please visit her blog, Writing in the Buff, at www.writinginthebuff.net.

**Martha Cotiaux** grew up in Ohio. Moving to New York City to pursue her advertising career, she married the boss and settled on Long Island to raise four children. She and her husband now live in Connecticut. E-mail her at m.cotiaux@cox.net.

**Valerie Coulman** writes for both children and grown-ups in a variety of places, including magazines, newsletters, web content, stage scripts, award-winning picture books and more. And she still enjoys a cup of hot chocolate when her toes are cold.

**Tammy Crosby** lives and writes in Ontario. Her son George's constant antics keep her short on time but never on writing material. She's dedicating this piece to her husband Chris, as without him, she'd never have found the time to get to the rink. Check out Tammy's other literary adventures at tammywrites.wordpress.com.

**Shane Daneyko** is a thirteen-year-old seventh grader who recently signed a record label and is featured on a soon-to-be released Kidz Bop album. He thanks God for giving him the strength and courage to rise above negativity and find happiness in his life.

**Bruce Davidsen** began his career in the 1960s as a bass player in Montreal. He went on to become a concert and theatre producer and personal manager who has travelled the world and worked with the biggest names in the entertainment business. His first love... Hockey! Les Canadiens! E-mail him at brucedavidsen@gmail.com.

**Moira Rose Donohue** (www.moirarosedonohue.net) is a children's author living in northern Virginia. She recently penned six biographies for State Standards Publishing (April 2012). She has also written two picture books, *Alfie the Apostrophe* and *Penny and the Punctuation Bee*, as well as children's plays, articles, and poems.

**Matt Duchene**, a Haliburton, ON native, was a first-round NHL draft pick in 2009 at age eighteen and plays centre for his childhood dream team, the Colorado Avalanche. During the 2010-2011 season, Matt led the team in games, goals, points, and shots — and is the youngest player in Avalanche history to lead the team in scoring. In a game ten days after his twentieth birthday, Matt became the youngest player in team history to score 100 career points. When not playing hockey, Matt likes to fish, play his guitar and spend time with his family and friends. Follow him on Twitter @Matt9Duchene.

**Cathy Elliott** writes a syndicated weekly NASCAR column, and is the co-author of *Chicken Soup for the Soul: NASCAR*. A native of North Carolina's Outer Banks, she loves Beagles, the beach, and University of North Carolina basketball... not necessarily in that order. E-mail her at cathyelliott@hotmail.com.

Born in Los Angeles in 1993, **Jack Ettlinger** now lives in Toronto. A total sports enthusiast, Jack's passion is hockey and he recently scored the winning goal to capture first place in his high school city championships. In 2012, Jack sang his way to the semi-final round on *Canada's Got Talent*.

An American by birth, **Mark Ettlinger** spent twenty-five years in Los Angeles and worked in various parts of the movie business. Currently a writer living in Toronto with his Canadian wife and two children, Mark especially loves the lakes found in cottage country a couple of hours north of Toronto.

**Laura Fabiani** lives in Pennsylvania with her husband and three children. She has a story in *Chicken Soup for the Soul: Messages from Heaven*, and has been published in *Exceptional Parent* magazine. A long-time Flyers fan, she looks forward to the day when Lord Stanley's Cup returns to Philly.

**Lori Fairchild** is the author of the Everyday Truth blog (www. everydaytruth.net), which focuses on helping parents teach their children about God. She is both a hockey mom and a soccer mom for her two girls. She has also written the e-book *Everyday Christmas*. E-mail her at ldfairchild@comcast.net.

**Ailish Forfar** attends Dartmouth College, the Ivy League university, in New Hampshire. She aspires to become a teacher overseas or work as a journalist. Her goal is to play hockey for the Canadian Women's Olympic Team in her future. She enjoys travelling, playing sports, and spending time with her family.

**John Forrest** is a retired educator who writes about the exceptional events and wonderful people that have enriched his life. His second book, *Home for Christmas*, will be out in the fall of 2012.

**Ken Freebairn** loves to write and had been married for over forty years to his childhood sweetheart. They have two wonderful children and three of the cutest grandchildren you have ever seen.

**Donna Firby Gamache** is a writer/retired teacher from Manitoba. Her publications include short fiction for adults and children; short nonfiction and poetry; and three novels: *Sarah, A New Beginning* and *Spruce Woods Adventure*, both for children; and *Loon Island*, for teens. Donna enjoys reading, camping, traveling and cross-country skiing.

**Arlene Rains Graber** is a freelance writer in Wichita, KS and a graduate of the University of Memphis. She is the author of three books: *Devoted to Traveling*, *A Plane Tree in Provence*, and *Angel on My Shoulder*. Visit her website/blog at arlenerainsgraber.com.

**Peter Green** was born in Canada and lives near Niagara Falls, NY. He has spent a lifetime as a musician and, more recently, a storyteller leading groups through Niagara Falls, western New York, southern Ontario and beyond with the tourism business he runs with his wife, Danielle.

**William Halderson** lives in Cookeville, TN with his wife Monica and his dog Max. He writes a newspaper column about life, family, pets and wild animals. Playing hockey outdoors at fifty below zero is a true but long past memory. E-mail him at billandmonica1943@frontiernet. net.

**Jeff Hamilton** resides in Spruce Grove, Alberta and his many passions include writing, photography, book collecting, and traveling. His story, "The Twelve Years of Christmas," was published in *A Chicken Soup for the Soul Christmas*. Contact him or read more of his writing at theduffzone.blogspot.ca.

**Christopher Harder** is a freelance writer and editor living in New Jersey with his wife and son. He may have left his native Montreal many years ago, but the city ingrained in him an ongoing affection for hockey.

**Carol Harrison, B.Ed** is a distinguished Toastmaster, motivational speaker and author of the book *Amee's Story*. She also has stories in five other *Chicken Soup for the Soul* books. She enjoys time with family and friends, reading and scrapbooking. E-mail her at carol@carolscorner.ca or visit her website www.carolscorner.ca.

**Lori Hein** is the author of *Ribbons of Highway: A Mother-Child Journey Across America*. Her freelance work has appeared in numerous publications and in several *Chicken Soup for the Soul* books. Visit her at LoriHein.com or her world travel blog, www.RibbonsofHighway. blogspot.com.

**Jimmy Holmstrom** is a professional musician and OCT educator. He grew up in Toronto, Canada as a steadfast Toronto Maple Leafs fan. Upon "retirement" after seventeen years on the road, Jimmy was hired by the Leafs organization as their organists/music director in 1988, a position he maintains today.

**Jennie Ivey** lives in Cookeville, TN. She is the author of various works of fiction and nonfiction, including stories in several *Chicken Soup for the Soul* books. Visit her website www.jennieivey.com.

**Phyllis Jardine** is a hockey grandmother who enjoys writing stories for and about her grandchildren. She lives in the Annapolis Valley, Nova Scotia, Canada with her husband, Bud and black Lab, Morgan. This is Phyllis's third story in the *Chicken Soup for the Soul* series.

**Leighton Kemmett** is a member of the Society of International Hockey Research. He is also a volunteer at the Hockey Hall of Fame working as an archivist at the D.K. (Doc) Seaman Hockey Research Centre. In addition, he takes great delight in his family, playing baseball, gardening and history.

**Sharon and John Klassen** are the proud parents of two children: Nicholas who is featured in this story and his older sister Natasha. Both enjoy sports, reading, biking and friendships. Living with abilities and disabilities has enhanced their view and appreciation of life.

**Teresa Kruze** is a broadcaster and journalist. She got her start in television as one of the first female sports reporters and anchors in Canada. Teresa currently hosts and produces a weekly television talk show and writes a national newspaper column called "The In-Credibility Factor." Visit her website at www.teresakruze.com.

Born in Montreal in 1976, **Georges Laraque** fought against racism to achieve his dream to play in the NHL with Edmonton, Phoenix, Pittsburgh and Montreal. One of the most feared players in the NHL

Georges retired in 2010 to focus on humanitarian efforts. He works with World Vision, the Green Party of Canada and is the co-owner of two vegan restaurants named Crudessence.

**Jennifer Litke** is happily married to her husband of fifteen years. Together they have three sons and they live and play in the small town community of Prince Edward County. Jennifer is the author of *Conceived: Encouragement and Hope for Young Single Moms*. Learn more at www.conceived.weebly.com.

Fourteen-year-old **Aedyn MacKenzie** plays rep hockey for the Wilmot Wolverines. When not listening to her iPod, she spends her time writing, snowboarding, playing soccer, and visiting with friends. She enjoys writing and hopes to be an architect when she grows up.

**Cynthia Mallick** began her writing career after teaching dance for twenty years and yoga for six. She works as a make-up artist in Tampa, Florida, enjoys swimming in the Gulf of Mexico, and is seeking representation for her young adult novel and other works.

**Shawn Marie Mann** is a trained geographer and freelance writer living in central Pennsylvania. She spends her free time writing and visiting amusement parks. This is Shawn Marie's fifth story published in the *Chicken Soup for the Soul* series. You can reach her through her website at www.shawnmariemann.com.

**Irene Maran** is a retired high school administrator living at the Jersey Shore. She writes children's stories, humorous essays and a bi-weekly newspaper column for *The News-Record* of Maplewood/South Orange and *The Coaster* in Asbury Park. Irene enjoys nature and art and creating jewelry. E-mail Irene at maran.irene@gmail.com.

**David Martin's** humor and political satire have appeared in many publications including *The New York Times*, *Chicago Tribune* and *Smithsonian* magazine. His latest humor collection, *Dare to be Average*, was published in 2010. David lives in Ottawa, Canada with his wife Cheryl and their daughter Sarah.

**Julienne Mascitti-Lentz** is a writer, speaker, wish granter, and Mrs. Claus for the Make-A-Wish Foundation/children's hospitals. She was previously published in *Chicken Soup for the Soul: Living Catholic Faith* and her book, *Opened Our Hearts*, will be published in 2013. Julienne sends out inspirations from juleslentz@wowway.com and blogs at mymomandmethelastchapter.blogspot.com.

**Hank Mattimore** was born and raised in Buffalo, NY and now lives in Santa Rosa, CA. He has been a surrogate grandpa for The Children's Village, an intergenerational home for abused children, in Santa Rosa for five years. E-mail him at hmattimore@yahoo.com.

**Dennis McCloskey** has a journalism degree from Ryerson University in Toronto. He has been a full-time freelance writer since 1980 and is the author of several books, including the 2008 award-winning biography, *My Favorite American*. He lives in Richmond Hill, Ontario with his wife, Kris. E-mail him at dmcclos@rogers.com.

**Sarah McCrobie** received her Bachelor of Art's degree, with honors, from SUNY Oswego in 2006. She has worked for nearly six years as a reporter and editor for a small daily newspaper in upstate New York. She enjoys spending time with her family and friends. E-mail her at smccrobie@gmail.com.

**Brian McFarlane** has been a player, an author and a broadcaster of the game for over fifty years. For twenty-seven years he was a commentator on Hockey Night in Canada. He has also been a broadcaster for CBS, NBC and ESPN. He has authored over eighty books on hockey and is a media member of the Hockey Hall of Fame.

**Michelle McKague-Radic** lives in Peterborough, Ontario with her husband and son. She has recently completed her Bachelor of Arts in History degree and is now working on a second bachelor's degree. Michelle would love to work in the publishing industry in the future. E-mail her at misha_beth@yahoo.com.

**Cara McLauchlan** enjoys writing stories about the beauty of life's ordinary moments. She is a writer, wife and homeschooling mom from North Carolina. To read more, visit her blog, Joy Goggles, at www.joygoggles.blogspot.com.

**Audrey McLaughlin** lives in Pittsburgh, PA with her husband Tom, spending her winters in Florida. She retired after working twenty-seven years in early childhood education. She enjoys writing what she has learned from working with young children, their families, and her personal life experiences. E-mail her at audreylengyel@comcast.net.

**Bruce Mills** is a civil engineer living in Boise, ID. Born in Michigan, he has also lived in Colorado, Utah, Washington, Idaho, and Ireland. Seeing new places is an obvious passion, along with howling out tunes with his guitar, hiking and spending time with family. E-mail Bruce at brucegmills@gmail.com.

**C.G. Morelli** plucked his roots from the cozy, northern soil and buried them in the sun-baked clays of North Carolina. His work has appeared in *Philadelphia Stories, The Ranfurly Review, Jersey Devil Press, Pink-Eye Lemonade, Monkey Puzzle Press,* and *Fiction at Work.*

**Christa Holder Ocker**, a published author and poet, likes to write about everyday life. Her memoir *auf Wiedersehen* — a 2009 Finalist in the *ForeWord Reviews'* Book of the Year Award — has been added to the Holocaust collection at Yeshiva University, the Leo Baeck Institute, the New York Society Library, and the Goethe-Institut.

**David K. Overlund** received a B.A. degree in history from St. Olaf College in 1958. He and his wife Marg, also an "Ole," have been married for fifty-three years. Both are retired, enjoy traveling, maintaining their yard, fishing and being active in the lives of their children and grandchildren.

Born in Kingston, Ontario, **Leanne Fanning Pankuch** received her Bachelor of Arts degree in English from North Central College, IL. She currently lives in Illinois with her husband, children, and dogs. She is an accomplished vocal musician and writes middle-grade fiction and humorous picture books. Visit her website at www.leannepankuch. com.

**Emily Papsin** is a Toronto native who, having just completed high school, plans on attending Dalhousie University in the fall where she will major in biology. She's an ever-faithful Leafs fan with an eclectic list of passions including songwriting, science, and of course, hockey.

**Alana Patrick** attends St. Olaf College in Northfield, MN, where she is a member of the varsity hockey and club lacrosse teams. Majoring in English with a concentration in biomedical studies, she hopes to one day become a physical therapist (and writer on the side). E-mail her at patrick@stolaf.edu.

**Judi Peers** has published many children's books (*Brontosaurus Brunch, Home Base, Shark Attack, Sayonara Sharks, Guardian of the Lamp*), and contributed to several anthologies. She is a speaker, literacy advocate, avid sports fan, and engaging Bible study leader. Judi and her husband Dave make their home in Peterborough, Ontario.

**Cathy Pendola** graduated from Northern Illinois University and resides in Flower Mound, TX with her husband Manny, daughter Francesca and their dog Scooter. She feels blessed to have stories published in the *Chicken Soup for the Soul* series. She is working on getting her first book published. E-mail Cathy at sascmp54@verizon. net.

**Jill Pertler** writes the syndicated column, "Slices of Life," which is printed in over 120 newspapers across the U.S. She is also a playwright and the author of *The Do-It-Yourselfer's Guide to Self-Syndication*. Find her columns on Facebook at Slices of Life; visit her website at marketing-by-design.home.mchsi.com.

**Mary C. M. Phillips** is a caffeinated wife, mom, and writer. She blogs at caffeineepiphanies.wordpress.com and is working on her first novel.

**Daniella Porano** is currently a student at McMaster University. She loves hockey, reading, writing, and traveling. E-mail her at daniella_porano_13@hotmail.com.

**Václav "Vinny" Prospal** is a Czech professional ice hockey left winger currently a member of the Columbus Blue Jackets. He has previously played for the Anaheim Ducks, Florida Panthers, Ottawa Senators, Tampa Bay Lightning and the Philadelphia Flyers. He has played over 1,000 regular season games with the NHL.

**Jennifer Quasha** is a freelance writer and editor who is the co-author of *Chicken Soup for the Soul: My Dog's Life*, *Chicken Soup for the Soul: My Cat's Life*, *Chicken Soup for the Soul: I Can't Believe My Dog Did That!* and *Chicken Soup for the Soul: I Can't Believe My Cat Did That!* Learn more at www.jenniferquasha.com.

**Bill Reay** received a B.S. degree in pharmacy in 1979, a Doctor of Pharmacy degree with honors in 1987, and Masters in Healthcare Administration in 1999. He is currently the Chief Pharmacy Officer and Senior Director for Physicians Plus Insurance Corporation in Madison, WI. E-mail him at wreay7475@charter.net.

**Tara Reyelts** attends St. Olaf College in Minnesota (class of 2014), where she majors in English and African Culture and Colonialism. She plays varsity hockey and track and field for the Oles. She plans to travel the world and write fiction novels after graduation. E-mail her at reyelts@stolaf.edu.

**Chris Robinson** is a jazz saxophonist and teacher in the Toronto area. He graduated from Humber College in 1993 and recorded his award-winning CD, *Pleased to Meet You*, in 2002. Recording more of his original compositions is his current goal, and to continue making beautiful music. E-mail him at chrisrobinsonjazz@gmail.com.

**Amanda Romaniello** graduated with honors from Syracuse University in 2010. This is her third story in the *Chicken Soup for the Soul* series. She writes about life, running, cooking, and love in her blog, Simple Girl, Simple Pleasures. She also is a contributing writer for HooplaHa. E-mail her at amanda.romaniello@gmail.com.

**Theresa Sanders** is honored to be a frequent contributor to the *Chicken Soup for the Soul* series. An award-winning technical writer, she lives in suburban St. Louis, where she and her husband have four grown children, a precious new grandson, and are passionate about their St. Louis Blues!

**Leigh Anne Saxe's** passion is to inspire others to be happier and healthier. She is an independent consultant with Arbonne International and is a happiness coach and inspirational speaker. Leigh Anne loves to downhill ski and spend time up north with her family. Learn more at www.leighannesaxe.myarbonne.ca.

**John Scanlan** is a 1983 graduate of the United States Naval Academy, and retired from the Marine Corps as a lieutenant colonel aviator. He currently resides on Hilton Head Island, SC and is pursuing a second career as a writer. E-mail John at ping1@hargray.com.

**Justin Schlechter** grew up playing ice hockey on Long Island and is an Islanders fan to this day.

**Annabel Sheila** writes poetry, fiction and nonfiction for grown-ups and children. Her work has appeared in print and online magazines. She lives with her soul mate, Rick, and loves spending time with family and travelling. Her precious grandson, Max, inspires her to be the best grammy ever! E-mail her at annabelsheila@live.ca.

**Brandi South** lives in Pennsylvania with her family and their dog, Buddy. She works at Hagerstown Community College and is pursuing her degree there as well. Brandi would like to thank God for giving her the courage to share her story, and her family and friends for their encouragement.

**Mark Spangler** is a freelance writer and poet. He is also an educator at Mankato West High School in southern Minnesota. He lives with his wife, Terry, son Garrison, and two dogs in Mankato. He is a graduate of Minnesota State University, Mankato and can be reached via e-mail at steelerstwin@juno.com.

**Diane Stark** is a former teacher turned stay-at-home mom and freelance writer. She loves to write about the important things in life: her family and her faith. She is the author of *Teachers' Devotions to Go*. E-mail her at DianeStark19@yahoo.com.

**Robert J. Stermcheg** retired from the Winnipeg Police Service in 2006, enabling him to devote more time to what he loved to do—writing historical fiction. He recently wrote his father's memoir, *POW #74324*. Among skiing, cycling, reading, Robert also enjoys traveling with his wife. Contact him at www.robertstermscheg.com.

**JC Sullivan** marketed ice hockey in Milan, Italy and was thrilled when the Kings won their first Stanley Cup. A beach girl, her only regret is that they do not have the sport in her current base, Puerto Vallarta (Mexico). Please visit her bilingual blog www.backpackingpoet.com, or write her at backpackingpoet@yahoo.com.

**Michael Sullivan** is an award-winning writer, a storyteller, and a pediatric nurse. He has performed songs and stories throughout the country in libraries, schools, bookstores, and museums. He lives in Richmond, VA, with his wife and two children. For more information, please check out his website at www.msullivantales.com or www. eyeballinmygarden.com.

**Beverly A. Suntjens** lives in Stony Plain, Alberta with her wonderful husband, three amazing kids, and two neurotic dogs. She is a recreation therapist and Program Chair at a community college. She believes everyone has a story to tell, and confirms this each time she boards a plane.

**B.J. Taylor** and her husband are fervent fans at hockey games. She is an award-winning author whose work has appeared in *Guideposts*, thirty *Chicken Soup for the Soul* books, and numerous magazines and newspapers. You can reach B.J. through her website at www. bjtayloronline.com. Check out her dog blog at www.bjtaylorblog. wordpress.com.

**Lisa Trovillion** earned a degree in Russian in 1979, and later a Master of Liberal Arts degree. When not at her job with the Federal Government, she enjoys training her two dressage horses, posting to her book review blog, spending time with family on their farm, and, of course, writing.

**John P. Walker** was born in Toronto and grew up along the shores of Georgian Bay. He is a freelance writer who now resides just outside of Harrisburg, PA with his wife, Bonnie. John married into a dedicated hockey family in 1984 and has prayed for mercy ever since. E-mail him at john1walker24576@yahoo.com.

**Jennifer Walter** graduated on the Dean's List with a B.A. degree in English literature from the University of Guelph. She is a writer, editor, speaker, hockey wife, hockey mom, nana, Twin Peaks Cancer

Foundation rep, and business partner to her husband, Ryan. Learn more at www.jennwalter.com, @jennijingles, www.sanctityinthecity. com/about/meet-our-experts and jennwalter.blogspot.com.

**Ryan Walter** played fifteen seasons and over 1000 games in the NHL. He was an All-Star, Stanley Cup Champion, and the youngest captain in NHL history, and is now a speaker, writer, and President of an AHL team. Contact Ryan at www.ryanwalter.com or buy his newest book at www.hungryfuellingyourbestgame.com.

**Hayley Wickenheiser** is a women's ice hockey player from Canada. She was the first woman to play full-time professional hockey in a position other than goalie. Hayley has represented Canada at the Winter Olympics four times, capturing three gold and one silver medal and twice being named tournament MVP. She is widely considered the greatest female ice hockey player in the world.

**Bobbie Wilkinson** is a writer, artist, and musician who works from her home in northern Virginia. She and her husband Tom have three married daughters and two grandchildren. They also run a home business that sells Bobbie's inspirational jewelry, cards and artwork. Visit her at theflipflopheart.com.

**Susan Winslow** lives with her husband Scott, children Lexie, Sam and Keelie and assorted horses, donkeys, cats and dogs. She is a therapeutic horseback riding instructor and writes for four magazines in the equine industry.

**Kate Zamboni** received her Bachelor of Art's degree, with honors, from the University of Richmond, and her Juris Doctor, with high honors, from George Mason University School of Law.

**Lori Zenker** attempts to understand her kids' hockey games, in Elmira, Ontario, Canada, where hockey is worshipped. She also has a story in *Chicken Soup for the Soul: O Canada*, and a children's book titled *Promiseland*. She is a pastor's wife, artist and writer, and buys and sells old junk. E-mail her at burmiethegreat@gto.net.

# Meet Our Authors

**Jack Canfield** is the co-creator of the *Chicken Soup for the Soul* series, which *Time* magazine has called "the publishing phenomenon of the decade." Jack is also the co-author of many other bestselling books.

Jack is the CEO of the Canfield Training Group in Santa Barbara, California, and founder of the Foundation for Self-Esteem in Culver City, California. He has conducted intensive personal and professional development seminars on the principles of success for more than a million people in twenty-three countries, has spoken to hundreds of thousands of people at more than 1,000 corporations, universities, professional conferences and conventions, and has been seen by millions more on national television shows.

Jack has received many awards and honors, including three honorary doctorates and a Guinness World Records Certificate for having seven books from the *Chicken Soup for the Soul* series appearing on the New York Times bestseller list on May 24, 1998.

You can reach Jack at www.jackcanfield.com.

**Mark Victor Hansen** is the co-founder of Chicken Soup for the Soul, along with Jack Canfield. He is a sought-after keynote speaker, bestselling author, and marketing maven. Mark's powerful messages of possibility, opportunity, and action have created powerful change in thousands of organizations and millions of individuals worldwide.

Mark is a prolific writer with many bestselling books in addition to the *Chicken Soup for the Soul* series. Mark has had a profound influence in the field of human potential through his library of audios, videos, and articles in the areas of big thinking, sales achievement, wealth building, publishing success, and personal and professional development. He is also the founder of the MEGA Seminar Series.

Mark has received numerous awards that honor his entrepreneurial spirit, philanthropic heart, and business acumen. He is a lifetime member of the Horatio Alger Association of Distinguished Americans.

You can reach Mark at www.markvictorhansen.com.

**Laura Robinson** is a Canadian actress/inventor/producer and married mother of two. She co-invented the classic, best-selling board game *Balderdash*, which has sold over twenty-five million copies worldwide. Laura launched a new game, *Identity Crisis*, to great success in 2010. Along with well-known celebrity partners, she recently developed and sold a pilot for a one-hour prime-time television game show based on the game to a major U.S. network.

Laura has enjoyed a successful and varied career as an actress, with many roles in film and television, both in Los Angeles and Toronto. She was a regular on the long-running CBS show *Night Heat*, played the title character in Lifetime Television's original detective drama *Veronica Clare*, and guest-starred on many hit shows, including *Cheers* and *Frasier*.

In 2009, Laura had the honor of becoming a Chicken Soup for the Soul author with the book *Chicken Soup for the Soul: Count Your Blessings*, all about the transformational power of gratitude, and co-created an inspiring family board game of the same name.

She was featured in the book *Women Invent* and has been a keynote speaker and host at numerous events in Los Angeles and elsewhere. She has appeared as a guest on *Entertainment Tonight Canada*, *Rogers Daytime*, and on CBC TV.

Laura has so enjoyed the process of co-authoring *Chicken Soup for the Soul: Hooked on Hockey*. She is a proud hockey mom herself and has spent many hours in rinks across Ontario watching her son Jack play, her husband Mark coach, and drinking hot chocolate with her daughter Julia!

Laura also consults and advises inventors on the trademark/copyright process and creating cohesive brand strategies. She can be reached at laurarobinson@rogers.com.

# Thank You

T
hank you to all the fabulous hockey players and families who contributed to this inspiring and entertaining book! I owe huge thanks to every one of you who shared your stories. I loved hearing all the wonderful memories and could almost feel the crisp, winter air on my face as I read about the outdoor rinks, the pond hockey games, and the nearly morning rituals. I thrilled to the stories of NHL Play-offs and Olympic victories—all the dreams and games and fun. But most of all I delighted at reading about the love between sons, daughters, moms and dads. I know that you poured your hearts and souls into the thousands of stories and poems that you submitted. Thank you. All of us at Chicken Soup for the Soul appreciate your willingness to share your lives with us.

We could only publish a small percentage of the stories that were submitted, but we read every single submission. Even the stories that do not appear in the book influenced us and affected the final manuscript.

A special thank you goes to Amy Newmark, Chicken Soup for the Soul's brilliant publisher, who guided me with deft expertise and constant contact. Assistant Publisher D'ette Corona managed the whole production process, and advised and assisted me every step of the way. This book could not have been made without her help. I also want to thank Chicken Soup for the Soul editor Kristiana Glavin for all the fabulous quotes and her innate knowledge of what makes a great Chicken Soup for the Soul story. She was an integral part of the production process, especially in the final crunch. Many thanks to editor Barbara LoMonaco for her proofreading assistance as well.

Lastly, I send a very special thanks to our creative director and book producer, Brian Taylor at Pneuma Books, for his wonderful cover and interior design.

~Laura Robinson

# Improving Your Life Every Day

Real people sharing real stories—for nineteen years. Now, Chicken Soup for the Soul has gone beyond the bookstore to become a world leader in life improvement. Through books, movies, DVDs, online resources and other partnerships, we bring hope, courage, inspiration and love to hundreds of millions of people around the world. Chicken Soup for the Soul's writers and readers belong to a one-of-a-kind global community, sharing advice, support, guidance, comfort, and knowledge.

Chicken Soup for the Soul stories have been translated into more than forty languages and can be found in more than one hundred countries. Every day, millions of people experience a Chicken Soup for the Soul story in a book, magazine, newspaper or online. As we share our life experiences through these stories, we offer hope, comfort and inspiration to one another. The stories travel from person to person, and from country to country, helping to improve lives everywhere.

# Share with Us

We all have had Chicken Soup for the Soul moments in our lives. If you would like to share your story or poem with millions of people around the world, go to chickensoup.com and click on "Submit Your Story." You may be able to help another reader, and become a published author at the same time. Some of our past contributors have launched writing and speaking careers from the publication of their stories in our books!

Our submission volume has been increasing steadily—the quality and quantity of your submissions has been fabulous. We only accept story submissions via our website. They are no longer accepted via mail or fax.

To contact us regarding other matters, please send us an e-mail through webmaster@chickensoupforthesoul.com, or fax or write us at:

Chicken Soup for the Soul
P.O. Box 700
Cos Cob, CT 06807
Fax: 203-861-7194

One more note from your friends at Chicken Soup for the Soul: Occasionally, we receive an unsolicited book manuscript from one of our readers, and we would like to respectfully inform you that we do not accept unsolicited manuscripts and we must discard the ones that appear.